Jazz Religion, the Second Line, and Black New Orleans

Jazz Religion, the Second Line, and Black New Orleans

RICHARD BRENT TURNER

Indiana University Press

Bloomington & Indianapolis

This book is a publication of

Indiana University Press
601 North Morton Street
Bloomington, IN 47404-3797 USA

www.iupress.indiana.edu

Telephone orders   800-842-6796
Fax orders   812-855-7931
Orders by e-mail   iuporder@indiana.edu

♾ The paper used in this publication
meets the minimum requirements of
the American National Standard for
Information Sciences—Permanence
of Paper for Printed Library Materials,
ANSI Z39.48-1992.

Manufactured in the United States of
America

Library of Congress Cataloging-in-
Publication Data

Turner, Richard Brent.
   Jazz religion, the second line, and Black
New Orleans / Richard Brent Turner.
      p. cm.
   Includes bibliographical references and
index.
   ISBN 978-0-253-35357-3 (cloth : alk.
paper) — ISBN 978-0-253-22120-9
(pbk. : alk. paper)
   1. Jazz—Religious aspects—
Louisiana—New Orleans. 2. Jazz—
Religious aspects—Voodooism.
3. African Americans—Louisiana—
New Orleans—Music—History and
criticism. I. Title.
   ML3921.8.J39T87 2009
   305.896'073076335—dc22
                              2009014084

1 2 3 4 5 14 13 12 11 10 09

FOR THE ANCESTORS

Lynn Burks
Shawn Burks
Eric Claytor
Richard Claytor
Kelsie Foreman
Lamonte Foreman
Ophelia Foreman
Zedock Foreman
Reginald Gougis
Andre Jones
Shirley Kennedy
James London
Horace Maxie
Ruth Maxie
Shirley Maxie
George Parker
James Turner Jr.
Mavis Turner
Evelyn Tynes
Jackie Tynes
Catherine Weaver
David Weaver
Horace Weaver

FOR

Social justice in New Orleans after Hurricane Katrina

CONTENTS

PREFACE

The inspiration for this book can be traced to Sidney Bechet's reflections about New Orleans music in *Treat It Gentle: An Autobiography*: jazz is "there in that bend in the road" in the American South and "you gotta treat it gentle."[1] Like the saxophonist Bechet, I have traveled many roads to understand New Orleans music and the joy and pain "alongside it."[2] I owe thanks to the city of New Orleans, my home from 1996 to 1999, for an extraordinary culture and community that I will never forget. The beautiful sounds of jazz and African drumming floating in the air and the joyful experience of the second line are always waiting for me on the road home to the Crescent City. My mother's death in 1997, the Parker family's love, and the spirit world of African American religion led me to that "bend in the road" along the Mississippi River that is the "music itself."[3]

The road to the music in *Jazz Religion* began in my hometown, Boston, Massachusetts, in the 1950s with the fascinating stories of the southern branch of my family in North Carolina that my mother, Mavis Turner, and my aunt, Kelsie Foreman, recited to me when I was a young boy. The exciting and mysterious life of my grandfather, Zedock Foreman, the handsome child of a former slave and former slave owner was at the crossroads of those southern stories that eventually brought me back home to the South, to my family's roots.

My teachers at Princeton University also enabled this book's publication with the excellent resources they provided in the 1980s. Thanks to John Wilson, who directed my Ph.D. program in the religion department, for including seminars in African religions with James Fernandez in anthropology and Ephraim Isaac at Princeton Theological Seminary. A reading course with Albert Raboteau in 1983 introduced me to his brilliant book, *Slave Religion: The "Invisible Institution" in the Antebellum South,* Melville Herskovits's *The Myth of the Negro Past,* and a career-long fascination with African continuities in African American religions.

I have been blessed with the advice of several brilliant extramural colleagues in the field of New World African religions. Claudine Michel at the University of California, Santa Barbara, and Patrick Bellegarde-Smith at the University of Wisconsin, Milwaukee, published shorter versions of my book chapters in the *Journal of Haitian Studies.* They welcomed me to the Board of Directors of KOSANBA, a scholarly association for the study of Haitian Vodou, in 2007, and provided critical feedback for the papers I read at KOSANBA's international colloquia in Boca Raton, Florida; Detroit, Michigan; and Boston, Massachusetts. Special thanks are due to George Lipsitz at the University of California, Santa Barbara, who read my book manuscript for Indiana University Press and provided important suggestions to improve the final product. To Lindsey Reed, I express thanks for brilliant editorial assistance, and Mitch Coleman did a great job with the word processing of the manuscript. It is always a professional pleasure to work with Robert Sloan, the editorial director of Indiana University Press.

DePaul University in Chicago awarded me a Faculty Research and Development Committee Grant, a Competitive Research Grant, and a Humanities Center Fellowship to begin the archival research for *Jazz Religion* from 1999 to 2001. The University of Iowa, one of the leading public research institutions in the United States, provided generous support to complete the research and writing of this book. During my years on Iowa's faculty, I received two Arts and Humanities Initiative Grants (2002–2003 and 2005–2006) from the Office of the Vice President for Research and a Career Development Award (fall 2006) from the College of Liberal Arts and Sciences that gave me the funds and release time from teaching to conduct research at William Ransom Hogan Jazz Archive at Tulane University, the Historic New Orleans Collection, the New Orleans Public Library, and the Backstreet Cultural Museum. My second Arts and Humanities Initiative Grant allowed me to travel to

New Orleans to attend Big Chief Allison Tootie Montana's jazz funeral in July 2005—a few weeks before Hurricane Katrina devastated the city.

Finally, blessings go out to all the brave New Orleanians who survived Hurricane Katrina. I am still a New Orleanian, and I love my city!

Jazz Religion, the Second Line, and Black New Orleans

Follow the Second Line

No matter where it's played, you gotta hear it starting way behind
you. There's the drum beating from Congo Square and there's the
song starting in a field just over the trees. The good musicianeer . . .
he's finishing something . . . that started back there in the South. It's
the remembering song. There's so much to remember.

SIDNEY BECHET, *TREAT IT GENTLE*

Personal Introduction

I arrived in New Orleans on a hot Saturday evening in August 1996 to
begin a new job in the theology department at Xavier University. I was
not a total stranger to the vibrant culture of the Crescent City. The Parkers, a large African American family that had befriended me during my
years in San Francisco and Santa Barbara, California, had introduced me
to their extensive New Orleans family network. Their New Orleanian
relatives found an orange shotgun house for me to rent on Cambronne
Street, in the heart of the uptown riverbend neighborhood where the
St. Charles streetcar line turns into Carrolton Avenue. This neighborhood is famous for its graceful architecture, Creole restaurants and coffee houses, and its music. Across the street from my new residence was
St. Joan of Arc, a small black Catholic Church with a gospel choir that

often sang so irresistibly that their practice sessions drew me out of the house and into the street to celebrate the spirit of their soulful sounds.

As I walked up Cambronne Street at 10 o'clock on my first night in New Orleans, my senses were overcome with the smells of southern-fried cooking from André's Creole Restaurant, and the sounds of live music in the air. When I reached dark and narrow Oak Street, I saw where all the noise was coming from, and I entered the Maple Leaf Bar. The Maple Leaf is one of those old neighborhood clubs where New Orleanians of every race, color, and style gather on certain nights of the week to party and dance to the music of the Dirty Dozen and Rebirth brass bands. Members of these bands perform in what are known as "second lines," the jazz street parades and processions of black New Orleans that follow the "first procession" of church and club members, secret societies, and grand marshals. On that Saturday, I partied all night and into the wee hours of Sunday morning.

The next day, after a Sunday brunch of hot beignets (freshly fried donuts sprinkled with powdered sugar) and café au lait at Café du Monde in the French Quarter, my friends led me to a second-line performance in the streets of Tremé—New Orleans' oldest black neighborhood, which begins on the far side of Rampart Street, at the edge of Louis Armstrong Park and Congo Square. We walked in funky rhythm with hundreds of black people who danced and partied to the music of a neighborhood jazz brass band that wound its way through the city for several hours in the humid afternoon heat. When we came to Esplanade Avenue, I asked a native New Orleanian in the crowd where the parade was going, and he said, in a melodic southern accent, "Just follow the second line, baby, and you'll see." Much later, the second line dispersed in front of the Circle Seven Market on St. Bernard Avenue, where people had set up their grills to sell barbeque, ribs, sausage, potato salad, and red beans and rice.

Although baptized as an infant in the African Methodist Episcopal Church, but confirmed as a young adolescent in the Catholic Church and brought up simultaneously in both traditions in Boston, for the next three years in New Orleans I added to my religious experience as I sought the musical and religious rituals performed outside of churches in second-line street parades, jazz funeral processions, and private homes.[1]

In my second New Orleans residence on General Pershing Street (which runs parallel to Napoleon Avenue, where the uptown Mardi Gras parades begin), I often learned from my friend, Elaine Brown, how to perform healing spiritual work at an altar in my home, where I placed pictures of a person's deceased family members and of saints, smelled the exotic fragrances of holy incenses and oils, recited biblical prayers from the Book of Psalms, and lit votive candles at specific times of the day for the Holy Spirit, St. Michael the Archangel, or the Spirit of Black Hawk.

Sometimes I spent whole Saturdays and Sundays from late morning to dusk running after second lines, photographing their dance performances, and often experiencing personal spiritual cleansing after absorbing their powerful energy and music. For some participants, a second line was "nothin' but a party goin' on" (also the title of a famous second-line brass band song); for others, however, it was a profound expression of New Orleans' African diaspora past, an experience of communal meditation or even trance that re-created the historic nineteenth-century performances in Congo Square, where black New Orleanians had reinterpreted the sacred music and dances of Vodou in weekly public African festivals every Sunday until the Civil War.[2] I followed the second lines of the social and pleasure clubs, Mardi Gras Indian tribes, and serviteurs of Vodou in an annual cycle of performances that included Super Sundays, the annual New Orleans Jazz and Heritage Festival, the Louisiana Black Heritage Festival, the Reggae Riddums Festival, the Essence Music Festival, jazz funerals, and black "Mardi Gras under the bridge" on Claiborne Avenue during the Carnival season.

Eventually I was drawn into a circle of African diasporic spiritual workers by friends and associates who were initiates of Vodou, for example, jazz musicians, visual artists, black Christian ministers, and church people who spoke of New Orleans as a magical city with a special religious and musical heritage deeply connected to the spirits of African ancestors from its slave past. As I spent time with friends and associates in late-night rap sessions about religion, spirituality, and music, and participated in the rich cultural experience of black New Orleans as a resident of the city—sometimes taking my Xavier students on historical fieldtrips to the French Quarter and Congo Square—I came to love New Orleans both for its rich culture combining unique spirituality and pleasure, and because it was a laboratory for learning through direct experience about the African diasporic roots of African American religion, music, and culture.

Personal involvement with friends, associates, and extended family increased my knowledge and understanding of second lines, the religion of Vodou, Mardi Gras Indian performances, and jazz funerals, and inspired me to write this book about "jazz religion": an exploration of theoretical perspectives on the history and contemporary significance of African diasporic religious traditions and identities celebrated in the jazz street parades and processions of black New Orleans. This volume uses popular religious culture to survey interactions from past to present between New Orleans, Haiti, and West and Central Africa; between African diasporic religions and Christianity; and between urban religion and music. New Orleanians who shared with me their knowledge about this culture include Elaine Brown, a Vodou princess I met at a Parker family funeral who blessed my house many times and offered me valuable spiritual advice to deal with the unexpected death of my mother, Mavis Turner, in the summer of 1997; my good friend Miles Parker, a jazz musician and aspirant to the Vodou priesthood, who, in frequent late-night sessions with musicians, artists, and scholars at P.J.'s Coffee House and Café Brazil on Frenchmen Street—offered me rich insights into Creole culture and the deeply interconnected spiritual roots of jazz and Vodou in New Orleans; Ava Kay Jones and Margaret Gross, Vodou queens and priestesses who explicated aspects of the spiritual philosophy of their religion for my Xavier students and me in the classroom and during fieldtrips to the Historic Voodoo Museum in the French Quarter; the late Big Chief Allison "Tootie" Montana and his son, Chief Darryl Montana, who, during a fish fry on Good Friday in 1997 at his dining room table, first explained the history, music, and artistic traditions of the Mardi Gras Indians; Jesse Clarence Brown, a wonderful friend, Baptist minister, and lawyer whom I met periodically at Café Mocha, a midcity coffeehouse, to discuss the unique spirituality of black New Orleans; my students at Xavier University, who shared with me, both in the classroom and during office hours, rich stories of their families' religious histories; members of St. Peter Claver Catholic Church on Governor Nichols Street, with whom I worshiped on Sundays and experienced a unique Afrocentric mass reflecting the dynamic musical and spiritual traditions of black New Orleans; and Sylvester "Hawk" Francis, founder of the Backstreet Cultural Museum on St. Claude Street in Tremé and the black community's official photographer of jazz funerals.[3] Above all, however, my research for this project was enriched by my participant observation in the rhythm, sounds, spirit, and movement of the second lines in Tremé and uptown neighborhoods that featured the social and pleasure clubs and the Mardi Gras Indians.

Statement of the Problem

Jazz Religion is an exploration of the historical and contemporary roots of the relationship of jazz to indigenous religion and spirituality in the culture and performances of New Orleans' second lines. The second-line theme also allows me to investigate how African diasporic religious identities and musical traditions from Haiti and West and Central Africa were reinterpreted over time in New Orleans jazz and popular religious performances. This theme provides strong evidence "that the African religious heritage was [not] lost" in New Orleans and that the religious experience of the past and present black communities in that city are not completely embodied in the "visible" institutions of Christianity.[4] The African spiritual energy and power of jazz street parades, Vodou ceremonies in domestic spaces, Mardi Gras Indian masking, and jazz funerals—which all belong to the second-line culture—demonstrate that black New Orleanians have an African diasporic spiritual life that interacts with Christianity but is largely unknown by the mainstream order because its communal rituals are performed by jazz musicians and initiates of secret societies and social and pleasure clubs.

Through the interweaving of narratives, history, and photo documentation, *Jazz Religion* explores the multicultural African diasporic spiritual world of second-line participants—the jazz musicians, dancers, artists, and community folk who periodically create their own sacred space in the streets of New Orleans—and analyzes the religious traditions of Vodou, the Mardi Gras Indians, jazz funerals, and black Catholic, Baptist, and Spiritual churches in New Orleans, which all inform the communal identity of the second lines. The book also examines the larger musical tradition of jazz, exemplified by the second lines, and highlights the ideas and identities that New Orleans jazz musicians have constructed to articulate the interaction between religion, music, and the African diaspora in their city. From the early twentieth century to the present New Orleanian musicians from Sidney Bechet to Los Hombres Calientes have discussed jazz music and its spiritual roots in second-line culture and Congo Square; specifically, they looked at how the participants in second lines, inspired by Congo Square (the oldest site of continuous African cultural and social memory in the U.S. and the birthplace of jazz), created their own social space and became proficient in the arts of political disguise, resistance, and performance. These issues are addressed by bringing together current work in the humanities, studies of popular urban religions, performance studies, and diasporic jazz research (The Black Atlantic).

The area of New Orleans called Congo Square—originally a sacred Indian site, now at the edge of the French Quarter—is also a significant theme in *Jazz Religion*. Congo Square was the only public space in the antebellum United States where African drumming was performed every Sunday. It therefore speaks to the continuity of the African spirit world and the religion of Vodou, both of which revolve around sacred drumming and are central to my inquiry into the origins of second-line culture.

The title *Jazz Religion, the Second Line, and Black New Orleans* is derived from my major argument, briefly noted above, that the second-line jazz street parades and related performance cultures in black New Orleans re-create "flashes" of memories, rhythms, and rituals that evoke the spirit world of the African diaspora and that periodically move the black community into the sacred realm of introspection about the legacy of circum-Atlantic slavery and its ancestral culture in Congo Square, Haiti, and West and Central Africa. The healing power of these performative meditations and transformations is evoked by the rhythms of jazz, or what many New Orleanians call "Congo Square music"—the sounds and rhythms that were first performed by slaves in the nineteenth-century Congo Square gatherings in New Orleans. In these public gatherings, the African-descended community re-created the spiritual power of the West African festival and Vodou through drumming, masking, iconography, music, and dance.[5]

After the Congo Square gatherings officially ended in the late nineteenth century, selected aspects of the West African festival and Haitian and New Orleanian Vodou were subversively re-created and performed over time not only in the second-line culture of jazz funerals, street parades, and Mardi Gras Indian masking but also in the spiritual work of early-twentieth-century Vodouists such as Zora Neale Hurston, who was inspired by the Congo Square legacy of the famous nineteenth-century Vodou queen Marie Laveau. The explication of the religious domain of second-line culture includes a discussion of Hurston's "performative representations" as an initiate observer of early-twentieth-century New Orleanian Vodou, as well as the link between her work and the Haiti–New Orleans African diasporic connection. Hurston is one of the most important New Orleanian Vodouists in the twentieth century and the first African American to have left a written record of her initiation. Integral connections exist between her spiritual journey in her book *Mules and Men* and the musical and religious performances of second lines. In fact, New Orleanian second liners and Vodouists from Hurston's time to the present have often used the same sacred spaces and African diasporic spiritual resources to gain proficiency in the arts of resistance and performance, and Hurston's re-creation of black vernacular religious culture in *Mules and Men* is central to understanding how second-line culture incorporates aspects of the religious tradition of Vodou.[6]

Another important theme in *Jazz Religion* is the link between New Orleans Mardi Gras Indian tribes, second-line participants, and "the sacred arts of Haitian Vodou," such as the sequin artists and Rara bands of Haiti.[7]

This book is motivated by several basic research questions. What are the historical and contemporary roots of the relationship of jazz to indigenous religion and spirituality in New Orleans? How are African diasporic religious identities and musical traditions from Haiti and West and Central Africa reinterpreted in New Orleans jazz and popular religious performances? How do the participants in the second lines—the musicians, secret society members, and anonymous dancers—create their own social space and become proficient in the arts of political disguise, resistance, and performance? *Jazz Religion* addresses all these questions.

Review of the Literature

I am indebted to Joseph Roach, who, in *Cities of the Dead*, analyzes the provocative relationship between memory, performance, and the re-creation of history in New Orleans. He writes:

> Memories of some particular times and places have become embodied in and through performances.... To perform ... means ... often secretly to reinvent. This claim is especially relevant to the performances that flourish within the geohistorical matrix of the circum-Atlantic world.... The concept of the circum-Atlantic world (as opposed to a transatlantic one) insists on the centrality of the diasporic and genocidal histories of Africa and the Americas, North and South, in the creation of the culture of modernity.... This interculture may be discerned most vividly by means of the performance tradition and the representation of performance that it engendered ... because performances so often carry within them the memory of otherwise forgotten substitutions—those that were rejected, and even invisibly, those that have succeeded.... The pursuit of performance does not require historians to abandon the archive but it does encourage them to spend more time in the streets ... reconstructing historic performances ... [such as] second line parades in New Orleans ... that have a continuous history since the eighteenth century in the celebrations of African-American social clubs and burial societies.[8]

As scholars both in the humanities and the social sciences suggest, the antebellum history of black culture in New Orleans is central to our understanding of the African diasporic roots of African American religion and music in the United States. Michael A. Gomez's *Exchanging Our Country Marks* is a groundbreaking study of the African origins of the antebellum African American community that explores the origins and development of Creole language and religion in New Orleans as the keys to one of the most important "African-derived cultures" in the United States.[9] Daniel E. Walker's *No More, No More* analyzes the African performances in Havana's El Día de Reyes (Day of the Kings festival) and New Orleans' Congo Square as two of the most important "multidimensional life-affirming" resistance traditions in the nineteenth century "that allowed the participants a form of reconnection with a host of social, familial, and spiritual networks that had been severed as a result of the slave trade."[10] John Storm Roberts, in his ethnomusicological study of the impact of Latin music on the history of jazz, *Latin Jazz*, sees "the Latin influence in nineteenth-century New Orleans music . . . [as an] underrated [paradigm] . . . for the U.S. as a whole."[11] The research of David E. Estes on Zora Neale Hurston's "literary imagination" in her fieldwork, described in "The Neo-African Vatican," establishes the Crescent City as "the essential location for understanding the origins of black culture in this country . . . because of the indigenous folkways of its African American residents."[12]

Moreover, scholars in American religious studies share a renewed interest in urban religions and the history, ethnography, and complex rhythms of folk communities, as exemplified in the work of Walter F. Pitts Jr. (*Old Ship of Zion*), Anthony B. Pinn (*Varieties of African-American Religious Experience*), and Robert A. Orsi (*The Madonna of 115th Street, Gods of the City,* and *Between Heaven and Earth*). Pitts and Pinn focus on the dynamic African diasporic roots of contemporary African American popular religious practices, music, and worship traditions, and Orsi explores the community themes, creativity, demography, and topography of urban religious culture, focusing on Italian Catholic popular devotions that constructed a "theology of the streets."[13]

Jazz Religion fills an important gap in the religious studies scholarship on both urban folk religions and on New Orleans religion and music. No one has systematically utilized this new wave of scholarship in religious studies to analyze the significance of New Orleans culture in the African diaspora. This book unites two traditions and situates the study of the religion and music of black New Orleans in the mainstream of exciting work in American and African American religious studies. All these perspectives underline the importance of New Orleans in American religious history as a sacred city in the African diaspora—the crossroads for African, Caribbean, and American religions and musics, the center for Vodou, and the birthplace of jazz in the United States.

Organization of the Study

Jazz Religion is an example of a new genre of scholarship in African American studies that intentionally moves across boundaries and paradigms of the humanities and social science disciplines to explore the complex interactions between cultures, religions, music, and community life in a particular location—the black community of New Orleans. This book should appeal to readers with special interests in religious studies; African, African American, and Africana studies; performance studies; music; urban culture; ethnohistory; and Caribbean religions. By focusing on performance as an important locus for religious and musical re-creations of the African diaspora, I emphasize the significance of the narratives and the ethos of ordinary people in "little communities," and, in the spirit of Zora Neale Hurston, I recognize the extraordinary knowledge and power of black people who construct strategies to resist oppression outside large institutions—in the realm of the "spirit world."[14]

Jazz Religion includes three chapters, an interlude, and an epilogue. Chapter 1 presents Hurston's early-twentieth-century anthropological fieldwork in New Orleans and her journey as an initiate observer of Vodou as a case study of the African diasporic religious domain of second-line culture. I trace the origin of that religious domain to the public music and dance performances in nineteenth-century Congo Square and to the spiritual work of the Vodou queen Marie Laveau and her descendants. The chapter also discusses the historical, spiritual, and artistic interactions between West African, Haitian, and New Orleanian Vodou from the eighteenth century to the present. Chapter 2 examines the African diasporic links between Carnival performance cultures in New Orleans and Haiti and their confluence with the spiritual philosophies of Central African religious traditions. Included is a case study of the Montana family of New Orleans, a family with deep roots in the Mardi Gras Indian tradition from the late-nineteenth-century to the present.

The interlude is more personal and considers how the crisis of my mother's death in 1997 prompted my own participation in the healing experience of jazz funerals and African diasporic religion. This experience provides another important perspective regarding the living traditions of second-line culture and its interactions with Vodou.

Chapter 3 looks at jazz funerals as the culmination of second-line culture and traces the roots of the Crescent City's African American funeral processions to the West African Yoruba concept of rituals as transformative journeys; the music and burial traditions of the Black

Church; and Haitian Vodou's ancestral spirits—the Gede family—that deal with the cemetery and "life and death struggles." The chapter describes the jazz funeral of the Mardi Gras Indian Chief Allison "Tootie" Montana—which I attended in 2005—as a case study of this venerable second-line tradition.

The epilogue analyzes the future prospects of New Orleans' black community and its musical and religious traditions two years after Hurricane Katrina. Finally, the epilogue offers my deeply felt personal, spiritual, and historical reflections about Congo Square, where American popular music and African American performance cultures were born in the early nineteenth century, as hundreds of slaves re-created every Sunday the spirit of African drumming, trance, and dance in a public forum. Indeed, the memory of "the drum beating from Congo Square" inspired Sidney Bechet's eloquent saxophone improvisations and will always call me back to New Orleans to "follow the second line."[15]

ONE

The Haiti–New Orleans Vodou Connection: Zora Neale Hurston as Initiate Observer

> The Negro has not been Christianized as extensively as is generally believed. The great masses are still standing before their pagan altars and calling old gods by new names.
>
> ZORA NEALE HURSTON, *THE SANCTIFIED CHURCH*

The story of Zora Neale Hurston's journey as an initiate observer of Vodou and her "introspection into the mystery" of the religion is an extraordinary religious narrative. Hurston interprets the key themes of Vodou, taps the magical-spiritual wisdom of her elders and ancestors, and records what Haitian adepts call *konesans*—the esoteric spiritual knowledge of ordinary black folk who create transformative healing rituals in the communities of the African diaspora. These ancestral, esoteric, and healing elements in Hurston's spiritual journey are also the essence of the religious domain of second-line culture.

The chapter explores the religious significance of Hurston's initiation and fieldwork in Vodou in the 1920s for the construction of a Haiti–New Orleans African diaspora cultural identity with provocative historical, spiritual, and artistic linkages that began in the nineteenth century and persist today. Hurston's publications on New Orleans Vodou, *Mules and Men* and "Hoodoo in America,"[1] offer important primary source material for analysis of this Haiti–New Orleans Vodou connection and its significance for the second-line theme of this volume.[2]

Through the memory of folklore, Hurston explicates in *Mules and Men* the complex religious domain of second-line culture, namely, the secretive world of early-twentieth-century New Orleans Vodou. She uses the highly original strategy of "folkloric performance" to re-create the rich vernacular language "rhythms" of the black community (which are central to second-line musical performances) and their connections to the geo-historical roots of New Orleans as an important circum-Atlantic city. Her narratives of the nineteenth-century Vodou queen Marie Laveau and the weekly Congo Square festivals—with their roots in Haitian and West and Central African spirituality—embody historical memories of slave resistance in New Orleans that continue to influence the political expression in second-line performances. Hurston's "performative representations" of her own initiation in *Mules and Men* is a powerful case study of how second-line culture encompasses and expresses significant aspects of the religious tradition of Vodou.[3]

Recently Hurston's work has been the subject of critical analysis in African American theological and religious studies. Katie G. Canon analyzes Hurston's use in her novels of the folk culture and values of the black church as a model for "black theological ethics" and "the moral wisdom of black women."[4] Donald H. Matthews explores Hurston's research methodology as an early model for "the African-centered approach to the interpretation of African-American" cultural, theological, and literary studies.[5] Theophus Smith demonstrates how the Bible served as "a magical formulary" in Hurston's folklore research.[6] And, finally, Anthony B. Pinn sketches the history of Vodou in Benin, Haiti, and New Orleans, and discusses Hurston's fieldwork as a way to rethink the canon of black religion in black theological studies.[7]

Pinn's *Varieties of African-American Religious Experience*, which reveals the "rich diversity of black religious life in America" by focusing on non-Christian "popular religious practices and sites," informs the African diasporic orientation of this volume. Two canonical issues that orient Pinn's research are central for understanding Hurston's unique contribution to black religious history in her time: the "narrow agenda and resource base of contemporary" black religious studies; and the "contention that African-American religious experience extends beyond . . . [the] institutional and doctrinal history" of Protestant Christianity to include Islam and African diasporic ancestral traditions.[8] Indeed, these key issues are reflected in the religious meaning of Hurston's research and initiation into Vodou in New Orleans and Haiti. She was seventy years ahead of her time in her exploration of the enduring connections between American religions and African diaspora traditions, and in her analysis of the power and richness of urban folk religions and Creolized synthetic-religious identities that stand on their own ground. Hurston's interests reflect the current paradigmatic shift in religious studies toward an "ethnographic description of individuals and the groups with which they affiliate," as exemplified in the works of Walter F. Pitts, Karen McCarthy Brown, and Robert Orsi.[9]

Zora Neale Hurston and New Orleans Vodou: The Haitian Concept of Knowledge, *Konesans*

> New Orleans is now and has ever been the hoodoo capital of America. Great names in rites that vie with those of Haiti in deeds that keep alive the powers of Africa.
>
> ZORA NEALE HURSTON, *MULES AND MEN*

In 1928 Hurston received a bachelor's degree in anthropology from Barnard College, and in August of that year she traveled to New Orleans to begin six months of intensive fieldwork among the city's Vodou adepts. She was a student of the renowned anthropologist Franz Boas at Columbia University. It was her spiritual experiences in New Orleans Vodou, however, that transformed her from a mere participant observer and collector of folklore to an initiate observer, deeply involved in the key themes and esoteric knowledge and rituals of the religion.

Previous studies of Hurston's New Orleans fieldwork minimized the depth of "her angle of vision" as an initiate to focus on her work exclusively "as anthropological documents . . . and literary texts."[10] Although I do not contest the validity of prior scholarship, I look to another provocative subject of analysis that is embedded in the study of Vodou as an African diasporic religious tradition with deep roots in

Haitian spirituality. I analyze *Mules and Men* as a parallel expression of the Haitian *konesans*, which originates in the spiritual experiences of initiates and mystics and is expressed intuitively in the healing and magical rituals of the religion. Hurston's record of esoteric knowledge in both *Mules and Men* and "Hoodoo in America" is an important primary source of information about New Orleans Vodou in the early twentieth century and its connections to Haitian Vodou.[11] This esoteric magical and healing practice is also central to our understanding of the religious domain of second-line culture and its relations to circum-Atlantic performance in West Africa and Haiti.

The Haitian scholar Milo Rigaud sheds light on Vodou's magical, esoteric practice embedded in the meaning and idea of the word "Voodoo":

> Voodoo encompasses an exceedingly complex religion and magic with complicated rituals and symbols that have developed for thousands of years . . . everything essential to the knowledge of the mystery is implicit in this word. . . . Vo means "introspection" and Du means "into the unknown." Those who indulge in this "introspection" into the mystère (mystery) will comprehend not only the Voodoo gods, but also the souls of those who are the adepts and the servants of these gods. This is the only way in which the fruitful practice of the rites is possible to produce supernaturally extraordinary phenomena or magic.[12]

In *Mules and Men* Hurston clearly views magic as the centerpiece of New Orleans Vodou:

> Belief in magic is older than writing. The way we tell it, Hoodoo started way back there before everything. Six days of magic spells and mighty words and the world with its elements above and below was made. And now God is leaning back taking a seventh day rest.[13]

This statement situates New Orleans Vodou in the realm of the profound and ancient mysteries of the religion that Haitian adepts such as contemporary visual artist André Pierre acknowledge as "a world created by magic."

> The Vodou religion is before all other religions. It is more ancient than Christ. It is the first religion of the earth. It is the creation of the world. The first magician is God who created people with his own hands from the

dust of the Earth. People originated by magic in all countries of the world. No one lives of the flesh. . . . The spirits of Vodou are the limbs of God.[14]

In Hurston's religious narrative, *Mules and Men,* Moses is the first and most powerful Vodou spirit, because he received God's magic rod and acquired knowledge of ten of God's powerful words from the snake resting under God's feet during the creation of the world. This narrative is not just a folkloric transformation of a biblical story into "a conjure story,"[15] as Theophus Smith writes, but instead is another path— "performative representations" of black vernacular oral tradition— through which Hurston establishes the Haiti–New Orleans Vodou connection in the realm of *konesans.*[16]

David Todd Lawrence contends that Hurston's "performative representations," namely, "her 'between story' exchanges" and interpretations in *Mules and Men,* "are the most valuable part of the entire book because they represent the performer in context in the act of performing for an audience . . . and enable us to understand the possibility of when and where a particular kind of folklore element might be employed over a long period of time."[17] Thus Hurston's information about the oral tradition of New Orleans Vodou in her time establishes "a predictive cultural pattern"[18] essential to an understanding of how subsequent second-line performance groups express important aspects of the oral culture of African diaspora religions over time.

In her later work, *Tell My Horse,* she explains the religious meaning of the folk stories of Moses's magic as "Damballah Ouedo . . . the supreme mystère" whose "signature is the serpent." From the time of the nineteenth-century Vodou queen Marie Laveau[19] to the present in New Orleans Vodou, Danbala Wedo has been a constant lwa (Vodou spirit) involved in rituals as "the ancient sky father [arched] across the sky as a snake beside his rainbow wife, Ayida Wedo. He is the origin of life, and the ancient source of wisdom." According to Hurston, however, in Haitian Vodou Danbala Wedo always has been one of the pantheons of lwa:

> In the Voodoo temple or peristyle, the place of Damballah, there also must be the places of Legba, Ogun, Loco, the cross of Guedé who is the messenger of the gods, of Erzulie, Mademoiselle Brigitte and brave Guedé.

Damballah resides within the snake on the altar in the midst of all these objects.[20]

The current scholarly consensus established by Patrick Bellegarde-Smith's research and other groundbreaking studies of Haitian Vodou is that a synthetic, not syncretic, relationship exists between Vodou as a powerful African diaspora religion of resistance to Western hegemony and Christianity.[21] Vodou stands alone, independent of mainstream Christianity. Hurston acknowledged this important synthetic quality of Vodou in New Orleans and Haiti, as she writes in *Tell My Horse*:

> The Haitian gods . . . are not the Catholic calendar of saints done over in Black. . . . This has been said over and over in print because the adepts have been buying the lithographs of saints, but this is done because they wish some visual representation of the invisible ones, and as yet no Haitian artist has given them an interpretation or concept of the lwa. But even the most illiterate peasant knows that the picture of the saint is only an approximation of the lwa.[22]

In *Mules and Men*, the African ancestral tradition, called "hoodoo" and "conjure" by early-twentieth-century New Orleans black folk, is not a mere footnote to African American religious history. In Hurston's work, the secrecy and centrality of Vodou in the religious life of New Orleans suggest that the religion's esoteric knowledge and power is just as strong there as in Haiti:

> Hoodoo . . . is burning with all the intensity of a suppressed religion. It has thousands of secret adherents. It adapts itself like Christianity to its local environment, reclaiming some of its borrowed characteristics to itself. . . . It is not the accepted theology of the nation and so believers conceal their faith.[23]

In her Vodou trilogy—*Mules and Men*, "Hoodoo in America," and *Tell My Horse*—Hurston maps New Orleans as a significant religious site not only because of its relationship to black southern conjure and root work but, more important, for its connection to the Creolized fragments of Haitian culture and spirituality that lie deep in its history. Thus New Orleans is writ large on the map of black religion as a magical African diaspora city, which, like Haiti, has successfully resisted the efforts of mainstream Christianity to absorb its esoteric African ancestral knowledge.[24]

Haitian and New Orleans Vodou:
Early Historical Connections in Congo Square

In "Hoodoo in America," Hurston traces the early historical encounters between Haitian and New Orleans Vodou in the eighteenth and nineteenth centuries:

> [Vodou] has had its highest development along the Gulf Coast, particularly in the city of New Orleans and in the surrounding country. It was these regions that were settled by the Haytian emigrees at the time of the overthrow of French rule in Haiti by L'Ouverture. Thousands of mulattoes and blacks, along with their ex-masters were driven out, and the nearest French refuge was the province of Louisiana. They brought with them their hoodoo rituals, modified of course by contact with white civilization and the Catholic church, but predominantly African. These island Negroes had retained far more of their West African background than the continental blacks.[25]

My analysis here is based on the work of scholars who followed Hurston's lead and provided detailed background about the African diasporic religious and musical performances in nineteenth-century Congo Square. This information is essential to understand the origins of second-line culture and the world into which Hurston came when she arrived in New Orleans.

Approximately twelve thousand Haitian immigrants arrived in New Orleans from the 1790s until 1810, seeking refuge from the black revolution in the former French colony, St. Domingue. They arrived in a city that already had a distinctive African heritage and religion. According to Gwendolyn Midlo Hall, the Afro-Creole imprint on New Orleans culture was dynamic and constant in the 1700s under French and Spanish rule. Colonial New Orleans culture revolved around the Louisiana Creole language that slaves from Senegambia and the Kongo created in the early 1700s. These Afro-Creole slaves also created rich religious, musical, and folklore traditions influenced by significant cultural and social interactions with Choctaw, Houma, and Chickasaw Indians, French and Canadian Catholic settlers, and pirates. The predominant African-ized culture of New Orleans was not accidental, as African slaves who arrived in the city on the same ships maintained their strong kinship bonds. By the 1730s the African population of southern Louisiana was twice as large as the white population. The unstable conditions of the French settlers; the resistance and creativity of the Bambara, an ethnic group primarily from Mali; the size and significance of the Native American communities; and the physical terrain of swamps and bayous that facilitated runaway slaves all created strong and unique African-Amerindian maroon communities in southern Louisiana in the eighteenth century. Vodou, brought directly to the city from West Africa by Yoruba and Fon slaves from the Bight of Benin and by slaves from the Kongo, certainly played a major role in this dynamic African diaspora culture in the eighteenth and nineteenth centuries.[26]

Slaves from the Kongo, although outnumbered by Bambara slaves, had a profound impact on African religious practices, music, dance, and Carnival celebrations through their festival processions and funerals. Beginning in the late 1750s New Orleans' African slaves, Native Americans, and racially mixed free people of color gathered every Sunday for communal trading and recreation in the Place des Nègres, an open area behind the city that earlier had been a sacred site for the Houma Indian corn feasts. The site, later called Congo Square, was noted for its interaction between African and Indian communities and for the African dances, drumming, and songs performed there by hundreds of New Orleanians of African descent. Certainly Congo Square was the most important site in the United States for the public performances of African dances—such as the bamboula, calinda, coujaille, and pilé chactas—all of which were related to Vodou rites and were reinterpreted by second-line performance groups in the twentieth century. It was also the marketplace for Afro-Creole Vodou charms, called "gris-gris" in New Orleans, a term from the Mende language of the Mandingo and Bambara peoples. The square's name recalls the healing rhythms of Kongo-Petwo tutila and ndungu drums that were brought to New Orleans from Haiti and from the many slaves who were brought from Kongo to Louisiana during the Spanish period.[27]

The *Code Noire*, "The Collection of Edicts, Declarations, and Decrees Concerning the Discipline and the Commerce of Negro Slaves of the Islands of French America," signed by Louis XIV in 1685, incorporated people of African descent in St. Domingue and New Orleans into a common French Catholic colonial culture that allowed the space for the liminal African festival rituals of Congo Square. Various articles of the *Code Noire* required owners to baptize and bury their slaves according to the Catholic religion and to excuse them from work on Sundays and holy days, and for funerals.[28]

The *Code Noire's* legal permission for African drumming in Congo Square was central to the establishment of New Orleans as the Vodou capital of the United States and to its attraction to Haitian immigrants who practiced Vodou.[29] Bobby Joe Neeley believes that in the context of the mass exodus of Vodou adepts from Haiti and Cuba to New Orleans in the early 1800s, "Voodooism and its sacred dance were institutionalized/acculturated in Congo Square."[30] His research sheds light on the importance of the drumming in Congo Square as the means by which the sacred rhythms of the lwa were invoked in the dances.

Furthermore, in the drawings of the English architect Benjamin Henry Latrobe, based on his observations of the Congo Square rituals in 1815, there is evidence of three different kinds of African drums—the Conga and Ogororo from the Yorubas and the "open-staved drum" from Dahomey. These drums were used in the public and private Vodou rituals of New Orleans performed by adepts from Haiti and the Crescent City in the nineteenth century.[31]

Michael Ventura's research shows that the Municipal Council's designation of Congo Square in 1817 as the only legal location in New Orleans for slave dancing was an official attempt to limit the power of Vodou, which had reached a high point of development with Haitian immigration and a succession of Vodou queens in the city. This official step to suppress the private music and dances of New Orleanian Vodou set the stage for the birth of jazz and its related second-line and Mardi Gras Indian performance traditions in the aftermath of Congo Square's heyday. Ventura writes:

> It was precisely by trying to stop Voodoo that for the first time in the world, African music and dancing was presented both for Africans and whites as an end in itself, a form of its own. Here was the metaphysics of Africa set loose from the forms of Africa. For this performance wasn't African. In the ceremonies of Voodoo there is no audience. Some may dance

and some may watch, but those roles may change several times in a ceremony, and all are participants. In Congo Square, African music was put into a western form of presentation. From 1817 until the early 1870s, these dances went on with few interruptions, the dance and the music focused on for their own sake by both participants and spectators. It is likely that this was the first time blacks became aware of the music as music instead of strictly as a part of a ceremony. Which means that in Congo Square, African metaphysics first became subsumed into music. . . . A possibility embodied by the music, instead of the music existing strictly as this metaphysic's technique. On the one hand, something wonderful was lost. On the other, only by separating the music from the religion could either the music or the metaphysics within it leave their origins and deeply influence a wider sphere.[32]

The American fears of Haitian Vodou had actually begun with the Louisiana Purchase from France in 1803. Napoleon's sale of Louisiana to the United States was related to his inability to control the religion of Vodou and the political revolution of its adherents against the French in Haiti. Because Napoleon was defeated in Haiti, he was unable to consolidate his French colonies in America. Later, the government of the United States was afraid of a similar black revolution within its borders and carried out several waves of persecution of Vodouists that included the Congo Square regulations.[33] Nonetheless, the black revolution in Haiti provided a powerful model of political resistance for people of African descent in New Orleans.

Political and cultural resistance was incorporated in the black community's efforts to subversively invoke various sacred Vodou values in the nineteenth-century Congo Square performances that continued to inform twentieth-century, second-line culture: the sacred nature of the universe; morality based on a fluid African ethos; a communal emphasis on biological and extended family; ritual as a bridge between human beings and their ancestors; respect for elders; wholeness of being—the interdependence of human beings with the forces of nature; a black aesthetics; initiation; healing and coping strategies; and resistance and continuity.[34]

Katherine J. Hagedorn's analysis of how sacred music and dances of Afro-Cuban Santeria were interpreted for secular folklore performances in late-nineteenth- and twentieth-century Cuba is also useful for understanding how secular and sacred performances continued to "inform each other" and "use each other"[35] in Congo Square; this musical influence emerged despite the separation of its music and dances from the metaphysics of Vodou that initiates might encounter in secret religious ceremonies. She clarifies how the "sacred intent"[36] of the participants and the language of African drums and dances influence the dynamic interaction between secular performance and sacred elements of African diasporic religious traditions:

> It has been through the lens of folklore performances that I have framed . . . the religious, and now it is through the lens of religious performance that I frame . . . the folklore. . . . [B]oth involve and invoke aspects of the sacred. What is sacred . . . is the connection of the utterances—created and received, gestural and musical—to constructs of the divine. This relationship is determined by intent, which in turn is negotiated among all the participants in performance, whether they are the audience members and musicians at a folklore performance or the ritual assistants and priests at a religious ceremony.[37]

The subtle angle of political agency in Hagedorn's focus on the "intent" and "utterances"[38] of the participants in African diasporic performances is connected to other theoretical writings about hegemony and resistance, or what has sometimes been called "the infrapolitics of subordinate groups."[39] There is a major discourse about what defines, and who gets to use, the spaces of a dissident culture. This discourse has been highlighted, in regard to Congo Square, above all by Daniel E. Walker. Walker considers the Congo Square performances to be "counterstatements to the social control designs of . . . slave societies,"[40] and he analyzes the interaction between sacred and secular in the performances, in the context of African diasporic "festival arts in the Americas during the period of slavery."[41] In his view, white domination and black subordination was emphasized in the various ways that nineteenth-century New Orleans slave owners assaulted the social, cultural, and psychological health of all African-descended New Orleanians to make their domination seem natural.[42]

The Municipal Council constructed the city's "public spaces"[43] so that people of African descent associated certain spaces with the terror and violence of slavery, which attempted to destroy the black family, positive images of African identity, and "group consciousness"[44] among free people of color (who were both black and racially mixed) and slaves.

New Orleans housed the largest slave market in the United States. In spaces on Chatres Street in the French Quarter and in the Central Business District, "100,000 men, women, and children were packaged, priced, and sold," and hundreds of slaves were imprisoned in slave pens surrounded by twenty-foot walls in the French Quarter during the selling season from September to May.[45] Another devastating assault on the black community that reified domination occurred in the Orleans Ballroom, where quadroon balls took place weekly. Here racially mixed women of African descent and white men danced and formalized plaçage, or institutionalized concubinage where sex was exchanged for money. According to Monique Guillory, "the fine cedar parquet of the quadroon balls amounted to little more than the rough planks of the auction block—each supporting a financial trade in raced bodies."[46] Finally, slave owners often sent their slaves to the New Orleans police jail on Chartres Street to be tortured in public spectacles in which slaves were beaten with whips until bloody strips of their skin were cut from the flesh of their quivering naked bodies.[47]

Walker writes that all these measures served as "barriers to the formation of conjugal units, the denigration of black men as potential partners, the objectification of the black female as an outlet for white male sexual desires, and the total disrespect for issues surrounding childbirth and parenting" in a city in which nineteenth-century black "women both slave and free, outnumbered their potential marital partners about two to one."[48] But these subordinate New Orleanians, faced with their seeming powerlessness, devised strategies for creating their own social space in Congo Square, and they became proficient in the arts of political disguise, perpetuating an infrapolitics of resistance to counter the assaults on their community.

The African festival arts in Congo Square focused on the communal family ethos of Vodou and the importance of black male-female relationships. These resistance themes were expressed through the performance of the bamboula and calinda dances by couples with gender-designated roles in dancing circles and lines.[49] According to Walker, these dances demonstrated a wish to reconstruct "the social landscape in a manner that directly contradicted the state of affairs dictated by the slave regime. . . . Despite the fact that many of their peers shunned any association with black men, these women who came to Congo Square embraced them."[50] Moreover, there was a dynamic interaction between the sacred and the secular in the "West and West Central African festival model"[51] that informed the performances in nineteenth-century Congo Square. Therefore, the resistance strategies of the men and women who danced with one another were also fraught with spiritual significance. In the Vodou religion, men and women dancing in sensual union are reminiscent of the African ancestral spirits who were married to each other at the beginning of time, such as Danbala Wedo, "the ancient sky father" and Ayida Wedo, "his rainbow wife."[52] Thus the dances of male-female couples symbolized sacred social values and rites of passage such as marriage, procreation, and the birth of children.[53]

West African festivals are "moving spectacles, kaleidoscope of colors in which the relationship between the secular and the spiritual is reinforced and the complementarities between art and life are reinvigorated."[54] In Congo Square's re-creation of these festivals, dance accompanied masking, iconography, and music, and had the potential in this context to initiate spirit possession and the animation of masks and icons that were important for the spiritual and social values of the black community. Through drumming, spirit possession, and the use of icons and masks (which embody ancestral spirits), performers in nineteenth-century Congo Square and twentieth-century second lines might pray to, communicate with, and receive guidance from the spirit world, remembering and reconnecting spiritually with African family networks destroyed by slavery.[55] These connections between dance, music, masking, and the ancestral spirit world are so powerful in the African diaspora that one Vodouist in Benin said, "It is our blood that is dancing."[56]

Indeed, the arrival of thousands of Haitian immigrants, particularly free persons of color and slaves in late-eighteenth- and early-nineteenth-century New Orleans, created a critical mass of black French-speaking people who resisted Americanization after the Louisiana Purchase in 1803 and continued the resistance strategies and traditions of Afro-Creole Vodou into a golden age of development that ended in the aftermath of the American Civil War in the 1860s. Despite the brutalities of slavery in Louisiana, and in the rest of the American South, black antebellum New Orleans, like Haiti, was predominantly Catholic and Creole with a fluid "three-caste racial system: whites, free persons of color, and slaves" that comprised a unique multicultural society.[57] As numerous black Haitians and black New Orleanians intermarried at the Ursulines Chapel and St. Louis Cathedral, many provocative spiritual exchanges undoubtedly occurred between Haitian and New Orleans Vodou adepts, and these exchanges created the environment for the ascendancy of the famous nineteenth-century New Orleans Vodou queen Marie Laveau (1801?–1881), a descendant of Crescent City slaves who inspired both Zora Neale Hurston's initiation and second-line performances in the twentieth century.[58]

Marie Laveau and the Vodou Priesthood

Marie Laveau is the great name of Negro conjure in America.

ZORA NEALE HURSTON, "HOODOO IN AMERICA"

I knew a conjure lady not long ago . . .
She was known throughout the nation as the Voodoo queen . . .
To the Voodoo lady they all would go—
The rich, the educated, the ignorant, and the poor.
She'd snap her fingers and shake her head
And tell them bout their lovers living or dead . . .
Marie Laveau, The Voodoo queen
Way down yonder in New Orleans.

DEJAN'S OLYMPIA BRASS BAND, *NEW ORLEANS' JAZZ!*

Marie Laveau's ancestral legacy and legendary spiritual powers are a central element in Zora Neale Hurston's twentieth-century religious narratives of Vodou and in the religious domain of twentieth-century, second-line bands such as Dejan's Olympia Brass Band as well as jazz musicians such as Sidney Bechet and Jelly Roll Morton, also Creole Catholics whose nineteenth-century descendants might have known Marie Laveau. Hurston notes in her narrative that three of the Vodou doctors with whom she studied were "New Orleans, Catholic" and had an ancestral connection to the powers of Marie Laveau.[59]

An autonomous Vodou priesthood, similar to the Haitian *manbos* and *houngans,* emerged in early-nineteenth-century New Orleans. Certainly the timing of the priesthood's emergence was connected to the arrival of thousands of Haitian immigrants in the Crescent City and their connections to Vodou. Numerous nineteenth-century New Orleans priestesses and priests, called queens and doctors, included Marie Saloppé, Sanité Dédé, Betsey Toledano, Marie Laveau, Doctor Jim Alexander (Charles Lafontaine), and Doctor John (Jean Montanée).[60]

Marie Laveau, a Catholic free woman of color and the most important spiritual leader in this group, was born in New Orleans probably in 1801. Her connection to Haiti began with her first husband, Jacques Paris, a free man of color who was born in St. Domingue; the couple married in St. Louis Cathedral in 1819 and had two daughters, Marie Angèlie and Felicité. Although the marriage lasted only a few years and Jacques disappeared mysteriously between 1822 and 1824, Laveau most likely developed a perspective about the power of Vodou as political resistance from her husband's experiences in his native land. Throughout her adult life she was known in the black community as a devout Catholic who attended daily mass at St. Louis Cathedral, which was one of the crossroads (i.e., community sites that are significant as sacred spaces) for the Haiti–New Orleans Vodou connection in the nineteenth century, as most of the city's free women of color were members of the congregation.[61] According to Ina Fandrich:

> This congregation [St. Louis Cathedral] was probably one of most integrated places in the world at the time and thus became a safe haven for free women of color who soon formed the majority of the parish membership. . . . It is not surprising that most New Orleanian Voodoo worshippers—including Marie Laveaux, and many other prominent priestesses, most of whom were free women of color—were also members of this progressive church. The Vodou religion, whether in its Haitian or its New Orleanian form . . . found a strange home under Catholic auspices where what appeared on the surface to be Christian symbols and rituals was abundantly filled and redefined with African spirit and meanings.[62]

Marie Laveau reigned as the Vodou queen of New Orleans from the 1820s to the 1870s, when Vodou reached its highest point of development as an organized religion in New Orleans under her extraordinary leadership.[63] According to Fandrich, Laveau was such a powerful priestess because she exemplified

> the Haitian concept of priesthood . . . [the head of a] spiritual house; i.e.,
> the worship societies similar to the humfor [spiritual house] societies in
> Haiti, and beyond [her] immediate followers . . . [she] served the larger
> community as a consultant in all aspects of life drawing from [her] divinatory skills and as public healer (because of [her] medicinal, psychological,
> and spiritual knowledge).[64]

We shall see later on that this model of leadership probably influenced the second-line secret societies of twentieth-century New Orleans Mardi Gras Indian tribes. Laveau's extensive spiritual work among prisoners condemned to death in the New Orleans parish prison, her nursing of yellow fever epidemic victims, as well as her individual spiritual consultations and distributions of gris-gris at her house on 152 St. Ann Street made her an extraordinary healer and spiritual head of a co-dependent, extended religious family network in New Orleans that included plantation slaves, maroons, free blacks, racially mixed people of color, and white women. Choctaw women camped in her backyard. Perhaps more than any other New Orleanian in her time, she was able to penetrate the boundaries of race, class, color, gender, and religion to establish a profound African spiritual presence in New Orleans that would continue to inspire Vodou adepts in Haiti and Louisiana in the twentieth century and participants in second lines.[65]

Indeed, in Hurston's initiation under Samuel Thompson, there is evidence of a continuation of the Haitian model of the "spiritual house," or humfor, society in early-twentieth-century New Orleans. Hurston's narrative noted the numerous initiates who worshiped in Thompson's house and participated in her initiation: "Many came into the room and performed ceremonial acts. But none spoke to me. Nor could I speak to them while the veil covered my face. Then Samuel entered and all the others retired."[66]

Finally, it was Marie Laveau's altars, rituals, and sacred dances consecrated to the lwa, particularly Danbala Wedo, at her first house on St. Ann Street and on Lake Pontchartrain in St. John the Baptist Eve ceremonies that created her strongest spiritual connection to Haitian

Vodou and inspired Hurston's initiation in the 1920s. Hurston wrote: "Every St. John Eve she [Marie Laveau] used to rise out of the lake with a huge communion candle burning on top of her head and one in each hand . . . as she rose from the bottom of the lake and walked to the shore upon the water."[67]

Hurston and second-line performers mapped the sites of Laveau's spiritual work as sacred ancestral spaces for twentieth-century New Orleans Vodou and for second-line culture. Hurston's initiation occurred in Samuel Thompson's House on Rampart Street (which intersects St. Ann Street and is across the street from Congo Square) and in the swamp along Lake Pontchartrain. She introduces these sites as important landmarks in the narrative of her initiation:

> On Thursday morning at eleven I was at the shuttered door of the ancient house. He let me in cheerfully and led me straight to the altar. There were new candles unlit. He signaled me to help. We dressed the candles and lit them and set three upon tumblers filled with honey, three filled with syrup, and three with holy water, and set them in a semi-circle upon the altar. A huge bouquet of flowers was in the center [and several days later] . . .
>
> Samuel led us on a truck . . . until a certain spot was reached . . . the swamp was dismal and damp, but after some stumbly walking we came to a little glade deep in the wood, near the lake.[68]

Laveau's spiritual and political power as a Vodou priestess, constructed from the Haitian concept of religious leadership, created a safe haven for New Orleans' Vodou adepts and neutralized the impact of police and Anglo-Protestant persecution of her followers until the end of her leadership in the 1870s. Thereafter a mysterious woman, mentioned in the Louisiana Writers' Project interviews as "Marie II" (probably not Laveau's daughter, Marie Heloise Euchariste Glapion), assumed leadership of the New Orleans Vodou community, but she was never able to reestablish the spiritual or political power that Marie Laveau had created. By the end of the nineteenth century, all the great Vodou doctors and queens were deceased, and New Orleans Vodou went underground as the federal, state, and city government and black and white American Protestant leaders attempted to destroy the folk religion of the African diaspora in Louisiana. This hostile political environment influenced the practice of New Orleans Vodou and the development of second-line culture in the era of Hurston's initiation.[69]

The Initiation of Zora Neale Hurston: Fragments of the Haitian Model of Initiation in New Orleans Vodou

I have landed in the kingdom of Marie Laveau
and expect to wear her crown some day.

ZORA NEALE HURSTON, "LETTER TO LANGSTON HUGHES"

A man or woman becomes a Hoodoo doctor in three ways: by
heredity, by serving an apprenticeship under an established
practitioner or by the "call" . . . there is general belief that the
power can be transmitted, and for this reason most of the old
doctors in New Orleans claim kinship with Marie Laveau.

ZORA NEALE HURSTON, "HOODOO IN AMERICA"

As the Americanization of Franco-Africans in New Orleans acceler-
ated and the white American Protestant racial order replaced the tripar-
tite racial system of antebellum Franco-Catholic New Orleans in the
last decades of the nineteenth century, the status and fortunes of the
New Orleans Creoles of Color declined rapidly, and some immigrated to
Haiti, France, or Mexico before the Civil War. Although multicultural
black New Orleanians entered the twentieth century compromised significantly by the new American Jim Crow system, they comprised half
the city's population. They thus found new ways to resist the assaults on
their African diaspora culture, including the termination of the Sunday
African dances at Congo Square in the 1860s, and to continue to practice Vodou.[70] The intimate exchange between Haitian and New Orleans
Vodou continued in the old downtown Creole neighborhoods, where
Hurston was later initiated and second-line culture developed. According to Ina Fandrich: "Since boats and secret messages constantly went
back and forth between the island [Haiti] and the metropolis in the Mississippi Delta, a secret traffic of Voodoo paraphernalia and supplies . . .
might have been among the underground exchange items."[71] The continuity of these secretive African diasporic exchanges reflected the need
for Vodou adepts and second-line performers to create their own social
space, to develop proficiency in the art of political disguise.

Hurston arrived in New Orleans in 1928 to begin her apprenticeship as a Vodou initiate:

> I was told that I must begin my novitiate. I must sleep for nine nights with my right stocking on. I must have clean thoughts. I must neither defile body nor spirit. Certain monies were necessary for the ceremony. I paid the sum. I was told to be seated before the altar and offer myself with absolute sincerity to the Great One. But once I was seated I was not to utter a sound. When the spirit was through with me I must leave in silence.[72]

As Hurston experienced her initiation, she found a religion that had undergone several profound changes since the beginning of the twentieth century. These changes occurred in the context of the Haiti–New Orleans Vodou connection and also affected the performance strategies of second liners who subversively incorporated elements of Vodou in their public and private rituals. Many New Orleans Vodou initiates were compelled to disguise their religion as spiritualism—"a technique for communication with the dead"—because of the American government's campaign to eradicate Vodou in Haiti and Louisiana.[73] The capstone of this campaign was the U.S. occupation of Haiti and the persecution of the nation's Vodou leaders from 1915 to 1934, actions motivated by American imperialism in the Caribbean and Central America. American stereotypes of Haitian Vodou expressed in sensational images of bloodthirsty orgies and human sacrifices provided part of the rationale for the criminalization of the Vodou religion in Louisiana. In October 1928 Hurston quickly moved from her first residence in Algiers (which is across the Mississippi River from New Orleans) because of police pressure on the Vodouists there. She found a new home in the city of New Orleans on 2744 Amelia Street.[74] Long has summarized the punitive actions levied against some Vodou leaders in New Orleans:

> Beginning in 1909, federal mail fraud laws were invoked against practitioners who conducted businesses by mail; conviction of mail fraud carried a penitentiary sentence. The Louisiana Board of Health, under the 1924 Medical Practice Act, prosecuted persons accused of practicing medicine without a license. A 1929 revision imposed a fifty-to-one hundred dollar fine or a sentence of ten to ninety days in the parish prison. In 1897, 1916, and 1924, the city of New Orleans instituted statutes against fortune-telling and obtaining money under false pretenses.[75]

Faced with these penalties, some Protestant Vodou initiates formed a protective shelter in the Spiritual churches of New Orleans. Hurston elaborates on this new synthetic layer of New Orleans Vodou: "Hoodooism is in disrepute, and certain of its practices forbidden by law. A spiritualistic name protects the congregation, and is a useful device of protective coloration."[76] Spiritual churches such as the Eternal Life Spiritual Church were first established by Mother Leafy Anderson in 1918. They included aspects of Vodou, Pentecostalism, Spiritualism, and Catholicism, with elaborate altars to ancestors, saints, and spirit guides, as well as worship services featuring female priests and mothers who prophesized and performed healings during ecstatic trances. Numerous twentieth-century Mardi Gras Indians also found a Christian refuge that resonated with second-line culture in Spiritual churches that revered the spirit of Black Hawk. At the same time some Catholic Creoles of Color disguised their connection to Vodou through spiritualist séances led by mediums who received detailed messages in French from the spirit world. René Grandjean, who was born in France and lived in Haiti for several years, kept written records of these Creole séances in New Orleans.[77]

Despite these restrictions, Hurston continued to experience the stages of her initiation:

> I sat obedient before the altar, shivering unknowingly. I knew when I was dismissed. I rose and turned from the altar. Then Samuel spoke "The spirit says you must bring three snake skins next time." I passed with bowed head. . . . At the end of the nine days I returned with the skins and again sat before the altar. . . . He prepared the skins and placed them before the Great One. He called him and admonished him to enter into the skins and give them life.[78]

Indeed, all these profound changes in the culture of black New Orleans and its connection to Haiti produced hoodoo.[79] This magical emphasis in Vodou attracted Hurston and also influenced the performances and rituals of second-line secret societies in her time. She studied with nine different Vodou doctors during her months in New Orleans. Speaking of one of these doctors, Luke Turner, she explains: "When I found out about Turner, I had already studied under five two-headed doctors and had gone thru an initiation ceremony with each. So I asked Turner to take me as a pupil."[80]

In *Mules and Men* and "Hoodoo in America," several of the doctors were assigned different names to protect them from prosecution. For example, Luke Turner, in *Mules and Men*, was called Samuel Thompson in "Hoodoo in America"; Anatol Pierre, in *Mules and Men*, was Albert Frechard in "Hoodoo in America"; Father Joe Watson, in *Mules and Men*, was also known as Father Sims in "Hoodoo in America"; and Kitty Brown, in *Mules and Men*, was called Ruth Mason in "Hoodoo in America." Drs. Duke, Samuel Jenkins, Strong, Grant, and Barnes, however, were assigned one name in both narratives. All these doctors were Vodou priests and priestesses,[81] and the most powerful of the group, Luke Turner, was a nephew of Marie Laveau, whose spiritual power came from that nineteenth-century ancestral connection. In *Mules and Men* Turner remembered his aunt, New Orleans' most powerful manbo in the Haitian model of priesthood, whose favorite lwa was Danbala Wedo, symbolized by the snake, and certainly his memories of Congo Square, which follow, were the inspiration for twentieth-century, second-line lyrics and tunes:

> Time went around pointing out what God had already made. Moses had seen the Burning Bush. Solomon by magic, knowed all wisdom. . . . And Marie Laveau was a woman in New Orleans . . . Alexander the great two-headed doctor felt the power in her and so he told her she must come to study with him. Marie . . . rather dance and make love, but one day a rattlesnake come to her in her bedroom and spoke to her. So she went to Alexander and studies but soon she could teach her teacher and the snake stayed with her always. . . . People come from all ends to America to get help from her . . . she hold Hoodoo dance in Congo Square every week . . . and everybody dance like they do in Hayti.[82]

In "Hoodoo in America," Hurston assigned Luke Turner the new name of Samuel Thompson and explicated the source of his ancestral wisdom and its roots in Haiti:

> Samuel Thompson is in his seventies, a Catholic Hoodoo doctor of New Orleans. He has a snake skin, which he says is the skin of the great snake that served her [Marie Laveau] altar. . . . Samuel Thompson always wrapped his snakeskin about him before attempting any serious work. His mother

was a Hoodoo worker and her mother before her. He says that his remote ancestors brought the power with them from "the rock" (Africa) and that his forbears lived in Santo Domingo before they came to the region of New Orleans.[83]

In the nineteenth century powerful Vodou priestesses such as Marie Laveau were spiritual heads of their own humfor societies or sanctuaries. The new restrictions on Vodou adepts in early-twentieth-century New Orleans forced some leaders and their initiates to form secret societies such as Mardi Gras Indian tribes like the Creole Wild West and the Yellow Pocahontas that continued selected aspects of Vodou traditions in their sequin art, Creole dance and musical rituals, and secret initiations in downtown neighborhoods. Their traditions were related thematically to those of Haiti's sequin artists who create the flags used in Vodou ceremonies. In addition, the Mardi Gras Indians' suits included sequined pouches, sometimes called "Congo pacquets," inspired by Haitian Vodou healers and embedded with spiritual power.[84]

In Hurston's mystical initiation into Vodou in Samuel Thompson's house, as well as in her spiritual work with the other priests and priestesses, there is evidence of a secret society of magic similar to the Haitian secret societies, specifically Bizango. Those Haitian societies were known for their powerful magic and administration of justice. They were "societies of the night . . . bound by oath" and magical rituals at the crossroads of life and death—in the cemeteries and the forests.[85]

Hurston's account of her initiation brings to light some of the themes of these secret societies, as well as some of the traditional aspects of initiation in Haitian Vodou such as separation, liminality, incorporation, fasting, abstinence from sexual relations, spiritual bathing in herbs, psychic experience, trance, apprenticeship, purification (couché, which means to become initiated), acquisition of knowledge of the lwa and magical rituals, and ritual sacrifice. Many of these themes undoubtedly were also incorporated into the initiations of other twentieth-century, second-line secret societies in New Orleans. However, the central theme in the final narrative of Hurston's initiation into New Orleans Vodou that follows is a relationship between religion and magic that Rachel Beauvoir-Dominique describes as at the heart of Haitian Vodou in the secret societies:

> Vodou emerged with a fundamental vision in which religion and magic, though autonomous, nevertheless constitutes a single body. . . . Each temple, even the most religious in outlook, is under the patronage of one or several . . . divinities destined to work, render service and even amass small fortunes for their possessors. During ceremony, these lwa are summoned, not worshipped. In exchange for periodic ritual feeding, the lwa are expected to protect and soothsay through regular sessions of divination. And they must also carry out therapeutic magic: lucrative treatments and exorcisms will fall under the responsibility of the Vodou divinities of which failings are hardly tolerated. . . . Ritual, medicine, and further techniques of manipulation intertwine informed by a common vision of self in which maneuverable human spiritual entities flow in relationship with other forces, all intermingling in the essence of a higher power. The vision emerges from a constantly evolving world and the possibility of adaptation, change, and amelioration.[86]

Beauvoir-Dominique's brilliant analysis of the spiritual and social realm of Vodou's magical practices speaks to the powerful spiritual philosophy of social justice, healing, and resistance to domination that continues to connect the rituals of Vodou initiates in Haiti and New Orleans with second-line performance groups such as the Mardi Gras Indians in the twenty-first century. In Hurston's final religious narratives we experience the wholeness of being, the co-dependence of men, women, plants, animals, and the spirits as Vodou initiates work the cosmic energies of the universe in magical healing rituals that affirm the humanity and central importance of ordinary black folk in spirit work. Although Hurston is silent about the details of her possession-performances and the identities of the lwa, the altars are the faces of the lwa and the crossroads of a powerful ancestral spirit world, shared by West and Central Africans, Haitians, and New Orleanians in their rituals.[87]

The following excerpt from Hurston's initiation narrative is important for students and practitioners of Vodou in Haiti and New Orleans as the first reliable record of a Vodou initiation in the United States:

> Then I rose from the altar and helped prepare the sacred couch, that is, the moccasin hide was fixed to green cloth and spread over the couch in the altar room. My sacred garments were made, including the crown. At three o'clock, naked as I came into the world, I was stretched face downwards with my navel to the serpent and a pitcher of water at my head that my spirit might not wander in search of it, and began my three day search for

the favor of the Great One. Three days I must lie silently, that is, my body would be there. My soul would be standing naked before the Spirit to see if he would have me.

I had five psychic experiences during those three days and nights. I shall not detail them here; but I knew that I had been accepted before the sixty-nine hours had passed. Strangely enough, I had no sense of hunger—only exaltation. At eleven o'clock on March 19, St. Joseph's Day, I arose and was led through the running water and again stretched upon my face upon the couch. Samuel approached me with a brother on either side of him. One held a small brush with red paint, the other a brush with yellow paint. With ceremony Samuel painted a lightning symbol down my back from my right shoulder to my left hip. This was to be my sign forever. The Great One shall speak to me in storms. I was now dressed in the new clothes, stockings, underwear, dress and veil. After I was dressed a pair of eyes was painted on my checks just below my eyes as a sign that I could see in more ways than one. The sun was painted on my forehead. . . .

At high noon I was seated at the splendid altar. It was dressed in the center with a huge communion candle with my name upon it set in sand, five large iced cakes in different colors, a plate of honeyed St. Joseph's bread, a plate of serpent-shaped breads, spinach and egg cakes fried in olive oil, breaded Chinese okra fried in olive oil, roast veal and wine, two huge yellow bouquets, two red bouquets and two white bouquets and thirty-six yellow tapers and a bottle of holy water.

Samuel seated me and stood behind me with his ceremonial hat upon his head, and the crown of power in his hand. "Spirit! I ask you to take her. Do you hear me, Spirit? Will you take her? Spirit, I want you to take her, she is worthy!" He held the crown poised above my head for a full minute. A profound silence held the room. Then he lifted the veil from my face and let it fall behind my head and crowned me with power. He lit my candle for me. But from then on I might be a candle lighter myself.

All the candles were reverently lit. We all sat down and ate the feast. First, a glass of blessed oil was handed me by Samuel. Drink this without tasting it. I gulped it down and he took the glass from my hand, took a sip of the little that remained. Then he handed it to the brother at his right who did the same, until it went around the table.

Eat first the spinach cakes, Samuel exhorted, and we did. Then the meal began. It was full of joy and laughter, even though we knew that the final ceremony waited only for the good hour of twelve midnight.

We all piled into an old Studebaker sedan. . . . Out road number 61 we rattled. . . . The sheets of typing paper I had been urged to bring were brought out and nine sheets were blessed and my petition written nine times on each sheet by the light from a shaded lantern. The crate containing the black sheep was opened and the sheep led forward into the center for the circle. He stood there dazed while the chant of strange syllables rose. I asked Samuel the words, but he replied that in good time I would know what to say. . . . A knife flashed and the sheep dropped to its knees, then fell prone with its mouth open in a weak cry. My petition was thrust into its throat that he might cry it to the Great One. The broom was seized and dipped in the blood from the slit throat and the ground swept vigorously—back and forth, back and forth—the length of the dying sheep. The sweeping went on as long as the blood gushed. Earth, the mother of the Great One and us all had been appeased. With a sharp stick Samuel traced the outline of the sheep then the digging commenced. The sheep was never touched. The ground was dug from under him so that his body dropped down into the hole. He was covered with the nine sheets of paper bearing the petition and the earth heaped upon him. A white candle was set upon the grave and we straggled back to the road and the Studebaker.[88]

This moving narrative of Hurston's ritual initiation reveals both her gifts as a writer and her professional talent as an ethnographer. Most striking about the narration, however, is Hurston's transformation into a servant of the spirits, one of the true spiritual folk who decided to enter the liminal territory of Vodou initiation that re-created the African ancestral bridge between black communities in Haiti and those in New Orleans in the twentieth century. As an initiate of Vodou, Hurston stripped herself naked, shedding her Western identities as a writer and anthropologist to assume the serious responsibility of introspection within the context of the African diasporic spirit world. The majesty and awe of the Vodou lwa inspire this narrative of Hurston's initiation. Clearly she was chosen to tap the wisdom of the ancestors and the healing powers of Danbala Wedo and Oyá.

Significance of Hurston's Initiation for the African Diasporic Spirit World

This analysis underlines the religious significance of Zora Neale Hurston's narratives of a lived religious experience. Her writings provide a record of her courage and insight as a woman of the spirit world and link her to the religious domain of early-twentieth-century second-line culture. She was the first African American scholar to launch herself into

the uncharted waters of Vodou initiation and to emerge from her profound experience as an authentically initiated adept. She is also the first
to have left a written record of her spiritual journey.

The spiritual journey of her initiation rites followed the three classic
stages of initiation—"separation," "transition," and "incorporation"—
formulated by Arnold Van Gennep.[89] The new sense of folk community
and collective consciousness established among the Vodou initiates in
early-twentieth-century New Orleans is a source of continuity between
Haitian and New Orleans initiation rites and inspires many second-line
performance groups.

Victor Turner's work is instructive here. Building on the ideas of
Van Gennep, Turner developed his theory of "ritual anti-structure,"
which focused on the "liminal period" of initiation when initiates were
considered "betwixt and between" social statuses in society.[90] Turner
regarded this period, where initiates learned new knowledge about the
structure of their community, "as a [transitional] process, a becoming,
and . . . even a transformation." He proposed that in the midst of the new
social energy that emerged among initiates during the liminal period,
"ritual often acted as a form of protest against the existing social structure and contributed to social change."[91]

Connected to this ritual anti-structure was "communitas," a new
sense of community among initiates during the liminal period. Turner
believed that communitas transformed the structure of society by generating new moods, feelings, and bonds among the initiates that infused
and revived the society with new anti-structural values during and after
initiation.[92] The ideas of communitas and liminality help us understand
the significance of Hurston's initiation and the public and secret rites
of second-line performers as transformative rituals that promoted racial self-definition, gender equality, healing, and resistance to negative
stereotypes of Vodou adepts and African diaspora culture in New Orleans and Haiti.

Finally, Hurston's initiation experience is a model for Beauvoir-
Dominique's vision of Vodou, "in which religion and magic . . . consti-
tute a single body."[93] In the last stage of the rituals in the swamp, the lwa
and mother earth are fed with the sacrifice of a black sheep,[94] clearly a
gesture of "therapeutic magic" to insure that Hurston's initiation will
promote protection, healing, and spiritual power for all the initiates who

performed the rites.[95] Here the provocative connection between Vodou adepts and the spirit world is highlighted in magical "techniques of manipulation" of the cosmic energies of the "Great One," who created the universe.[96]

Conclusion

In the late 1930s, Zora Neale Hurston resumed her research into the mysteries of Vodou with two years of fieldwork in Haiti and Jamaica. The result of that research, *Tell My Horse: Voodoo and Life in Haiti and Jamaica*, was published in 1938. Although she is celebrated primarily as a Harlem Renaissance literary figure and a folklore collector in Florida, her research and religious experience are also important for understanding the profound and enduring connection between Haitian and New Orleans Vodou and its relation to the religious domain of second-line culture.[97]

Today many black New Orleanians acknowledge the persistence of the Haiti–New Orleans Vodou connection into the new millennium: well-known New Orleans Vodou priestesses such as Ava Kay Jones have traveled to Haiti for initiation as manbos, "Haitian-style" Vodou services are conducted for initiates, and Haitian Vodou supplies are sold in botanicas in the city's downtown neighborhoods.[98]

Finally, in 1996, the annual New Orleans Jazz and Heritage Festival (which celebrates second-line culture and the West African festival values of Congo Square) re-creates the spiritual and musical connections between Haiti and Louisiana by showcasing the music and culture of Haiti in its first International Pavilion. Festival organizers explained their version of the Haiti–New Orleans connection:

> Several Haitian musicians, bands, and dancers are performing at this year's festivals, expressing the myriad of rhythms that distinguish their homeland: compas, the dance music genre . . .; Rara, carnival music highlighted by colorful parades that are similar to New Orleans' second lines; and racine, a musical genre that enhances Voodoo's rhythms with electric instruments. . . .
>
> Serving as master of ceremonies for the pavilion is Aboudja Derenoncourt, a respected priest and master drummer who leads audiences through an exploration of Haitian history and cultural traditions—traditions that New Orleanians will find complements those of their own.[99]

TWO

Mardi Gras Indians and Second Lines, Sequin Artists and Rara Bands: Street Festivals and Performances in New Orleans and Haiti

New Orleans is the most African city in the United States. . . . We have been playing music for generations that has its foundations in Africa.

IRVIN MAYFIELD, LOS HOMBRES CALIENTES

New Orleans' status as a sacred city in the African diaspora derives from the profound influences of two distinct cultures: the city's Mardi Gras Indian tribes, with their second-line street performances and festival parades, and the sequin artists and Rara bands of Haiti. The African diasporic connections between these two societies may be seen in their musical traditions and material art, the latter evidenced in the creative use of sequins, beads, and feathers sewn into flags and dancers' costumes. Both flags and costumes are important African diasporic symbols in the parades and festivals of secret societies of drummers, dancers, and chanters who perform in healing rituals and dance competitions at significant crossroads in the black communities of New Orleans and Haiti. The Black Indian "gangs" that were to become today's Mardi Gras tribes originated in late-nineteenth-century New Orleans as a Carnival performance tradition expressing the African diasporic memories of Congo Square (the birthplace of jazz) and the resistance strategies of African-Amerindian maroon communities during slavery.[1]

Two kinds of analysis are needed to understand the Africanisms—West and Central African traditions in the New World—specific to New Orleans. The first is a "triangular mode of inquiry" to explore how select aspects of the spiritual philosophies of Central African religious traditions are reinterpreted in the artistic and religious expressions of African diasporic performance cultures in New Orleans and Haiti.[2] This analysis examines relationships between African continuities in three different locations and draws on the creative research methods developed at the Center for Black Music Research, Columbia College, Chicago, and the work of art historian Robert Farris Thompson.[3] This approach contributes to a broader understanding of how the circum-Caribbean region has influenced African American performance cultures and also integrates analysis "of concrete historical connections" with spiritual "analogies across space and time" in New Orleans and Haiti.[4]

The second analysis develops the implications of the "circum-Atlantic performance" thesis that Joseph Roach brought out in his book, *Cities of the Dead*.[5] According to Roach:

> The concept of the circum-Atlantic world . . . insists on the centrality of the diasporic and genocidal histories of Africa and the Americas in the creation of the culture of modernity. . . . Memories of some particular times and places have become embodied in and through performances . . . to perform . . . means . . . often . . . secretly to reinvent. This claim is especially relevant to the performances that flourish within the geohistorical matrix of the circum-Atlantic world. Bounded by Europe, Africa, and the Americas, North and South, this economic and cultural system entailed vast movements of peoples and commodities to experimental destinations, the consequences of which continue to visit themselves upon the material and human fabric of the cities inhabited by their successors. . . . While a great deal of violence instrumental to the creation [of modernity] may have been officially forgotten, circum-Atlantic memory maintains its consequences; one of which is that the unspeakable cannot be rendered forever inexpressible. . . . Into the cavities united by the loss through death or other forms of departure . . . survivors attempt to fit satisfactory alternatives [through] . . . the process of surrogation.[6]

Roach's focus on memory, performance, and surrogation (the replacement of African memories) highlights New Orleans as the most important American city of the dead, where contemporary circum-Atlantic, second-line performances have had "a continuous history since the eighteenth century" and encompass important traditions in the secret societies examined in this volume.[7]

"Surrogation" defines the "mechanism of . . . [the] perseverance [of

Africanisms]."[8] To fully understand Roach's theory and the influence of Africanisms in the culture of New Orleans' Mardi Gras Indian tribes, it is essential to briefly examine an influential scholarly study that updates Melville Herskovits's groundbreaking work. Craig Steven Wilder's *In the Company of Black Men: The African Influence on African American Culture in New York City* proposes a crucial weakness in Herskovits's *Myth of the Negro Past,* the 1941 book that "sparked the modern debate by exposing West African influences in African American culture."[9] Wilder argues that Herskovits's research does not reveal the "mechanism" of the "reinterpretation of [African] culture" in the Americas, which is the latter's major theoretical contribution to the debate on Africanisms.[10] Joseph Roach's performance theory fills this theoretical gap in Melville Herskovits's *Myth of the Negro Past.* Roach's mechanism of surrogation "as enacted in performance" explains the system of connected processes through which New Orleanians of African descent "fill the voids left by the death and departure" of their ancestors who participated in the original nineteenth-century Congo Square performances.[11] Black residents of the Crescent City constructed new twentieth-century religious and performance identities, namely, the Mardi Gras Indian tribes that reinvented and performed "their pasts" at the crossroads "between history and memory" and "remembrance and forgetting."[12] These new identities and performances were expressed in the context of second-line secret societies founded after the death of the Vodou queen Marie Laveau in 1881.

Wilder, following Herskovits's and Roach's lead, also sheds light on an important dimension of second-line culture derived from the impact of Africanisms on black New Orleans, namely, the continuity of secret associations. From the African ethnic societies of the enslaved performers in Congo Square to the ritual houses of Zora Neale Hurston's Vodou initiation to the formation of Mardi Gras Indian tribes in late-nineteenth and early-twentieth-century New Orleans, secret associations have played a key role in the replacement and reinterpretation of African memories in New Orleans. Wilder argues that New World African "secret societies—defined by esoteric knowledge, structure, and ritual . . . provided the institutional foundation upon which African American religious, political, and social culture could flourish."[13] He traces the origins of subaltern secret societies, such as the Mardi Gras

Indians, to rebellious eighteenth-century "maroon villages . . . ruled by chiefs"[14] in St. Dominique (Haiti) and to powerful models in premodern West Africa:

> West Africans were familiar with numerous intergenerational, international, and intertribal secret societies, in Africa these bands ranged from benevolent, burial and religious associations to political, martial, criminal, and subversive societies. Some developed secret languages, and adopted signs and rites, imposed ranks with insignia, and kept meeting houses, shrines, and dormitories. . . . The "Society of the Magicians" claimed its genesis around 1600 bc and spread from North to West Africa in the following centuries. 'Si' mo and 'Oro' were the oldest indigenous West African organizations. Their warrior-priests carried them from Guinea and Nigeria to Angola and multiplied their power by spawning kindred associations. From 1100 to 1500 ad, Mande traders and smiths spread secret societies along the commercial roots of West Africa. . . . By the seventeenth century societies [were] the repositories of folklore, myths and history and the conceptions of art and culture and learning and wisdom that the tribes possessed. Moreover they became the teachers of these things.[15]

The second-line performances of the Mardi Gras Indian tribes express, as we shall see, a "ritualized memory" of subversive surrogation and also re-create select aspects of the secret societies of Haitian Vodou, Central and West African religious symbols, and "Afro-Amerindian maroon communities."[16] African and Native American cultural elements were integral to extraordinary Afro-Creole dance and musical traditions performed every Sunday in Congo Square until the late nineteenth century.[17]

The continuity of the Congo Square performances reflected both the significant influence of Haitian immigrants on the religious life of the city and the public acceptance of Creole New Orleans as the center for Vodou in the United States. However, the important point here is that the beginning of the Jim Crow era in the late nineteenth century marked a period of intense Americanization of New Orleans and the related criminalization and persecution of Vodouists. In this context, the Carnival performance tradition of the Mardi Gras Indians was born. The Black Indians used their secret societies to resist the city government's attempts to de-Africanize the spirituality and culture of New Orleans and to mask their political activities, which included violent confrontations with white mobs on Carnival day in the early twentieth century.[18] Building on the memories of Congo Square, contemporary performance expressions in second-line New Orleans street festivals continue to re-create flashes of African spiritual energy and political power and, in so doing, are strikingly similar to the performances of Haitian Rara bands and the work of sequin artists.

These considerations raise a number of important questions. How do the contemporary performances of Rara bands and second lines express historical African diasporic musical and spiritual unities and re-sistance strategies to oppression? How is the musical tradition of New Orleans jazz exemplified by second-line culture and Mardi Gras Indian performances? How did the early New Orleans Mardi Gras Indian tribes reinterpret Kongo and Haitian religious symbols and performance tra-ditions? And how do contemporary Mardi Gras Indians, exemplified by the case study of the Montana family, re-create aspects of the spiritual power of Haitian sequin artists in their festivals and performances?

Rara Bands and Second Lines:
African Diasporic Unities at the Crossroads

New Orleans is the last frontier ... because everything culminates here. The Mississippi River is the Nile. All these musics are cousins, and mother is Africa, and everyone comes and visits their cousin [New Orleans].

BILL SUMMERS, LOS HOMBRES CALIENTES

The musical and spiritual philosophy of the contemporary New Orleans music group Los Hombres Calientes—featuring percussionist Bill Sum-mers and trumpeter Irvin Mayfield—represents the spirit of the African diasporic links between Rara bands in Haiti and second lines in Loui-siana. The group's focus on the historical and spiritual crossroads be-tween New Orleanian and Haitian performance traditions highlights ways in which these two musical traditions encompass and express simi-lar African diasporic spiritual philosophies. Mayfield and Summers spent time in Haiti, Trinidad, Jamaica, Brazil, and Cuba to re-create "Congo Square music"—the music of the second lines, the Mardi Gras Indians, and the Vodou rites of Haiti and New Orleans because, according to Summers, "all these African people came together . . . [in Congo Square] and created what is known as jazz."[19] Analysis of these relationships between New Orleans and Haiti requires first a brief explication of the larger traditions of Vodou music and jazz exemplified by Rara and the second lines.

RARA AND THE MUSIC OF HAITIAN VODOU

Haitian Vodou music can be traced to the culture and resistance strategies of the African slaves brought to Saint Domingue from Dahomey and the Kongo during the colonial period. On the slave plantations and in maroon communities, these slaves, and "Creoles of African descent," developed the Kreyol language, the Vodou religion, and a complex musical tradition of dancing, drumming, and singing that reflected their devotion to the African spirit world and their resistance to oppression that culminated with the Haitian revolution and Haiti's independence in 1804.[20] The sacred music of Vodou includes ancient Rada rituals, based on the Fon culture of Dahomey; Kongo—Petwo rituals, rooted in the Central African culture of the ancient Kongo kingdoms; and Bizango, the Haitian secret societies that protect the community. Each of these primary Vodou rites has created a complex musical tradition with regional variations using specific dances, songs, drums, and other musical instruments to serve the spirits.[21]

The ultimate purpose of the music is devotion to and "direct communication" with the Vodou spirits. The range of the performance of this religious music includes the ritual dances of priests, priestesses, and initiates for possession by the lwa; music that accompanies people as they construct ritual items such as flags, drums, and altar decorations; and Haitian popular music from the 1950s to the present inspired by the spiritual work and political resistance of Vodou.[22] The popular music includes the dance music of compas, Vodou-jazz, and the contemporary "roots music" of groups such as Ram and Boukman Eksperyans, who perform songs called "Vodou Adjae."[23] Their songs mix musical traditions from "the dance floor and the Vodou temple."[24]

Elizabeth McAlister, who has done ethnographic research on Rara bands, one of the most vibrant aspects of Haitian Vodou music, describes Rara as

> the yearly festival in Haiti, that even more than carnival, belongs to the so-called peasant classes and the urban poor. Beginning the moment carnival ends, on the eve of Lent, and building for six weeks until Easter Week, Rara processions walk for miles through local territory, attracting fans and singing new and old songs. Bands stop traffic for hours to play music and perform rituals for Afro-Haitian deities at crossroads, bridges, and cemeteries. They are conducting the spiritual work that becomes necessary when the angels and saints, along with Jesus, disappear into the underworld on Good Friday. . . . Rara season is one of the few times that the poor assemble freely, in mass, relatively unharmed, in bands from around thirty people to several thousands. . . . During Rara season the religious and political tensions in Haitian society rise to the surface as religious ritual is brought into the public space, the popular classes confront the power-holders, and Rara bands confront one another.[25]

Rara is a complex Haitian tradition with several musical, dance, and political similarities to the second lines of New Orleans. Perhaps one of most striking African diasporic unities between the two traditions relates to the participants' spiritual work at important crossroads and cemeteries in Haiti and New Orleans. The playful, carnivalesque public dance and musical performances of both Rara bands and second lines often parallel a serious "inner core" of performative work that re-creates memories of slavery and the African past at the crossroads.[26] It is important that the Haitian and New Orleanian performers often dance and play their music on similar routes or sacred spaces.[27] These routes are danced "from home to streets to crossroads to the cemetery."[28] Crossroads, in Kongo culture, are the sites of powerful altars for introspection and prayer, where the ultimate crossroad, the cemetery, offers introspection into the spirit world. In both traditions the crossroads and cemeteries are liminal public spaces—intersections between the supernatural magical realm of African ancestors and spirits and the ritual work of their human descendants. These are also sacred locations where Rara bands and second lines can periodically re-create the substitutions of officially repressed memories of slavery and genocide and thus "infuse" their communities with the healing energies of circum-Atlantic performances.[29] Here, the liminal and healing aspects of these performances at the crossroads echo two themes of Victor Turner's work on "ritual anti-structure": first, "ritual often [acts] as a form of protest against the existing social structure and contributes to social change"; and, second, "communitas," a new sense of community generated during the liminal rituals, infuses and revives society with new anti-structural values.[30]

Certainly Kongoisms—African diasporic unities from Central Africa—animate the spiritual work of both performance traditions. Robert Farris Thompson believes that Kongo-Petwo rites from Central Africa "light up" the music and performances of Haitian Rara bands and also "turn up" as re-created African diasporic unities in early-nineteenth-century Congo Square. Thompson believes that the Kreyol term "Rara" originated in "wala," the Ki-Kongo word for "musicians perambulating in lines and circles."[31] Ethnomusicologist John Storm Roberts writes about the origins of the Rara parades:

> Parades...associated with dancing and...carnivals [of]...the rara bands of Haiti...[and] the New Orleans marching bands...seem to be part of a loose tradition associating dance, music, religion, social function, and royalty...[that] is to be traced to [central] African origins in royal and religious ceremonial.[32]

Thompson's work on Afro-Atlantic altars clarifies the significance of crossroads and cemeteries in the performances of Rara bands and second lines. The Ki-Kongo expression "impambu nzila" means "crossing of paths, crossing, ramification . . . point of reunion, point of separation." In the circum-Atlantic context, the concept of the Kongo crossroads was transported across the Atlantic Ocean to Haiti and New Orleans, where it was re-created in music, dance, and material art performances that consecrated special locations as sites for remembering slavery and the African spirit world.[33]

The spiritual work at the crossroads is a major theme in the lyrics of Rara bands, as illustrated by the following "prayer song":

> Mama asked me where I'm going
> I said to my father's house
> Papa asked me where I'm going
> I said to the crossroads
> Master crossroads asked me where
> I'm going
> I'm going to the cemetery.[34]

Boukman Eksperyans, a contemporary group that plays "roots music" inspired by the rhythms of Rara and Carnival and a reverence for the spirits of Vodou and the grassroots resistance of Boukman (the Vodou priest who organized the slaves during the Haitian revolution),[35] sings about the powerful political and spiritual transformations at the crossroads in the following lyrics: "When we have them at the crossroads, crossroads, judge these bad guys."[36]

The political perspective of this musical group echoes not only the spiritual power of Rara bands at the crossroads but also Rara's political empowerment of the masses to resist domination and define the African diasporic significance of their Haitian Kreyol culture. These ideas are expressed in the following excerpt from the song "We're Creole": "Yes. That's what we are, we're Creole . . . We're the people of the Kongo, let's not be ashamed of it Children of the Kongo, Guinea, Nago People of the Petwo way—People of Dahomey."[37] The political lyrics of Vodou jazz and Haitian roots music suggest provocative links to the themes of solidarity and resistance as expressed in the culture of late-nineteenth-century black New Orleans, and the emergence of the Mardi Gras Indian second lines.

The contemporary global popularity of groups such as Boukman Eksperyans and Ram has brought the spiritual and political energy of Rara bands to the United States. These bands rallied international support for Haiti's political struggles in the 1990s by performing outside the United Nations, in Brooklyn, New York, and on Capitol Hill in Washington, D.C.[38]

Rara performances, like the brass bands and social aid and pleasure clubs of New Orleans' second lines, are organized in several interactive musical and dance phases. The first phase of Rara, according to Elizabeth McAlister, is the "carnivalesque, pou plezi (for pleasure)" when residents of local households view or participate in the dancing and camaraderie of the procession as it passes through their neighborhoods.[39] Certainly this is similar to a familiar scene in New Orleans when second lines pass through black neighborhoods and residents fling open their front doors, run into the street, and synchronize their movements with the dance rhythms of the parading social and pleasure clubs.[40] Rara's second phase involves specific dance performances of "ochan" (musical salute), where the bands stop at important crossroads, such as cemeteries and religious houses, to pay their respects and solicit donations.[41] Similarly downtown and uptown New Orleanian second lines often stop at important crossroads with historical significance for the black community such as Bayou St. John, the intersection of Orleans Avenue and Claiborne Avenue, St. Augustine Church on Governor Nichols Street, the Tremé community center, and around Louis Armstrong Park, which surrounds Congo Square on Rampart Street.[42] The third phase involves the bands' performances during religious rites, including consecrations of musical instruments, spiritual baths for musicians, magical work, and Petwo and Bizango ceremonies in Vodou temples.[43] The religious rites of Vodouists in New Orleans' second lines also sometimes occur on the streets, such as at Chicken Man, Fred Staten's jazz funeral in 1998, when Vodou priestesses temporarily stopped the second line on St. Phillips Street in the French Quarter to pour libations for the famous New Orleanian Vodouist. Second-line parades focusing on Vodou usually conclude in front of the Vodou Spiritual Temple on Rampart Street, where private rituals are performed.[44]

Rara bands vary in their musical instrumentation. Like the second lines, they can be as simple as "a capella chargio-pye" (foot bands) with a tambourine and other simple hand-held percussion instruments, or, like the second-line brass band, they can include a complex orchestra composed of three portable Petwo drums, "vaksin" (bamboo tube instruments used in Bakongo hocketing music), trumpets, conch shells, and percussion instruments, a chorus of singers, and the "sanba"—the leader and songwriter of the band. Distinctive among the dancers in Rara are the "majo jon" (baton jugglers who wear sequined suits) and the "Wa Rara"—the Rara King.[45]

SECOND LINES AND EARLY NEW ORLEANS JAZZ

The connection between New Orleans jazz and second lines becomes clear when we look at diasporic jazz research that highlights the ideas and identities constructed by early-twentieth-century jazz musicians to articulate the interaction between religion, music, and the African diaspora in their city. Jason Berry, Jonathan Foose, and Tad Jones, in their *Up from the Cradle of Jazz*, trace the origins of jazz and second lines in New Orleans to the city's Caribbean location and its eighteenth- and nineteenth-century African diasporic cultural connections:

Scholars now consider New Orleans like Miami to be part of the Caribbean Basin, rimlands of the Gulf of Mexico that are cultural extensions of the Caribbean. Since the beginning of slavery, the inflow of Caribbean peoples has had a pronounced impact on custom and habit. . . . Long before the music [jazz] issued out of fin de siècle New Orleans, cultural seeds had scattered. A unique environment took root, nourished by different ethnic families, but more important was the city where the families settled.[46]

Up from the Cradle of Jazz defines the emergence of New Orleans jazz in the context of other African diasporic musical traditions—such as samba in Brazil and rhumba in Cuba—as a music of "working-class neighborhoods"[47] and street sounds:

In a sense, jazz was the articulation of a new cultural language: the African genius for improvisation, tonal, and percussive communication; advancing through European instruments and melodies, drawing liberally from ragtime, marching bands, church songs, and blues, a synthesis of varied musical expressions converging at the bottom of America. . . . The New Orleans sound refers to a distinct style: percussive piano rhythms; rocking vocally suggestive horns; and a parade-time backbeat on the drums. Its root is called the second line, the waves of marching dancers who engulf the brass bands and trail behind them, moving to the beat with their bodies gyrating in the streets. Before anything else, it is dance music: sounds to make you clap your hands, move your feet. . . . The family served as the main passageway through which these sounds merged into a common thread.[48]

Berry, Foose, and Jones also develop a provocative thesis about the African diasporic community that defines the New Orleans musical families that "sent forth jazz"[49] in the late nineteenth and early twentieth century. Their thesis is essential for understanding the history of second-line culture and the Mardi Gras Indians:

A partial list of Seventh Ward musical families includes Manuel Perez, Sidney Bechet, Joe and Buddy Petit, Chris Kelly, Lorenzo Tio, Sr. and Jr., the Renas, Barbarians, Louis Arthidore, two families of Fraziers, Dave Williams, Emile and Paul Barnes (cousins of the Marreros). The Barnses, Williamses, Fraziers, and Marreros intermarried. Then there was Barney Bigard, Albert Nicholas, Danny and his wife, Blue Lu Barker. These were the founding jazz families. . . .

In such early families were people who taught, played or simply lived for music. Theirs was a city of great ethnic diversity, where musical expression cut through obstacles of race and class. It was the North American city with the deepest African identity: Voodoo and a communal drum—and dance tradition among slaves flourished in the nineteenth century.... As the African sensibility overlapped with European and Latin musical tradition so did New Orleans become the cradle of jazz.[50]

The ceremonial significance of musical families with their networks of kinship, neighborhoods, bars, and clubs, along with the rituals, oral traditions, and African drumming of the Mardi Gras Indians, are the African diasporic "roots beneath the trunk of early jazz"[51] and the second-line culture explored in this volume. The musical families of early jazz musicians and Mardi Gras Indian chiefs functioned as New World African secret societies "to preserve African belief systems and customs, including music, dance, and masked ritual"[52] in second-line performances in late-nineteenth- and early-twentieth-century New Orleans. As in the religions tradition of Vodou, members of the community "tapped the wisdom of their elders"[53]—in this case, in the musical families—to learn the art, culture, myths, and history of their extended African diasporic kinship network. As the early jazz guitarist and banjo player Danny Barker recalled: "A party for some social event was planned and musicians came and played. There your elders would explain to you, at length, how and why different musicians were related to you—when you greeted each other after that, it was 'Hello Cuz.'"[54]

Memories and myths about nineteenth-century New Orleans Vodou and Congo Square were re-created in these founding musical families. The jazz saxophonist Sidney Bechet had a direct ancestral connection to the heyday of Congo Square through his grandfather Omar, a slave musician and Vodouist who performed in Congo Square every Sunday. In his autobiography, *Treat it Gentle,* Bechet often talked about the second lines as re-creations of musical and ritual memories of Congo Square's African diasporic culture in the early twentieth century.[55] The New Orleans jazz pianist Jelly Roll Morton was descended from Haitians on both sides of his family and believed in Vodou: "Nobody can convince me that there are no such things as spirits. Too many have been seen by my family. . . . When I was a young man, these hoodoo people with their underground stuff helped me along."[56]

The early-twentieth-century jazz trumpeter Oscar "Papa" Celestin still remembered the power of nineteenth-century New Orleans Vodou as he recited the following verses from a Marie Laveau second-line song on a 1951 radio program:

> Marie Laveau helped them in her hand,
> New Orleans was her promised land,
> Quality folks came from far and near,
> The wonder woman for to hear.
> They were afraid to be seen at her gate,
> And would creep through the dark to hear their fate.
> Holdin' dark veils over their head,
> They would tremble to hear what Marie Laveau said,
> Poor Marie Laveau, Marie Laveau,
> The Voodoo Queen from New Orleans.[57]

The previous discussion prioritizes "what musicians have had to say about" African diasporic culture in New Orleans jazz. In this context I draw on Eric Porter, who in his groundbreaking work, *What Is This Thing Called Jazz*, develops an understanding of jazz from the intellectual work of African American musicians as expressed in their writings, biographies, and "musical histories." This approach to the explication of jazz prioritizes "the self conscious aspects of black cultural production . . . [and] historical discussions of what African American musicians [and performance artists] have said publicly about their music, their positions as artists, the 'jazz tradition' in general, and the broader social and cultural implications of this music."[58]

Finally, Porter's study of jazz musicians "as creators, thinkers, and politically conscious individuals"[59] establishes the direction for new diasporic research on early New Orleans jazz that moves beyond the boundaries of scholars' fascination with the oft-repeated narrative of the tensions between the "uptown, English-speaking African American" Protestant musicians, such as the trumpeter Buddy Bolden and the downtown, Francophone[60] Creole Catholic musicians, such as Sidney Bechet and Jelly Roll Morton. Porter's focus on what African American musicians say about jazz will help us understand early-twentieth-century and present-day New Orleanian jazz musicians as conscious shapers of a powerful African diasporic-spiritual identity in the Crescent City.

Today the second line remains a treasured New Orleans tradition, unchanged in many ways since the days of Sidney Bechet—a musical blending of the Kongo-derived perambulating band tradition of Haitian Raras and the early African American performance cultures of New Orleanian jazz.[61] The following description of a contemporary second line provides nuances of the memories of Haitian Rara performances that were re-created in "the remembering songs" of jazz performance traditions that came out of Congo Square:

> Torey recognized the sound immediately . . . coming from down the street three or four blocks. It was the sound of the bass drum, the pulse of the neighborhood's many second-line jazz parades. . . .
>
> He ran towards the music. . . . He began to hear the sizzling snare and the bellowing tuba, the horns and percussion, the people yelling and partying. Up and down the street, doors opened and people of all ages spilled out of their houses, excitedly drawn towards the funky jazz. . . .
>
> He joined the rear of the parade that was longer than he expected . . . it covered the street and sidewalk completely with well over a thousand sweaty, dancing bodies. . . . The Social Aid and Pleasure Club that sponsored the parade, the Tremé Sport . . . led the affair in grand style, lithely stutter-stepping down the street, occasionally stopping to dance with each other in a series of choreographed steps and passes. . . .
>
> Dancing his way slowly up through the crowd . . . Torey could see the whole band: The snare drums, trumpets, trombones, and saxophones, at least a dozen total, not counting the people jamming away on cowbells and tambourines. . . .
>
> The Grand Marshall blew his whistle and he and his fellow Tremé Sports led the parade in a right turn onto Barracks Street. . . . When Mr. Riley played the phrase a third time, it was as though a switch was thrown. . . . People started jumping on top of the cars, dumpsters, anything in their path, dancing ecstatically, feverishly on the verge of abandon. Everywhere Torey looked, he saw bodies spinning, rocking, bumping, and grinding with high velocity, yet remarkably with perfect fluidity, as though they were woven right into the music.[62]

The Emergence of the Mardi Gras Indian
Tradition: Haitian and Kongo Continuities

The Kongo and Haitian origins of the sequin arts work of the early Mardi Gras Indian tribes had a great impact on the resistance strategies of jazz religion in late-nineteenth and early-twentieth-century New Orleans, thus emphasizing the Mardi Gras Indians' second-line performances as important loci for religious and musical re-creations of the African diaspora.

The first Mardi Gras Indian tribes appeared in the 1880s, a decade of profound changes for black New Orleanians. During this period the Americanization of the city was consolidated as the Jim Crow system eliminated the Francophone three-tier racial system of blacks, Creoles of Color, and whites. Suddenly the downtown Francophone Catholic Creoles of Color and uptown Protestant African Americans were grouped together, classified as Negroes, and segregated from whites. And at this momentous time one could say that jazz emerged through the musical interaction between Afro-Creole, classically trained musicians who were thrown together with the uptown African Americans who played the blues and spiritual rhythms of black Baptist and Methodist churches by ear. Both the uptown and downtown musicians had fresh memories of Congo Square and remembered the songs of Vodou and the African diaspora in their music. Wynton Marsalis writes:

> Jazz was sent out into the twentieth century like a probe. It's the first art of people negotiating their agendas through a form. . . . Our music was born out of forced integration. You can believe that the Creoles and the white people and black folks that lived in New Orleans around the turn of the last century definitely did not like each other. They were forced to deal with each other and that's what created jazz.[63]

The 1880s were also noteworthy for the establishment of numerous black brass bands, orchestras, mutual aid and benevolent associations, fraternal organizations, unions, workingmen's groups, military drill teams, sporting clubs, and social aid and pleasure clubs that sponsored second-line parades and funeral processions. In the early twentieth century the Zulu Social Aid and Pleasure Club became the major black Carnival organization in the city.[64]

In 1883 Chief Becate Batiste, who was of mixed African and Native American ancestry, began "masking Indian" on Mardi Gras day with his downtown seventh ward Creole Wild West Indian gang. Quickly the custom of "masking Indian" on Carnival day was adopted by numerous black New Orleanian tribes or gangs in downtown and uptown neighborhoods.[65] The tribes were secret societies, primarily male, that were organized in working-class areas like Tremé, the Ninth Ward, Gert

Town, and New Orleans housing projects.[66] According to an early news-paper account, they appeared in "bands from twenty to thirty . . . singing war songs and doing the war dance."[67] Their chants, composed of Cre-ole and African American vernacular, were sung to the percussion of sticks, bottles, tambourines, and hand clapping in rhythmic, trance-like dances.[68] Eventually, dressed in intricate hand-sewn Indian suits and crowns made with many pounds of feathers, beads, and sequins, each tribe interacted, fluidly and by improvisation, with second liners and brass bands as it paraded through the territory of its neighborhood and sometimes violently confronted members of different tribes with hatch-ets, swords, or knives. Certainly one remarkable aspect of this new per-formance tradition was the creation of a ritual space where black men could boldly express rebellious and politically resistant behavior similar to that of the nineteenth-century Natchez Indians. The tribes' behavior was also reminiscent of the "stickfighting bands"—parallel mock fight-ing Carnival traditions in the African diaspora of nineteenth-century Trinidad and capoeira in Brazil.[69]

However, the underlying spiritual philosophy of the Mardi Gras In-dians' circum-Atlantic performances originated in the "remembering songs" of Haitian Vodou and Congo Square. Jason Berry writes that the Congo Square rituals and "Voodoo cultists" maintained African drum-ming in New Orleans more or less covertly into Reconstruction. In the early 1880s the tribal percussion sensibility shifted to hand-held instru-ments with the emergence of Mardi Gras Indian tribes. Thus "masking Indian" was a performance strategy related to the spirit world of Vodou, for "masks" were "spirit faces of the ancestors, of deities." In this context Mardi Gras, a season of Christian devotion, was "a cultural opening" for performance that re-created memories of slavery and the African-Amerindian maroon communities of eighteenth- and nineteenth-century Louisiana when "blacks embraced the Indian persona."[70] They also sub-versively substituted the performance of the Native American spirit of rebellion for the overt reenactment of the Vodouists' resistance strate-gies in their performances in Congo Square.[71] The Mardi Gras Indians were not alone in performing Native American substitutions at the turn of the twentieth century, when the practice of Vodou was made illegal in New Orleans. The Spiritual churches of New Orleans—which com-bined aspects of Pentecostalism, Catholicism, and Vodou—often call on the spirit of Black Hawk, the rebellious Midwestern Native American leader of the 1830s, to fight their battles in the spirit world.[72] In both these fascinating communities, the Indians are utilized in performances to "restage events of circum-Atlantic encounters and surrogation in which European experience remains only obliquely acknowledged, if at all."[73] In the early twentieth century Native American substitutions for African ceremonial memories were a politically safe strategy; at that point Indians were no longer considered a threat to white supremacy in the United States, as most Indian communities had been subject to systemic genocide in the nineteenth century.

Robert Farris Thompson's provocative analysis of the Kongo origins of feather and sequin arts in Haiti and New Orleans explicates this "three sided [circum-Atlantic] relationship of memory, performance and surrogation" among the Mardi Gras Indians. He writes:

> As altar . . . the crossroads came with a thousand voices to the Americas. Haitian healers make "Congo pacquets," bags with feathers inserted at the top to indicate heaven and within them earths, embedding spirit. In Africa, Kongo healer diviners are known as "leopards of the sky"—i.e., predatory birds . . . hence their feathered bonnets. . . . The climax was New Orleans, city of Kongo Square. Here the all-over feather costumes of black Mardi Gras Indian groups compare directly with the all-over feather masks of the Loango region in Kongo.
>
> Sequins . . . mask an inner presence of Kongo bearing . . . through an outwardly Creole manifestation. . . . In Petwo (Haitian Kongo) context . . . they become ritual metallic dotting. Ritual dotting . . . associates with the secrets and the power of the dead in Kongo. . . . Sequins light up the flag which ushers in Vodou services. . . . Sequins translate into visual Creole, the ancient dotting patterns which in Kongo stood for spotted mediatory felines . . . moving between the two worlds, bush and village. The power of mediation returned in the scintillating flags bringing in the gods.[74]

In Haitian Vodou, "drapo"—ritual flags with sequins and beads—are one of the most important aspects of sacred art. Tina Girouard and Patrick Polk have studied the sewing and lifestyles of sequin artists, and the history and significance of the sequined flags. The flags are central because they signal the supernatural beauty of the spirits and their immanent presence in a religious ceremony. Because of the flag's ritual significance, sequin artists dedicate their lives to their art form.[75] Likewise, Mardi Gras Indian chiefs who have inherited African spiritual authority and power from Congo Square traditions spend thousands of dollars and most of their recreational and family time sewing the intricate sequined suits that they wear on Mardi Gras day and Super Sunday (usually the Sunday after St. Joseph's day). In their street performances the "spy boy," or tribal scout, and the "flag boy," who carries the gang flag, move ahead of the big chief, advise him about his movements, and signal to the second liners that the tribal banner will be followed by the chief's ceremonial performance. According to Allison Tootie Montana, the former Big Chief of the Yellow Pocahontas Tribe, "They used to carry real shotguns and hatchets. . . . If you want to get in any trouble you touch that flag."[76]

Polk explicates the use of sequined cosmograms ("vévé" or work emblems) and Haitian images on the ceremonial flags of Vodou:

> Each is normally dedicated to a specific lwa, incorporating the sacred colors and symbols of that deity. . . . Drapo often bear the trace—work emblems (vévé) of the lwa to whom they are consecrated. . . . Flashing colors and glittering ornaments catch the eye and direct attention to the advent of a supernatural encounter. In revealing the presence of the spirit, Vodou imagery depends on multiple levels of perception and the flexible symmetry of sacred space. . . . In their art, flag makers produce a kaleidoscopic perspective of sacred space and ritual movement through which the entire ounfo [the temple where Vodou worshipers perform ceremonies and rites] is translated into fabric.[77]

Similarly the Mardi Gras Indian chief, flag boy, and other secret society members create a kaleidoscopic effect in their performances, as they transform the streets of New Orleans into sacred spaces of interactive images and ceremonial dances reflected in the sequins, feathers, and materials of their spectacular suits and flags. In both Haiti and New Orleans, "the brilliant colors" and "intricate designs" of sequined flags and suits mirror "the elaborate choreography of their ceremonial use."[78] In the former context, the presentation of sequined flags begins the choreography of a religious ceremony in a Vodou temple; in the latter context, the appearance of the flag and sequined suit substitutes for memories of pre–twentieth-century Vodou ritual dances in Congo Square.

In Haiti the "salutary parading" of two sequined flags commences the Vodou ritual in a spectacular choreographed sequence. The flag bearers, who are initiated women, carry the flags into the peristyle and flank the master of ceremonies (who is second in Vodou society hierarchy) as he marches around the poto mitan (the center pole through which the spirits enter the ceremony) carrying the sacred weapon. The sword or saber invokes the lwa Ogou and his association with armed resistance and religious political "authority."[79] According to Maya Deren, the oungan (the priest and master of ceremonies) "engage in some strange mock battle" which is eventually resolved when the priest pays his respect to the sword, the flags, and the religious society and spirits they represent, and the master of ceremonies and flag bearers perform a sign of respect for the oungan.[80] Thus the sequined flag and mock battle express the hierarchy of the religious society and the "ritual power" of the spirits.[81]

In a similar fashion, the improvisational performances of the spy boy and the flag boy have re-created the "salutary parading" and the manifestation of the religious hierarchy of Haitian Vodou.[82] According to Larry Bannock, Big Chief of the Golden Star Hunters:

> There's different ranks—it's kinda loose—depending on the gang. Some have Spy Boy, Spy Flag, Gang Flag; some have First Flag, Second Flag, First Chief, Second Chief.... There's always going to be only one Big Chief though. The Spy Boy is in the front... he is ahead looking for trouble. Only a chosen few can be Spy Boy. It's his job to send a signal to First Flag when he sees other Indians. [The Spy Boy might chant]: "I'm the spy boy, spy boy like morning, spy boy like day, let the sun shine like morning."[83]
>
> The route on Mardi Gras is always secret. Nobody knows where anybody's gonna be... that's why Spy boy is ahead looking for Indians. If he sights a gang, he tells Flag boy that a gang is on its way. First flag signals back down the line to Big Chief. Big Chief has a stick that controls the Indians. When he hits the ground with the stick they better get down and bow to the chief.[84]
>
> [The Big Chief of the White Eagle tribe might improvise a chant when he meets the Golden Star Hunters]: "We gonna meet everybody gonna turn around. I'm pretty White Eagle gonna go to town. Mardi Gras morning we gonna weep and moan with pretty White Eagle when we leave home."[85]

Some tribes also include a queen, who dances with the chiefs, and a wildman or medicine man, wearing a headpiece with horns and armed with a weapon, who protects the big chief from harm.[86] The wildman's spear and the hatchet and gun fights of the late-nineteenth- to mid-twentieth-century Mardi Gras Indians are probably a reinterpretation of the opening ceremony in Haitian Vodou, when the master of ceremonies wields the sacred machete or saber in a mock battle as he dances between the flags in the temple. In both cases the weapons are related to "the warrior spirit" of Ogou, the lwa who "bestows the power to survive."[87] His sword symbolizes the strength of metal and thus the might of mankind, according to Tina Girouard.[88] Sallie Ann Glassman explicates his political significance: "Ogou is the force that guards your arm in battle. His power enables you to slay your enemies. He inspired the Haitian slave uprising in 1804 that led to Haiti's independence from France. His is the might that crushes oppression."[89] In the Mardi Gras Indian ceremonies the overt portrayal of such a magically resistant and powerful African spirit was probably too dangerous in the politically repressive environment created by the Jim Crow laws and legislation that criminalized the religion of Vodou in late-nineteenth- and early-twentieth-century New Orleans. However, the power of Ogou was absorbed into the mystical Black Indian persona, and this circum-Atlantic surrogation echoed the theme of the Afro-Haitian proverb—"When I'm right, my magic will prevail."[90] As Robert Farris Thompson has demonstrated, in the midst of pogroms against African faith, "Vodou remains ready to return,"[91] because the spirits are rooted in nature. Cemeteries, trees, the sky, and those who respect the spirit world have the "resiliency of guerilla warriors . . . [with] feints on the right, feints on the left, hiding motion and existence."[92] As we have seen, their feints are exemplified sometimes in Creole ceremonial garments and sewing traditions.

A member of the Golden Blades tribe describes the Creolized transformation and exchange between African-American and Native American resistance strategies experienced by Black Indians on Mardi Gras day:

> They shave their faces, his proudness, say his prayer in the morning. Refuse to bow to anyone but his chief. Each chief is like a minor form of an Indian nation. [Their Creole chant], hey pocky way, just a part of that natural rhythm that goes back to that Marie Laveau thing, that Vodou thing.[93]

The convergence of these resistance strategies and their re-created memories of Congo Square and the circum-Atlantic world are the political heart of the Mardi Gras Indian tradition. When people started masking Indian on Carnival days in the late nineteenth century, black New Orleanians were continuing a rich heritage of slave resistance that white Americans preferred to bury alive: a complex African maroon culture involving cultural exchanges with local Native American tribes; the cross-fertilization of Haitian and New Orleanian Vodou that happened in Congo Square; the reinterpretation of African ceremonial music and dance in new jazz performance cultures; and the survival of a beautiful Creole "gumbo people" caught up in a vicious color caste system that was a clear result of the rape and sexual exploitation by white men of African-descended and Native American women in the eighteenth and nineteenth centuries.

At the same time, the Crescent City was the epicenter of black resistance against legal segregation at the turn of the century. Homer Plessy, a Creole shoemaker in Tremé, became the civil disobedience test case for the new racial restrictions. Because he was an African American man who could pass for white, he was chosen by the New Orleanian Comité de Citoyens to ride in a "whites only carriage" to test the legality of the Jim Crow laws. When the Louisiana Supreme Court ruled against him in Plessy v. Ferguson in 1896, the "separate-but-equal doctrine" became the law of the land until 1954.[94] In the midst of these fascinating but trying times, the re-creation of African memories through surrogation is a powerful statement about the African American right to live in a land free of racial oppression. Roach explicates this political/utopian aspect of Mardi Gras Indian performances:

> I believe that one deep purpose of the gangs, their secret preparations, and their spectacular but nomadic performances is publicly to imagine a space, a continent, from which the white man and his culture have vanished or retreated to the peripheries. The tribes on this fictive continent are richly differentiated, uptown and downtown, friendly and unfriendly, but they all communicate through expressive performances across the shifting borders of their imagined community, the living and the dead. In other words, I believe that performance in New Orleans permits, through the disguise of "masking Indian," the imaginative re-creation and repossession of Africa.[95]

Case Study: The Montana Family—Mardi Gras Indian Chiefs and Sequin Artists of New Orleans

The repetitive act of sewing is similar to chanting a mantra—a transcendental meditation of sorts. The artists become one with their work, the work becomes an act of faith, each sequin a silent prayer. The triumph of spirit over despair is captured in . . . the sequin arts of Haiti.

TINA GIROUARD, *SEQUIN ARTISTS OF HAITI*

Tina Girouard's work focuses on the spiritual commitment and creativity of the sequin artists of Haiti—families and members of Vodou societies who create the sequined Rara costumes, flags, and bottles for religious ceremonies and parades. Inspired by their dedication to the spirit world, they support the belief system of Vodou by creating sequined images of the lwa for Vodou temples, museums, and art galleries in Haiti and abroad. At the heart of this tradition is the St. Louis family, which has been devoted continuously to sequin arts and Rara in the area of Port-au-Prince for generations ever since the late nineteenth century. The family patriarch, Ceus St. Louis (who was eight-one years old when Girouard conducted her fieldwork in 1993) has served as a kind of African chief of this tradition for most of his life. According to Girouard, he was a Vodou "priest, doctor, artist, architect, and performer," who mentored his relatives as they developed the Haitian sequin arts tradition from generation to generation in the twentieth century.[96] Because of their deep connection to Rara, Vodou societies, and the Afro-Creole performance tradition of ceremonial sewing, the sequin arts of Haiti are strikingly similar to the performance traditions of the Mardi Gras Indians of New Orleans. Sequin artists in Haiti and New Orleans have compared their sewing techniques and have found that they are almost exactly the same.[97] Just as the St. Louis family has for generations been instrumental to the development of the Haitian sequin arts, so the Montanas of New Orleans have functioned as the first musical family of the sequin arts and the Mardi Gras Indian tradition in New Orleans since reaching back to the late 1800s.

My perspective on the contributions of the Montana family to the origins and shaping of Black Indian traditions has been influenced by Maurice M. Martinez Jr. in his seminal essay, "Two Islands: The Black Indians of Haiti and New Orleans." Martinez compares circum-Caribbean Carnival Indian traditions and cultural exchanges between Haiti and New Orleans, and provides evidence that performance traditions in both locations have been nourished by "island isolation." He writes:

> The Black Indians of New Orleans have experienced island isolation. Their present-day cultural manifestations, costumes, rituals, and dances have strong roots in the most certain intermarriage of their oppressed and isolated forebears: Indians and Africans. Early slave trade of Indians and Africans by the French brought these two people together. They shared their beliefs, customs, and songs. They made the children of "mixed blood" who

in later years found "legitimate" opportunities in vehicles such as Mardi Gras to practice and display their cultural heritage. . . . Legislative acts such as the Black Code of 1724 prevented the intermarriage of whites and blacks and set the tone for legislative action that extends far into the twentieth century. Blacks and people of color were placed on an island of social segregation from whites. The Black Indians until recent years remained on that island, preferring to march on Carnival Day, through the "back" streets of their neighborhoods.[98]

Martinez's theory on the origins of the Black Indians sharply conflicts with Michael P. Smith's ideas outlined in his book *Mardi Gras Indians*. Although Smith acknowledges pre–twentieth-century African-Amerindian maroon communities as sources for masking Indian, he gives more credit to the Buffalo Bill Wild West show that appeared in New Orleans in the winter months of 1884–85 as the spark of inspiration for the Mardi Gras Indian performance traditions in New Orleans.[99] On the other hand, Roach explains the origin of the tradition as "patchwork amid exchange": each of the "creation narratives"—colonial connections between Africans and Native Americans, Caribbean and West African dance and music linkages, African American self-help groups, the belief in the spirit world, and the Buffalo Bill Wild West Shows—"contributes its own grain of truth" to the origins of the Mardi Gras Indians.[100] The following oral history from the Montana family clearly supports Martinez's ideas. This narrative includes important information about the early history, sequin/sewing art, oral traditions, and ethos of the Black Indians of New Orleans.

Tootie Montana was the Big Chief of the Yellow Pocahontas tribe for fifty years. Masking Indian began in his family with his grandmother's brother. He remembered that his "grandmother died at about 118 years old, her brother was older than her, so Mardi Gras Indian masking goes back to the time of slavery." His grandmother's uncle was Becate, the first Mardi Gras Indian chief of the Creole Wild West tribe. The tribe started downtown in the Seventh Ward and moved uptown when his uncle, Becate, moved uptown. The chief traced the original link between blacks and Indians in New Orleans through marriage, and there were marriages between the two groups in his family in the 1800s. Also, he explained, "blacks and Indians fought white people together." Montana's father was also a Mardi Gras Indian.[101]

According to Montana, the major difference between his sequin artwork and his father's is in the crown or headdress of the Indian suit. In an old family picture that the author viewed in the chief's home, this difference is clear. His father's crown was composed of feathers hung behind him. Tootie Montana's innovation was to bring the crown to the front so that vibrant multicolored feathers and sequins framed his face. This aspect of his sequin art explains the popularity of the Mardi Gras Indian chant: "Da Yellow Pocahontas Got the Golden Crown."[102]

In the 1930s Chief Montana and his wife "were members of the Roosevelt Social and Pleasure Club. The women dressed up as baby dolls in black tights and pink accessories. The men wore derbies and bow ties."[103] In the 1940s he became chief of the Yellow Pocahontas Indian tribe:

> I've made fifty suits. I draw suits out of my head. My money-making job is a carpenter but beadwork, sewing, creative work, that's my life. . . . You do a few beads and sequins, just do what I do. These suits take a whole year to create. They are created through a craft of design, sewing sequins and plumes and jewels which is passed down from generation to generation.[104]

According to the chief, the time, patience, and dedication that it takes to create a suit for masking transforms one's life and creates a lifestyle centered around work and home, so that one does not have time to spend in the bars or on the street corners. However, he remembered:

> When the tribes used to carry guns, during my daddy's time they didn't worry about how pretty the costumes were. People remember the time when it was about fighting. Today I'm the one that changed it from the fighting with weapons to fighting with the costumes. I'm choosy about who I take into my tribe. My time changing from carrying the guns.[105]

"When I was twenty-four years old I started masking Indian,"[106] said Montana, who was raised as a Roman Catholic and educated as a young boy at Holy Redeemer Church. He is critical of Roman Catholicism because of the racism he experienced in the church. He recalled that as a boy in Holy Redeemer catechism class he was beaten, slapped in the mouth, and almost had his ear pulled off by a nun, because "white nuns and priests did not like dark-skinned blacks." Although Holy Redeemer was a black parish, "it was ruled by white priests and nuns and the seating arrangements were racially segregated with the first two rows reserved for white Catholics." When Holy Redeemer Church was destroyed by

Hurricane Beatrice, the chief said "This was an act of God."[107] However, his mother is a devout Catholic who went to church every day and set a strong spiritual example for her children, and he is a member of St. Augustine Catholic Church in Tremé.[108]

LOUISIANA CREOLE AND THE
MARDI GRAS INDIAN ORAL TRADITION

Chief Montana speaks fluent Creole. His mother, who was about ninety-five years old at the time of the author's interview in 1997, had a stroke in the mid-1990s which left her paralyzed on her right side. However, Montana said, "she perks up and begins to speak when her son speaks" to her in Creole. This is the same Creole language that is spoken by Haitian sequin artists and members of Rara bands. Aspects of the language are a key to some of the call-and-response oral traditions of the Mardi Gras Indian second lines. Kreyol, now acknowledged as an official language in Haiti, is a secret language in New Orleans, spoken fluently only by a small number of elders in black families. "Humbah," a Creole word used frequently in the Black Indian songs and second-line culture, means to "bow down," according to Montana.[109]

Indeed, the earliest evidence of the Mardi Gras Indian oral tradition is in Creole, such as the following late-nineteenth-century account of a second line from the jazz pianist Jelly Roll Morton:

> They would send their spy boy two blocks on ahead—I happened to be a spy boy myself once so I know how this went . . . singing "T'ouwais bas q'ouwais"—and the tribe would answer—"Ou tendais."[110]

Eddie Richardson, who was the chief of the One-Eleven tribe "sometime around . . . 1915–1925"[111] recalled:

> We'd have rehearsals everybody'd be ready. . . . I'd come in with my tambourine up and shake it. . . . That draws their attention! I'd say: "Ha-Chi-Con-Nah Fay-Ah?" They'd say: "Aey-Ha." I'd say: "Ha-Chi Con Nah Fay-Ah, ooo-Pike-Ah Bid-Away?" That's "How you feeling?" When they'd say "Aey-Ha," that was "All Right!" Now I may tell 'em: "Ma Hon, No Hike-Ah Me, No Hike-Ah You, No Ha, No Man-Day-Hi." "Touch my Queen'n my ami'n I'll fight you mo-toe!" And then I'd say: "No Hike-Ah Me, No Hike-Ah You, No Hike-Ah Man-Day-Ha!" And they'd start to sing: "Xango

Mongo Lo Ha." [Xango is an alternate spelling for the Yoruba spirit of thunder, Shango.][112]

The use of re-created bits and pieces of the Creole language in the early Mardi Gras Indian oral tradition was a way of maintaining the memories of Congo Square's nineteenth-century heyday, when most black New Orleanians and Haitian immigrants in the Crescent City spoke the language. Although contemporary Mardi Gras Indian tribes are no longer fluent in Creole and do not sing "Xango Mongo Lo Ha," aspects of the Creole language are still interspersed in their vocal repertoire. "Indian Red," the Black Indian hymn sung at all tribal ceremonial gatherings, begins when the big chief sings: "Ma-Day, Cootie Fiyo and all present answer: Tee-Nah Aeey, Tee-Nah Aeey."[113] The hymn then continues: "We are Indians . . . of the nation . . . wild wild Creation. . . . We won't kneel down. . . . I love to hear them call my Indian Red."[114] The Mardi Gras Indian song "Iko Iko" became a part of the commercial repertoire of rhythm and blues music in the late twentieth century: "My spy boy and your spy boy was sittin' on the bayou. . . . Hey now . . . Iko Iko . . . Jacamo Fi Nah Nay."[115]

Donald Harrison, the late Big Chief of the Young Guardians of the Flame tribe, explained the significance of "Chong Chong," another traditional Black Indian song: "When two Indian gangs would meet . . . the chief of one of the gangs would call his best singer and the best singer would sing: 'My Big Chief, Chong Chong, don't like your Song Song,' and they overpower the other gang with their vocals."[116]

THE MARDI GRAS INDIAN TRADITION CONTINUES

In many ways the Montana family exemplifies the ethos of African traditional religions such as Vodou, as the family has continued the sequin arts and oral traditions of the Mardi Gras Indians in the twenty-first century by respecting the wisdom of elders and maintaining co-dependent relationships with family members and the Tremé community adjacent to Congo Square. In 1996 Tootie's son Darryl Montana became the new Big Chief of the Yellow Pocahontas tribe. Darryl, who is in his forties, sewed his first Indian suit when he was ten. He teaches sequin arts in the New Orleans public schools and has exhibited his Indian suits in major U.S. art venues such as the Whitney Museum in New York City, the New Orleans Museum of Art, and the Fourth International Biennial Exhibition in Santa Fe, New Mexico. He is also a community advocate for elderly citizens in New Orleans, inheriting from his father a serious communal and artistic philosophy about his ceremonial responsibilities:

> Mardi Gras Indian chiefs are like African chiefs and some have a connection or have been recognized by African chiefs. . . . Dance practices start up right after Christmas during Mardi Gras season. During the rest of the time, members of the tribe don't have picnics together or regular social functions because they are not social and pleasure clubs. Their main purpose is to be ready for Mardi Gras day and Super Sunday and on those occasions when some of them might be hired to perform like at the Jazz and Heritage Festival.[117]

Although Darryl's wife, Sabrina, does not mask Indian, she explained how the whole family is involved in the tradition during the Mardi Gras season:

> If you marry me, you marry what I do, what I am. If you have a mate who is pulling against you, there is no way a Mardi Gras Indian can mask. . . . The whole family would come together on Friday, Joyce would fry fish and we would sew and talk Indian stuff. It is so African-based in terms of the family structure. . . . My first experience in practice was an awakening for me. . . . Yellow Pocahontas does not use anything from the previous suit, they start from scratch each year. The drawing for the suit for next year begins the day after Mardi Gras. The Yellow Pocahontas is very traditionally based—their costumes are three dimensional. They sculpture pieces as well as doing beading and sequins. The sewing teaches patience and camaraderie because it is very tedious. The sewing involves commitment to a culture that no one pays them to do. Darryl's yellow suit cost $7000. It is not just about being out in the street but maintaining the culture and keeping it going truthfully. The exhibit of Tootie Montana at NOMA [New Orleans Museum of Art] was the second largest attended since King Tut.[118]

Approximately thirty-one Mardi Gras Indian tribes reside in the neighborhoods of New Orleans and include the Yellow Pocahontas, Creole Wild West, White Eagles, Mandingo Warriors, Young Monogram Hunters, Black Feather, Cheyenne Hunters, Ninth Ward Hunters, Seminole, Golden Star Hunters, Wild Magnolias, Young Guardians of the Flame, Carrollton Hunters, Comanche Hunters, Golden Eagles, Geronimo Hunters, Seventh Ward Warriors, Golden Arrows, Wild Apache, Creole Osceola, White Cloud Hunters, Black Eagle, Mohawk Hunters, Young Brave Hunters, Wild Bogacheetus, Seminole Hunters, Cheyenne, Trouble Nation, and Wild Tremé.[119] The Black Indians re-create their magnificent ceremonial performances every year during a ritual cycle in New Orleans that begins on Carnival day, continues the night of St. Joseph's feast day (St. Joseph is "the patron saint of families, working men, social justice"),[120] and culminates with elaborate down-town and uptown Mardi Gras Indian parades on Super Sunday. The Mardi Gras Indians' African diasporic spirituality and resistance strate-gies continue to resonate with the struggles of twenty-first-century black New Orleans. With a black majority population of 67 percent and me-dian African American family incomes that were half the median family incomes for white New Orleanians (before Hurricane Katrina), New Orleans is sometimes called "the city that care forgot."[121]

Beyond New Orleans: The Diaspora Continues

We gonna take it to New Orleans, the place that Ameri-can music was born, a place called Congo Square.

THE NEVILLE BROTHERS, *LIVE ON PLANET EARTH*

The New Orleans music critic, Kalamu ya Salaam, noted that the Cres-cent City was "the birthplace of jazz" and American music, and that Joseph "King" Oliver and Louis Armstrong brought jazz to the rest of the United States in the 1920s.[122] From that decade until the 1970s, how-ever, important new developments in jazz occurred outside New Or-leans.[123] Beginning in the 1970s several New Orleanian jazz and rhythm and blues groups, whose music was directly influenced by the perfor-mance traditions of the Mardi Gras Indians, second lines, and Congo Square, recorded albums that revitalized the world's interest in New Or-leans as the cradle of American music.

The commercial success of the Neville Brothers began with *The Wild Tchoupitoulas* in 1976, which featured their uncle George Landry,

Big Chief of the uptown Wild Tchoupitoulas tribe, singing his renditions of Black Indian classics such as "Indian Red" and "Big Chief Got a Golden Crown."[124] When the Neville Brothers became superstars in American popular music, they maintained their connections to the Afro-Caribbean rhythms of Congo Square with songs such as "Voodoo" ("You musta put Voodoo on me. You musta cast a spell. . . . You musta been burnin' candles to make the love so strong")[125] and "Congo Square" ("You can hear 'em in the distance, that's when those Voodoo people gather and play them drums at night in Congo Square").[126] At the same time a New Orleans house band, the Meters (George Porter, Leo Nocentelli, Joe Modeliste [also known as Zigaboo Modeliste], and Art Neville) brought the funky rhythms of the second lines to rhythm and blues music with national hits like, "Sophisticated Cissy," "Look Ka Py Py," "Chicken Strut," and "Be My Lady."[127]

The annual New Orleans Jazz and Heritage Festival began in 1970 and soon became the world's largest jazz festival. Every year it highlights the legacy of Congo Square and showcases the musical and spiritual traditions of the African diaspora from Haiti, Brazil, and Martinique to Senegal.[128] The 1970s also marked the first nationally acclaimed recordings of New Orleans second-line brass bands such as the Dirty Dozen and Rebirth Brass Band.[129] Their albums brought thousands of tourists to the Crescent City to hear second-line music, both in its indigenous contexts, such as jazz funerals and Mardi Gras Indian street festivals, and in local clubs, such as the uptown Maple Leaf on Oak Street and the downtown Funky Butt Bar on Rampart Street. At least sixteen street brass bands perform today in New Orleans.[130] The internationally acclaimed jazz trumpeter Wynton Marsalis has brought the "influence" of New Orleans ceremonial music to the jazz programs at Lincoln Center in New York City.[131]

Still, no contemporary musical group re-creates the ancestral memories of Congo Square and the spiritual and musical linkages between New Orleans and Haiti more effectively than jazzmen Bill Summers and Irvin Mayfield. They are Los Hombres Calientes—"the hot men"—who perform the hot music of "Afro-Caribbean soul." For their album, *Vol. 4: Vodou Dance,* they traveled to Haiti, Trinidad, Jamaica, Cuba, and New Orleans to record the ancestral music of the African diaspora that keeps alive the spirit of Congo Square and second-line culture. Their Haitian spiritual and musical journey took them to the outskirts of Port-au-Prince to musician Jean Raymond:

> Professor Bill immediately asked Jean Raymond if the group could document authentic Voodoo drumming. The house, which was without electricity, was wired within a few hours. . . . The hot men documented the ceremonial drumming in pure form. Rara songs are also provided in this album from that experience. . . . This CD was done in love and respect for our ancestors who left this rich spiritual, artistic, and scientific legacy.[132]

The current popularization of black New Orleans ceremonial music highlights the significance of space, place, and memory in the recognition of the Crescent City as the most important port of entry for African diasporic religious and musical traditions in the United States. "As we move away from a Eurocentric interpretation of American culture and begin to explore the African roots of all Americans," writes Gwendolyn Midlo Hall, "it is important to understand Louisiana Creole culture. It is the most significant source of Africanization of the entire culture of the United States."[133]

As this chapter has demonstrated, Haitian religion and music are important influences in the Africanization of New Orleans, and the second-line theme of *Jazz Religion* is a provocative way to analyze the vibrant African diasporic unities in Haitian and New Orleans performance cultures. This exploration of the rich musical and religious connections between the Mardi Gras Indians, second lines, sequin artists, and Rara bands is also a fascinating case study of "circum-Atlantic performance." Roach's thesis of the importance of memory, performance, and surrogation illuminates the remnants of Haitian language, spirituality, and material art that were re-created over time and are currently performed in Crescent City street festivals.

From Port-au-Prince to Congo Square, in the music and dancing of Rara bands and Mardi Gras Indian tribes, the memories of courageous African-descended ancestors who survived slavery continue to live in the "cities of the dead." The magical and healing flashes of the Afro-Creole spirit world that are re-created in Haitian and New Orleanian performances are evidence of the profound influence of African spirituality on the popular culture of America.

The Healing Arts of African Diasporic Religion

Nou fèt pou nou mouri—we are born or slated to die.

HAITIAN PROVERB

The crisis of my mother's death in the summer months of 1997 prompted my own personal involvement in the healing experience of jazz funerals and African diasporic religion, and revealed an important perspective about the living traditions of second-line culture and its interactions with Vodou.

Why do scholars of African diasporic religions "weave together"[1] analytical and personal writing in their accounts of healing traditions such as Haitian and New Orleanian Vodou? Karen McCarthy Brown writes about the extraordinary systemic suffering that poor and working-class people experience in Haiti and New Orleans, and how magical Vodou rituals make it possible to heal broken lives in unjust societies:

> There is no Vodou ritual small or large, individual or communal, which is not a healing rite. It is no exaggeration to say that Haitians believe that living and suffering are inseparable. Vodou is the system they have devised to deal with the suffering that is life, a system whose purpose is to minimize pain, avoid disaster, cushion loss, and strengthen survivors and survival instincts. The drama of Vodou occurs not within the rituals themselves but rather in the junction between the rituals and the devotees' troubled lives. Hoping to be healed, people bring the burdens and pains of their

lives to this religious system. If I persisted in studying Vodou objectively, I realized, the heart of the system, its ability to heal, would remain closed to me. I could understand the psychodrama of Vodou only by opening my life to the ministrations of Alourdes [Mama Lola].[2]

My first encounters with the Vodou world and second-line culture in New Orleans were far from academic; rather, they were part of a personal choice to express my grief and my hope through the healing arts of African diasporic religion. My individual experience with the religion ultimately brought a deeper understanding to my analysis of the African spiritual philosophy and the deeply felt healing rites that inform second-line culture.

It began on a hot summer night in early July when I walked into my mother's hospital room in the intensive care unit of Boston University Medical Center after a long flight from New Orleans. I was not prepared for the gravity of her illness. A few days before I arrived in Boston, she had been admitted to the hospital needing treatment for an infection, and her doctors had found that she had suffered a severe heart attack. The woman I loved more than anyone was hooked up to numerous tubes and machines, in a coma, and close to death. My legs quivered beneath me. A friend who had traveled with me from New Orleans propped me up in a chair close to my mother's bed, and her young doctor, patting me on the back, said, "I guess your family didn't tell you how sick she is."

Later that night I had drinks with several of my childhood friends in a dark corner of Richard's, a favorite nightspot of mine on Tremont Street in the South End of Boston. In the silent interludes of our conversation I came to understand that only prayer and meditation might miraculously awaken my mother from her coma and help my family face the strong possibility of her death in the sad days that were to follow. Sitting in the back of that bar, in shock, I knew that the only way I could maintain hope and cope with the grief I was feeling was to explore the relationships my family, close friends, and I had formed with God and the spirit world.[3] Only an extraordinary religious community that celebrates life and provides healing and coping strategies for "what we cannot control or imagine"[4] could help me recover my strength to deal with the final outcome of this crisis.

The next morning, at the rectory of the Jesuit Church of the Immaculate Conception, across the street from the hospital, I discussed my plight with a kind old priest who prayed with me at the altar of the dark candle-lit church and offered me beautiful old rosary beads from a box of religious items. In the afternoon I contacted the hospital's Protestant chaplain. For several days thereafter we prayed together over my mother's bed for a miracle that did not happen—that she would awaken from her coma and speak to me.

Soon numerous doctors made it clear to my family that my mother, Mavis Turner, who was eighty-one years old, would not live to see the month of August. In the middle of July I returned to New Orleans to put my business affairs on hold and prepare myself for my mother's imminent death. My father and I agreed that her funeral would take place in early August, which would give me time to pull together the additional financial resources I needed to return to my hometown for her wake and burial.

My mother died on July 24, 1997. Even before that day an extraordinary group of New Orleanians gathered around me to offer their strong support during the intense grief and mourning period which continued for a year after my mother passed away. My internist at Tulane University Medical Center gave me a thorough examination and vowed to see me through this difficult time. I found an excellent grief counselor in my uptown New Orleans neighborhood, and our weekly sessions were a lifesaver in the months that followed.

Friends in New Orleans also provided consolation and showed me new ways to handle grief. My personal involvement with Vodou began when I first met two sisters—Elaine Brown and Ceola Burks—and Ceola's husband Shawn, at a Parker family funeral at the Majestic Mortuary Service on Oretha Castle Haley Boulevard in New Orleans in June 1997. Elaine and Ceola are cousins of George Parker, who was my housemate in New Orleans. The funeral for one of their cousins, Pop, only in his early twenties when he died, was an extraordinary affair. Most of the mourners at the funeral home service were younger than thirty and showed their respect for the dead by wearing elegant dresses and handsome light-colored suits, even though the temperature outside was over ninety degrees, with high humidity. Several young people also wore T-shirts emblazoned with Pop's photograph and his dates of birth and death.[5]

After Pop's burial service at the cemetery numerous family members and friends from New Orleans and California arrived at his mother Hilda's shotgun house on Dumaine Street for a family reunion and repast in remembrance of her deceased son. One by one, everyone went into her bathroom, changed out of their funeral clothes, and emerged wearing shorts, tank tops, and T-shirts, reflecting the relaxed celebratory mood of the gathering. Bonds of family and friendship were renewed and lots of delicious Creole cooking consumed as everyone grooved to the sounds of soul music into the early evening.

In the weeks after Pop's funeral, I became close friends with Shawn and Ceola, who lived in New Orleans East with their four children, and Elaine, who lived downtown with her mother. They welcomed me into the intricate and supportive network of cousins, aunts, and uncles in the New Orleans branch of the Parker family. Every weekend there was a party, family reunion, barbecue, crawfish boil, or fish fry to attend, new people to meet, and love and good times to enjoy. Shawn, who was like a big brother to me, said, "Rich, we're your family here. People in New Orleans ain't nothin' pretty to mess around with. We party with our family—it's safer that way." In the 1990s New Orleans was known as the murder capital of the United States because of its daily homicides and its violent and corrupt police department. Extended family, friends, community groups, churches, black colleges, clubs, associations, and secret societies functioned as a safety net against crime and corruption and also made "the patterns of life" in black New Orleans "more varied and complex than those in any other city in the United States."[6]

The day after Pop's funeral, Elaine visited her cousin George at our house on General Pershing Street. During the next week the three of us made several trips to the bayou in St. Bernard Parish, just outside New Orleans, to catch fish and crabs in the tropical afternoon heat. In the early evening we returned home to fry the fish we had caught, and Elaine would cook wonderful Creole dishes like crab stew as we played cards, danced, and talked into the wee hours about our love of New Orleans. About a week later I realized that a photograph of Elaine was in a New Orleans book I owned, Michael P. Smith's *Spirit World*. The photo was taken in 1980, and she wore a dark-colored choir robe, sunglasses, and a cross around her neck as she prophesied in front of a statue of the Indian spirit guide, Black Hawk, at a Spiritual Church service. I showed the image to Elaine, who was unaware that she had been photographed, but she did remember that particular night in 1988 at the Black Hawk service.

We then engaged in deep conversations about black Christianity and Vodou in New Orleans, and that was the beginning of my long friendship and spiritual relationship with Elaine, who revealed to me that night that she is an initiated Vodou princess. Raised in the Spiritual Churches of New Orleans, Elaine acquired a reputation, in the 1970s and 1980s, as a powerful healer and prophesier in the family and community networks in the neighborhoods around the St. Bernard and St. Thomas housing projects. Her stories revealed the powerful roles that black women have as leaders and healers in the Spiritual Churches and the synthesis that has occurred there between Christianity and Vodou in the religion. According to Elaine, many of the ministers, bishops, and healers in those churches are also devotees of Vodou and use sacred incense, oils, herbs, and candles to influence their congregations. Some of them are even possessed by African and Indian spirit guides during their church services. Because of our mutual interest in New Orleans' black religious world, on Saturday afternoons we often walked through the French Quarter, visiting stores that sold incense and candles used in the spiritual work of New World African religions, and Elaine explained to me the power of landmarks of slavery in the French Quarter, which drew Vodouists to that part of the city to tap the spiritual energies that remained there from the time of Marie Laveau.

All this intrigued me for several reasons. First, I was gathering materials for a new Xavier University course on the history of African American Christianity, which included a segment that my students enjoyed on Vodou in New Orleans. At the end of the course we visited the Historic Vodou Museum in the French Quarter and Congo Square on Rampart Street, and we ended up at Café Du Monde, across from St. Louis Cathedral, which is famous for its beignets and café au lait. Also, at least once a week, I visited my friend Miles at his workplace in Kate Latter's Candy Store, which sold pralines and tourist souvenirs in the French Quarter. Miles, who is a Creole jazz musician, was also studying for the Vodou priesthood, and we often had long and fascinating conversations about the synthesis of African music and religion in the Crescent City. Those discussions stimulated my interest in knowing more about Vodou in New Orleans. Finally, I attended my first jazz funeral in the winter of 1997 for the Mardi Gras Indian Chief Donald Harrison, at St. Augustine Church in Tremé. Thousands of black people participated in the second line for his funeral, including groups with connections to African religions that I wanted to know more about. My friendship with Elaine began to clarify my knowledge of New Orleans' rich contemporary African religious and musical heritage which, she explained, was the spiritual inheritance of all people of African descent in the United States.

When my mother's health crisis began in July, Elaine became an essential part of my support system, introducing me to the healing practices of Vodou in many hours of individual consultations. We talked about the family tensions that had kept me from returning home to Boston for so long. I was impressed when Elaine described a dream to me in which she saw details of the serious arguments that had estranged me from my family. Healing and coping strategies that mend dysfunctional relationships in family and community, particularly at the time of death, are the hallmark of Vodou's power as a living religious tradition. To provide me with the spiritual and emotional strength to deal with my mother's illness and family tensions in Boston, Elaine blessed and prayed in every corner of my New Orleans residence on General Pershing Street to remove the negative energies she sensed there. For spiritual strength, she marked several psalms in my Bible that I was to read in Boston, most prominent Psalm 64:1–2, "Hear my voice, O God, in my prayer: preserve my life from fear of the enemy. Hide me from the secret counsel of the wicked; from the insurrection of the workers of iniquity." Though I was familiar with Psalm 23, which I had memorized and frequently used in my prayers since childhood, Elaine expanded my sense of the Psalms' power, informing me that they were revered for their special magical and healing qualities in Vodou and in the Spiritual churches. After my return to Boston at the time of my mother's death, I functioned more effectively with my family and mended some of the deep tensions in our relationships largely because of the healing energy of the Psalms and my therapeutic conversations with Elaine in New Orleans.

After returning to New Orleans, knowing that my mother would die soon, every day was painful as I awaited the inevitable phone call and struggled to budget money so I could return to Boston in August for the funeral. Elaine's sister, Ceola, and her husband Shawn were very kind, offering to lend me $300 to pay for my second airline ticket to Boston that summer. Shawn's mother had died when Shawn was my age, and so he was empathetic and wanted to be helpful.

On the evening of July 24 Shawn suddenly interrupted our telephone conversation and said: "Maybe we should cut [this] short, your people from Boston may be trying to get through." Immediately upon hanging up the phone, it rang; Karl, a close family friend in Boston, was calling to tell me that my mother had died earlier that day. A few minutes after that phone call, I had a significant spiritual experience, a vivid and colorful vision similar to one I had experienced in Santa Barbara, California, in 1994, on the day my cousin Lamonte died. The earlier vision had also occurred directly after a phone call with family in Boston. In both cases I attempted to discuss these incidents with Protestant ministers and Catholic priests, but they dismissed these profound spiritual experiences as manifestations of shock and imagination at the time of a loved one's death. Discussing these visions with Elaine, however, brought me great comfort and clarity, as visions, dreams, and possession trances are at the heart of Vodouists' spiritual experiences. Dream analysis became important to me directly after my mother died; I wanted her to appear in my dreams to help me understand her death and to answer questions about her life.

In the following months Elaine's counseling and friendship helped me to understand this phase of my mother's spiritual journey. Death, she explained, allowed a soul to travel to its final destination, heaven. Her soul needed her son, her loved one, to "set lights"—spiritual candles— on an ancestral altar with holy incense—frankincense or myrrh, which are mentioned in the Bible—alongside her picture to give her a sign that I loved her and would help guide her with the light to her resting place in heaven. Thereafter, every evening for many years, I looked forward to the comfort of praying, meditating, and lighting sweet-smelling incense and candles on an altar in my living room as I meditated on the mysteries of life and death.

Elaine's description of Vodou as a healing religion of introspection into the mysteries of the universe helped me get through this difficult time in my life. One Saturday afternoon she took me to St. Jude's Shrine on Rampart Street, next to Congo Square, where hundreds of black people prayed for miracles in novena masses every day. In the religious gift shop next to the shrine, she picked out a Christian religious book for me about the extraordinary healing powers and supernatural abilities of angels. Elaine explained that the supernatural qualities of angels are similar to those of the lwa or spirits in Vodou and that St. Michael, the archangel, is the most important angel/spirit to call on to help "fight your battles in the spirit world." Thereafter, red novena candles lit for St. Michael became a central feature of my religious life at home and helped me focus my prayers and work through grief about my mother's spiritual journey and to understand the healing power of God and the spirits.

Although I declined Elaine's invitation to learn more about the deeper mysteries of the religion of Vodou with the possibility of eventual initiation, I remain grateful to the Vodouists who unselfishly shared with me their friendship, religious knowledge, and healing techniques in the year after my mother's death. Vodou provided me with fascinating healing perspectives about the mystery of death. From 1997 to 1999 I attended many second lines and several jazz funerals and began to understand these community rituals on a continuum with other New Orleanian African diasporic traditions, such as the Spiritual churches and Vodou. Participating in ecstatic music and dance, as I photographed second-line performances in the streets of New Orleans, provided great comfort and helped me to heal.

Jazz funerals in New Orleans are the epitome of second-line culture, as they synthesize aspects of the healing arts and music traditions of Vodou, African religions, and African American Christianity, and it is to the analysis and description of these sources that we now turn.

Second Line, Chicken Man Jazz Funeral, 1998

Second Line, Chicken Man Jazz Funeral, 1998

Second Line, Chicken Man Jazz Funeral, 1998

Second Line, Big Chief Donald Harrison Jazz Funeral, 1997

Second Line, Big Chief Donald Harrison Jazz Funeral, 1997

Second Line, Skeleton Man, Super Sunday, 1999

Big Chief Allison Tootie Montana, Super Sunday, 1999

Second Line, New Orleans Jazz and Heritage Festival, 1999

Second Line, New Orleans Jazz and Heritage Festival, 1999

Congo Square Village, New Orleans Jazz and Heritage Festival, 1999

Congo Square Village, New Orleans Jazz and Heritage Festival, 1999

Second Line, Mardi Gras Indian Jazz Funeral, 1999

Second Line, Jazz Funeral, 1999

Second Line, Jazz Funeral, 1999

Second Line, Big Chief Allison Tootie Montana Jazz Funeral, July 9, 2005

Second Line, Vodou Priestess Ava K. Jones, at
Big Chief Allison Tootie Montana Jazz Funeral

Second Line, Skeleton Man, Big Chief Allison Tootie Montana Jazz Funeral

Jolly Bunch Funeral, Olympia Brass Band, February, 1970.
Courtesy of The Historic New Orleans Collection

Jolly Bunch Funeral, Second Line, February, 1970.
Courtesy of The Historic New Orleans Collection

THREE

In Rhythm with the Spirit: New Orleans Jazz Funerals and the African Diaspora

Four centuries ago the Dahomeans and the Yoruba of West Africa were laying the foundation for one of today's most novel social practices on the North American continent—the jazz funeral. Their secret societies assured individual members of a proper burial at the time of death. Many of the associates had the features of a cooperative where through pooled resources individuals were able to accomplish what they couldn't by themselves. When black men were brought to America either direct or via the West Indies, one of the things many retained from their past was this belief in secret societies and their benefits.

JACK V. BUERKLE AND DANNY BAKER, *BOURBON STREET BLACK: THE NEW ORLEANS BLACK JAZZMAN*

New Orleans' African American jazz funerals are the culmination of second-line culture. These funeral processions have roots in at least four rich sources: the West African Yoruba concept of rituals as transformative journeys; the music and burial traditions of New Orleans black brass bands, social aid and pleasure clubs, and the Black Church; Catholic street processions and religious celebrations; and Haitian Vodou's ancestral spirits—the Gede family of spirits who "are the guardians of the dead and . . . embrace the dual domains of human frailty and mortality, the creation and the conclusion of life."[1] To heal the African American community during the crisis of death, contemporary participants in jazz funerals draw on fragments of historical memory and religious and musical traditions based in circum-Atlantic slavery in the Americas as well as in the experience of working-class, post-industrial, urban blacks in the United States. Thus the spiritual and political philosophies that under-lie these public musical ceremonies surrounding death in New Orleans draw on the survival and resistance techniques of "the vanquished" that Patrick Bellegarde-Smith calls "fragments of bone."[2] He writes:

> For me "fragments" means these bits of words, uttered vibrations trans-ported on a wing and a prayer, in the air and on the winds, transposed from a tropical continent onto tropical islands. A new discourse was achieved and new worlds created from (dis)membered segments.... One speaks of shards—in French, échardes or éclats—of those elusive remembrances, always incomplete and altered in passage and in the retelling, erected, re-enacted, and re-creating spiritual systems and religions from fragmentary esoteric knowledge, the whole from the particle. These formed a proto-, pseudo-, and neo-African gestalt in which patterns appear so unified that properties cannot be derived from the parts alone, and the whole cannot be divided easily, into component parts that might make "sense."[3]

The fragments and remembrances that Bellegarde-Smith discusses come together in the traditional communal rituals of jazz funerals. These rituals periodically move the black community into the sacred realm of introspection concerning the legacy of its ancestral culture in Congo Square, Haiti, and West and Central Africa. The power of these per-formative meditations and transformations is evoked by the rhythms of jazz, or what many New Orleanians call "Congo Square music"—the sounds and rhythms that slaves first performed in the nineteenth-century Congo Square gatherings in New Orleans. To illustrate these themes, I analyze my participation in the wake service and jazz funeral of Allison "Tootie" Montana, the former Big Chief of the Yellow Poca-hontas Mardi Gras Indian Tribe, in July 2005, and the most famous Mardi Gras Indian leader in twentieth-century New Orleans.[4]

Big Chief Allison "Tootie" Montana's Jazz Funeral: Prelude

"This has got to stop!" Connugh/Fais! [Stop!]

BIG CHIEF ALLISON "TOOTIE" MONTANA, NEW
ORLEANS CITY COUNCIL MEETING, JULY 7, 2005

Allison "Tootie" Montana (1922–2005), affectionately called "Chief of Chiefs" by his associates in the Mardi Gras Indian culture, and his family, made significant contributions to the music, sewing, and spiritual arts of the Black Indian tradition for more than one hundred years. He died following a heart attack as he testified before a meeting of the New Orleans City Council with Mayor Ray Nagin on June 27, 2005. The hearing focused on the New Orleans Police Department's harassment of the Mardi Gras Indians' parade on St. Joseph's night on March 19. St. Joseph's Feast Day is an important religious festival for Italians in Louisiana and is also a significant day for the Black Indians, as they roam the streets of historic black downtown neighborhoods at night celebrating their music and dance traditions, wearing their colorful Indian regalia. As noted earlier, Super Sunday, their biggest parade and festival day after Mardi Gras, is usually on the Sunday after St. Joseph's night. Montana, surrounded by his fellow chiefs, discussed the police brutality against the Mardi Gras Indians that he had experienced during his fifty-two years of participating in the tradition and told the City Council, "This has got to stop!" Moments later he collapsed at the City Council podium and was dead when he arrived at Charity Hospital.[5]

On July 8 and 9, 2005, Chief Montana's Friday evening Visitation Celebration (wake), Celebration of Life Service, and Saturday afternoon jazz funeral brought together thousands of black New Orleanians to remember his brave spirit of resistance to police brutality against black citizens and his dedication to second-line culture. One community leader proclaimed, "He gave his life for his demands. That's dying with your boots on!"[6] The following narrative and analysis of these events are based on my own participation in, and research into, the African diasporic rituals of these "living" traditions.[7] Jazz funerals, in addition to providing consolation to mourners, re-create "flashes" of memories, rhythms, and rituals that evoke the spirit world of the African diaspora and that periodically move the black community into the sacred realm of introspection about the legacy of circum-Atlantic slavery and its ancestral culture in Congo Square, Haiti, and West and Central Africa.

Fragments of West African Ancestral Memory from Congo Square: Yoruba Influences in Montana's Visitation Celebration and Celebration of Life Service

Yoruba peoples of southwestern Nigeria conceive of rituals as journeys—sometimes actual, sometimes virtual. In elaborate funeral rituals, the elders transfer the deceased's spirit to its otherworldly domain.... In masking rituals, trained specialists bring spectacles of cloth, dance, and music into the world from their otherworldly domain and send them away again to close the performance.... Wherever Yoruba religion thrives—Brazil, Cuba, the United States—this practice has persisted. Cast in performance in a myriad of ways—as a parade or a procession, a pilgrimage, a masking display, or possession trance—the journey evokes the reflexive, progressive transformative experience of ritual participation.[8]

MARGARET THOMPSON DREWAL, *YORUBA RITUAL: PERFORMERS, PLAY, AGENCY*

Joseph Roach describes the fragments of "memory, performance, and substitution"[9] that control the creation of second-line performances. Selected features of "Yoruba ritual," Roach maintains, were chosen for jazz funeral performances because they can evoke the memory of the West African spirit of New Orleans in Congo Square in the past and influence ritual improvisation in the present. Margaret Thompson Drewal's analysis of the transformational power of improvisation and play in Yoruba rituals sheds additional light on improvisational strategies and the interactions between musicians and dancers in New Orleans' second lines. It also illuminates Chief Montana's Visitation Celebration and Celebration of Life Service. Drewal writes:

By improvisation, I mean more specifically moment-to-moment maneuvering based on acquired in-body techniques to achieve a particular effect and/or style or performance. In improvisation each move is contingent on a previous move and in some measure influences the one that follows. Improvisation requires a mastery of the logic of action and in-body codes... together with the skill to intervene in them and transform them.... Each performance, each time is generated anew. Periodically repeated, unscripted performance—including most ritual, music, and dance in Africa—is improvisational. Most performers—maskers, dancers, diviners, singers, and drummers alike—have been trained from childhood in particular techniques enabling them to play spontaneously with learned in-body formulas.... Whenever improvisation is a performative strategy in ritual, it places ritual squarely within the domain of play. It is indeed the playing, the improvising, that energizes people, drawing them into the action, constructing their relationships, thereby generating multiple simultaneous discourse.[10]

The following description of Montana's Visitation Celebration and Celebration of Life Service on Friday, July 8, 2005, from 6 PM to 10 PM in the Mahalia Jackson Auditorium for the Performing Arts in Tremé brings to life both Drewal's theory of improvisation and play in Yoruba ritual and the performances of jazz funerals that re-create fragments of memory, music, and ritual from Congo Square. The descriptions of Montana's traditional celebrations highlight my overall thesis that jazz funerals evoke introspection about the African spirit world and ancestral culture in Congo Square. Indeed, the Mahalia Jackson Auditorium is adjacent to the sacred space of Congo Square and the historic St. Louis Cemetery No. 1 on Basin Street, where the nineteenth-century Vodou queen Marie Laveau is buried.

In the early part of Montana's service, Reverend Dwight Webster, pastor of Christian Unity Baptist Church, performed the invocation and the pouring of libations to the ancestors, and he led a processional of clergymen that included Father Jerome G. Le Doux, pastor of St. Augustine Catholic Church; Reverend Donald Jeanjacques, pastor of True Vine Baptist Church; and Reverend Elijah Melancon, pastor of Elijah Christian Ministries. Musical selections were performed by Desman Barnes and the Soul Heirs, Patricia Montana, the Elijah Christian Ministries Praise Team, Willie Tee, Anita "Miss Lollipop" Bowers, John Boutté, and the Tremé Brass Band. Presentations and speeches of remembrance were delivered by the Montana family, the Mardi Gras Indian Hall of Fame curator Cherice Harrison Nelson, Xavier University administrator Sybil Morial, scholars of New Orleans music Kalamu Ya Salaam and Maurice Martinez, civil rights activist Lolis Elie Sr., and Poet Laureate of Louisiana Brenda Marie Osbey.[11]

Times-Picayune reporter Lolis Eric Elie Jr. discussed the significance of the Yoruba praise singers who performed in Montana's Celebration of Life Service and their link to the African spirit world of Congo Square:

> In the Yoruba religious tradition of West Africa, the spirit Oya is guardian of the gates of the cemetery. She is also the spirit who rules the winds and the hurricanes. And she is the spirit to whom the dancers danced as they entered the Mahalia Jackson Theatre of the Performing Arts for Allison "Tootie" Montana's memorial service Friday evening. Nine is Oya's number. Though clad in white, each dancer also had nine sashes of different colors draped from his or her waist. The praise singer at

the microphone sang a simple two-line phrase. Perhaps she sang in litur-
gical Yoruba, the sacred variation on that West African language. What-
ever the origins of the sounds she employed, her two-line phrase ended
in two words, the English speaking audience understood well: "Chief
Tootie." . . .

Who can say whether Oya deigned to intervene in such human affairs
as Montana's funeral? But we do know this: the hurricane that threatened
to disrupt both the funeral and Saturday's second-line memorial parade
disturbed neither. . . .

Fred Johnson, who masked as the spy boy with Montana in the 1970s
and 80s, quietly intoned one of the standard songs of the Indian repertoire. "Golden crown, golden crown," he sang, "My Big Chief got a golden
crown." Soon he was joined on stage by other Indians, including Montana's son Darryl. "You know the one thing that makes them mad," he
sang. "We got the Big Chief they wish they had."

When the song was over, Johnson spoke directly to Montana's widow,
Joyce. He may not have known it but Oya is the female warrior in Yoruba
cosmology. Though her husband Shango is the warrior king, she is considered a fiercer fighter than he. Though Tootie Montana may have been the
center of attention, his wife was always at his side, whether they were sewing or socializing. So in memory of Tootie Montana and in praise of Oya,
it was entirely appropriate that Johnson's remarks included the statement,
"I just wanted to say, Joyce, for every great man there is a great woman."[12]

In the first phase of the Celebration of Life Service, the Black Indian
Chiefs on the stage sang an emotional rendition of the Mardi Gras Indian hymn, "Indian Red." Thereafter the second line began in the auditorium, and their performances resonated with Drewal's analysis of the
in-body codes, spontaneity, and transformative relationships generated
by improvisation and play in Yoruba ritual. The Indian Chiefs onstage
shook their tambourines in honor of Tootie Montana, "Chief of Chiefs."
The Chiefs, the Yoruba dancers, the African drummers, and members
of the Montana family began to dance off the stage and through the auditorium as hundreds of people in the audience formed a second line
to dance and follow them to the front lobby. The second-liners reached
one of their highest points of energetic dancing and chanting, "Big Chief
Got a Golden Crown," in the lobby as they were surrounded by African
drummers and beautiful photographic images of Chief Tootie Montana. The participants moved in rhythm with the spirit of the powerful
African drummers, as they proceeded out of the auditorium into the
grassy courtyard in front of the building. Hundreds of second-liners, im-

provising dances in African rhythms to large and small African drums, cowbells, tambourines, and rattles, surrounded the front and sides of the theater, as dancing images were highlighted in the moonlight and reflected dramatically in the water of the small pools and fountains outside the building. The joy and exuberant spirit of the second line was so profound that one man shouted, appropriately, "This is Mardi Gras in July."

The "domain of play"[13] in the second line for Chief Montana's Celebration of Life Service culminated when the masked African dancers on high stilts appeared and began to dance playfully in the midst of several hundred second-liners outside the auditorium. The dancers were dressed in deep yellow and gold skirt-like ritual clothing with stringy brown masks hanging down to their shoulders and hiding their faces. They danced not only in perfect rhythm to the African drummers but also back and forth in rhythm with the second-liners, interacting with them in multidimensional and self-reflexive patterns of play and performance.[14]

The masking spectacle in this second line recalled the Egungun masks that represent "the spirits of the ancestors . . . in the play segments of [Yoruba] funerals." In the Yoruba context, masked "ritual specialists" use performance to transform the consciousness of mourners by enabling the journey of the ancestral spirits "from their otherworldly domain . . . into the world . . . and send[ing] them away again through their performances of spectacles." The play of the Egungun performer is also intended "to cheer up the community" at the time of death.[15]

Ritual specialists who organize jazz funerals in New Orleans have the power to select African rituals and themes from various sources that illustrate Joseph Roach's process of surrogation, as they stimulate contemporary memory of African performances in the Crescent City's past. For instance, at the jazz funeral for New Orleans' Vodou priest Chicken Man Fred Staten, on January 31, 1999, the dominant African rituals and themes came directly from the Vodou religion, as the second-liners who were Vodouists carried large banners emblazoned with the vévés, or cosmograms of Vodou spirits. The vévés evoked powerful memories of the performances and rituals of Marie Laveau, who in her time lived along the same route in the French Quarter followed by the second-liners at Chicken Man's funeral.[16]

At around 10:30 PM the procession for Chief Montana in front of the Mahalia Jackson Auditorium began to thin out, as small groups of second-liners followed different bands of African drummers who danced out of the gates of the performing arts complex into the adjacent Louis Armstrong Park, which includes the grounds of Congo Square on Rampart Street. I was in a group of approximately twenty second-liners who danced, strutted, and followed the music of a band of five drummers into Congo Square. The performances that followed evoked the African ancestral spirit world of Congo Square. The drumming was hypnotic and so intense that its power pulsed through my body like a heartbeat. One by one, several of the second-liners who were part of the drumming and dance circle stepped into the center of the ring of performers and improvised frenetic African dance solos. Several dancers in this group went into trances—their eyelids fluttered, their pupils slid to the back of their eyes, and at least one person temporarily lost consciousness. A beautiful, slender, young African American woman, wearing white jeans and a turquoise tank/ top, was caught twice when she momentarily lost consciousness as she performed an intricate African dance that possessed both her and the crowd surrounding her. A tall young black man with thick black curly hair who was attired in baggy blue jean shorts and a large blue and white striped polo shirt then danced into the center of the ring. He appeared to be possessed by the drum rhythms, as he danced first upright, then with his body close to the ground, and finally with his body prostrated on the ground, moving in perfect rhythm to the African spirit of the drums. Finally, a young white woman with reddish hair under a black hat adorned with a large feather, and dressed in a black short-sleeve top and black jeans, performed an aggressive, high-kicking African dance with wide slicing arm movements that accentuated the rhythms of the drums and suggested the warrior dance of the Vodou lwa Ogou.[17]

Were the majority of these second-liners Vodouists or devotees of Yoruba religion? I do not know, and I did not ask. But I do know that their second line expressed both the cultural memory and subconscious knowledge of drumming, singing, and dancing in those African diasporic religions. Yvonne Daniel's analysis of "the powerful aesthetic, emotional, physical, spiritual, and mental consequences of a unified ritual community with huge numbers of performers performing in unison"[18] in Haiti, Cuba, and Bahia elucidates the spiritual power embodied in the performers of Chief Montana's second line in New Orleans. She writes:

> In the ritual contexts of Haiti, Cuba, and Bahia, strong belief systems initiate regular, routine ceremonial performances among African Americans. The ceremonies that have developed concentrate heavily on either the human or the suprahuman body; that is, a human body that has been transformed by a spiritual incorporation. The communities meet according to a ritual calendar, and whenever they come together, they are a mass of dancing bodies. They are expressive dancing bodies in the same space at the same time performing the same movements to the same rhythms. The dancing bodies accumulate spirit, display power, and enact as well as disseminate knowledge. Worshipping performers reenact what they have learned, what they have been told, what they feel, and what they imagine. . . . The communities dance and support the transformation of a few for the benefit of the many. A suprahuman body is the result of spiritual transformation, when the worshipping, believing, and dancing human body is prepared for or overwhelmed by the arrival of spiritual force. The dancing human body proceeds to unfold spiritual energy, or, in the believers' understanding, to present or manifest divinities, who are aspects of a Supreme Deity.[19]

I left the second line when it disbanded at around 11:15 PM. One of the drummers, an African American man in his forties dressed in a black suit with an unbuttoned white shirt, shook my hands and thanked me for my participation in the performances. I walked out of dark, grassy Louis Armstrong Park and crossed Rampart Street, which was bustling with the excitement of people on their way to nearby clubs. I walked down St. Ann Street into the French Quarter, stopped in a bar to have a couple of beers, and returned to my hotel room on Canal Street to sleep before the Saturday morning jazz funeral at St. Augustine's Church in Tremé.

Fragments of Black Christian Ancestral Memory from Congo Square: St. Augustine Catholic Church and the Sanctified Church

I felt the world swallow me up when I heard that Fred was gone. . . .
They brought him back to be buried at our little church and the crowd

that turned out for the funeral was a sight to see. . . . The wake went on all night long and lodge bands formed outside the church and played until I thought my heart would break. After the funeral was over, the bands began to blow it out without charge. People from everywhere formed "the second-line," and they paraded back to the Sixteenth Ward—all the men who'd been Fred's lodge brothers and the men and women who had known him—and took all the saloons apart in one big spree. Everybody said Fred would have loved it if he'd been there.

MAHALIA JACKSON, *MOVIN' ON UP*

The central issue considered in this section is how St. Augustine Catholic Church and Sanctified Churches in New Orleans have influenced performative meditations of historical memory and ecstatic music and dance derived from Congo Square and West Africa in the second lines of jazz funerals. Jason Berry calls churches "the missing link in jazz history"[20] because of the paucity of research on the synthesis of black religion and black music in the Crescent City. Although jazz funerals are dynamic, improvised performances that change over time to reinterpret new substitutions of religion, music, history, and politics from black America and the African diaspora, analysis of selected narrative accounts of the connections between churches and the Africanisms in early jazz funerals reveals the historical significance of St. Augustine Church as a site for Congo Square music and the ancestral rituals in Big Chief Tootie Montana's contemporary jazz funeral. As we shall see, the historical memory of jazz funerals and Congo Square music and religion has been influenced by Black Christianity in New Orleans.

Mahalia Jackson, an iconic figure in the history of gospel music, was born in New Orleans in 1911, and she still remembered, in 1966, the healing power of the Black Church and African American community in the jazz funeral and second line for her favorite cousin Fred in the late 1920s. The procession for Fred, whose nickname was Chafalaye "after the river in the country near where he'd been born,"[21] began at Mount Moriah Baptist Church. According to Jackson, in her childhood,

they didn't play jazz at the funerals. The band would play as solemn as a choir on a big pipe organ—right out in front of the church where the funeral service was being held. Then they would march behind the hearse—

all the way to the cemetery. They didn't play jazz on the way either—
that's the bunk. After the family had left and the man was buried, then on
the way back they would jazz it up. The musicians had been paid so they
would play coming back from the cemetery, full of spirit—blow it out free
of charge—and the folks along the way would have a good time. That's the
way a funeral band was.[22]

Jackson's story typifies the corpus of fragmentary narrative accounts
of early jazz funerals, in which churches are important, but rarely explored, in the effort to understand the fragments of African ancestral
memory from Congo Square in these community healing rituals.

Mahalia Jackson's narrative re-creates in my memory the opening
scene of Chief Montana's jazz funeral. Hundreds of second-liners, musicians, and spectators assembled outside St. Augustine Church waiting
for his casket to be released from the Catholic funeral mass in order to
begin the long processional to the graveyard. The dirges of brass horns
warming up and the rhythms of African drums, Congo Square music,
and second-line dancers rehearsing their steps echoed in the humid
air around the church on that Saturday morning, July 9, 2005. St. Augustine, a black Catholic Church on the corner of St. Claude Avenue
and Governor Nicholls Street in Tremé, is one of the most historically
important black churches in the United States. Established in 1841 by
African-descended free people of color and slaves, it is also one of the
oldest black parishes in the U.S. The church, in the 1850s, was home to
the second oldest religious order of African American Catholic women
in the nation, the Sisters of the Holy Family. Near the church, and linked
to its historic mission to African Americans, is the Tomb of the Unknown Slave, a shrine with a large fallen cross constructed with "iron
balls," "shackles," and "marine chains welded together."[23] Father Jerome
Le Doux, the African American priest and community leader who conducted Chief Montana's funeral mass, explains the fragments of ancestral African memory (from Congo Square) that is re-created in the
shrine:

> The Tomb of the Unknown Slave, of course, is analogous to the tomb of
> the unknown soldier in Arlington, Virginia. It's pretty much the same
> idea. And the big difference is that it's slaves, and what we do know is that
> all over this country, there are many slaves buried, and nobody knows

who they are or where they are, and especially in this part of the country, here in Tremé, where there was a . . . concentration of slaves. We know a number were murdered and when people murder you, they don't tell anybody where the body is. . . . They bury it secretly. So there are many secret burials.

The other problem is plague, things like malaria, yellow fever, in particular here, so you get thousands of people dying on occasion. There's no place to bury them. The cemeteries won't hold them. And so, we know they're buried around the city. And we know exactly where they are, choose someplace. What better place than on the side of a church where slaves actually worshipped, where they had their own seats on the two-side aisles, seats bought for them by the free people of color, and given them to be their own in perpetuity.[24]

St. Augustine Church is also an important site of political resistance that looms large in historical memory, because a member of the church was Homer Plessy, the African American Creole citizen of New Orleans who challenged the legality of racial segregation in public accommodations in the landmark U.S. Supreme Court case *Plessy v. Ferguson* in 1896. On May 19, 1996, Father Jerome Le Doux, pastor of the church, blessed Plessy's tomb in St. Louis Cemetery No. 1 in a large public ceremony following a jazz funeral in Plessy's honor in the streets of Tremé that lead to Congo Square.[25]

St. Augustine was the church of the great early-twentieth-century jazz saxophonist Sidney Bechet, whose slave ancestor, Omar, was a Vodouist and musician in nineteenth-century Congo Square. It is an important landmark for jazz funerals and second-line culture because of its location in Tremé, New Orleans' "oldest fauburg (suburb)."[26] Tremé was established in 1812 and ever since the late 1700s was "the home of many skilled artisans [and] gens de couleur libre (free people of color)"[27] of African American, Haitian, and Cuban origin. Tremé is historically significant for Congo Square music and religion, and for its architecture, nightclubs and bars, second lines and street culture, and numerous jazz musicians who resided there before Hurricane Katrina; indeed, according to the New Orleans musician Milton Batiste, Tremé is the "very epitome of where blues and jazz actually was born."[28]

St. Augustine Church is across the street from an important second-line institution—the Backstreet Cultural Museum at 1116 St. Claude Avenue. Sylvester Francis, the black community's official photographer of jazz funerals since 1980, established the museum in 1999 to exhibit the culture of jazz funerals and second lines with displays of Mardi Gras Indian suits and the original clothing and material art of the social aid and pleasure clubs. Francis's exhibits are housed in the former Blandin Funeral Home, a historic landmark for jazz funerals and jazz musicians for many generations in New Orleans.[29]

In this context, St. Augustine Church is an important site for jazz funerals not only because of its Black Christian traditions but also because of its significance for "the process of 'surrogation' . . . in new performances of ideas from the past"[30] that originated in fragments of the African spirit world and the Congo Square culture. The performances for the dead that take place on the streets surrounding the church are as important for second-line culture and the ancestral memory of Congo Square as what goes on inside the church. Two significant aspects of the funeral ritual—the Black Catholic Church and the Congo Square–derived second line—were synthesized in a seamless performance in Big Chief Tootie Montana's jazz funeral. It is important to note that these aspects of the funeral express separate but interactive realms of religious and musical experience in the formation of the African American community of New Orleans.[31]

Although numerous jazz funeral processions in New Orleans begin their journey to the graveyard at the powerful Afro-Creole crossroad at St. Augustine Church, the Sanctified Church—another black Christian tradition with a storied history in the Crescent City—has also profoundly influenced fragments of West African–derived memory and performance from Congo Square in the music and dance traditions of jazz funerals. Mahalia Jackson, queen of gospel blues and a devout Baptist, emphasized the profound African ancestral influence of the Sanctified Church on African American vernacular music in early-twentieth-century New Orleans:

> I know now that a great influence in my life was the Sanctified or Holiness churches we had in the South. I was always a Baptist, but there was a Sanctified church right next door to our house in New Orleans.
> Those people had no choir and no organ. They used the drum, the cymbal, the tambourine, and the steel triangle. Everybody in there sang and they clapped and stomped their feet and sang with their whole bodies. They had a beat, a powerful beat, a rhythm we held onto from slavery

days and their music was so strong and expressive it used to bring the tears to my eyes.

I believe the blues and jazz and even rock and roll stuff got their beat from the Sanctified church.[32]

Another great African American musician of twentieth-century New Orleans, Louis Armstrong, the king of jazz (the contemporary park surrounding Congo Square was named in his honor), was deeply influenced by the music of the Sanctified Church. Jackson and Armstrong both talked about the connections between the African ancestral memory of the music of the Black Church and the music of jazz funerals. Regarding the "uptempo rejoicing" in the brass band hymns of the funeral, Armstrong said, "Yeah Pops—jazz actually arose from the dead . . . the real music came from the grave. That was how jazz began. That's why it brings people to life."[33]

Both Armstrong's and Jackson's parents were part of a wave of forty thousand migrants who moved from numerous plantations in Mississippi and Louisiana to settle in the Crescent City in the late nineteenth century. Thomas Brothers notes that these migrants were initially different in religion and culture from the downtown Catholic Afro-Creoles in Tremé and "brought with them a culture that had been strongly shaped by the legacies from various parts of Africa."[34] Their memory and performance of West African–derived religious and musical traditions had a profound impact on jazz and second-line culture from Congo Square. By 1900 these ex-slaves and their families found "common ground at Funky Butt Hall, where both the blues and sacred music were performed, in storefront churches and in street parades and funerals."[35] Much of their music and religion was influenced by the dynamic and vernacular oral tradition of poor blacks who were primarily Protestant and lived uptown, as Mahalia Jackson's family did.

Although Louis Armstrong lived downtown and was baptized at birth at the Catholic Sacred Heart of Jesus Church, he later wrote that Congo Square music—jazz and second-line culture—"all came from the old Sanctified churches."[36] During his childhood in New Orleans, his mother, May Ann, sent him to the Sanctified Church,

that featured communal focus on a direct experience of the Holy Spirit, the one that cultivated vigorous rhythms that made your body move and deeply felt melody that made your heart pour out—the tradition that in many ways transmitted the core values of vernacular African-American culture in the South.... Music for them ... fostered wholeness by bringing spirituality, communality, and politics into the same performing circle. Their musical-social-spiritual practice was a technique for resisting pressures to fragment and reify experience, just as it had been for their ancestors in slavery and Africa.[37]

Jessie Charles, another black New Orleanian who observed the ritual connection between second-line culture and the Sanctified Church, focused on the dances of the second-liners and said, "Second-line—that's the life of parade and a funeral. . . . Dancing in Sanctified churches is like the second-line."[38] Thus the communal music, the African ancestral memory, and the trance-inducing worship style of the Sanctified Churches influenced second-liners in jazz funerals in Louis Armstrong's youth in the early twentieth century. Together these influences brought the ecstatic "circle-dance traditions of West Africa"[39] into the realm of the street processions of black New Orleans. By the 1950s Roland Wingfield saw the same West African dance features in the second line of a New Orleans jazz funeral: "The dancers moved with pelvis thrown forward, the upper body slightly tilted back, loose and responding freely to the rhythm, legs slightly apart and propelling a shuffling step with a subtle bounce—a step characteristic of Africa and found often in Brazil and the West Indies."[40] Certainly these African-derived performances of ecstatic dance were also integral to the second line of hundreds of performers, Black Indians, and musicians who danced and posed for photographs in the streets outside St. Augustine Church as they waited for Chief Montana's funeral mass to end and his jazz funeral to begin. These ritual elements evoked introspection about the African spirit world and ancestral music in Congo Square.

A final note is in order about the complex synthesis of West African music and dance in New Orleans Spiritual Churches and their ties to the African ancestral memory of jazz funeral processions. In these churches, which combine Roman Catholicism, Spiritualism, Vodou, and Pentecostalism in ecstatic worship, "members may be filled by the Holy Spirit, as in Pentecostal churches, or 'entertain' spirits or spirit guides, as in Spiritualism or Voodoo. Prophecy and healing are presented as the markers of this faith, and the Native American figure Black Hawk as a major symbol of empowerment."[41] According to Jason Berry, "their founder, Mother Leafy Anderson, was a faith healer and medium of African and Native American ancestry who summoned spirits of the dead to commune with the living. In 1920 she came from Chicago to establish the denomination led by women and gladdened by jazz bands."[42] These small churches, with names such as Guiding Star Spiritual Church, St. Lazarus Spiritual Church, St. Daniel Spiritual Church, St. Christopher Spiritual Church, and Israelite Universal Divine Spiritual Church, were also influenced by the religious work of Mother Catherine Seals, who founded the Temple of the Innocent Blood in the late 1920s and who housed numerous young black women and their babies in her compound in the Lower Ninth Ward of New Orleans.[43]

A significant Black Christian tradition is seen, therefore, in the interactions between, fragments of sacred space, African-derived music, and burial traditions, and also between the performances of jazz funerals and Congo Square music and religion since the formative years of Mahalia Jackson and Louis Armstrong in New Orleans. Celebrated musical and religious traditions from St. Augustine Catholic Church and the Sanctified Church have continued to influence the sacred realm of introspection about African ancestral culture in contemporary New Orleans jazz funerals. This powerful synthesis between Black Christianity and African-derived traditions in the Crescent City is rooted in Haitian and New Orleanian Vodou, and it is to the analysis of the considerable influence of this religious tradition on jazz funeral performances that we now turn.

Re-creating the Congo Square Beat: Healing Fragments of Vodou and West African Secret Societies in Montana's Jazz Funeral

[Vodou] rituals do, actually, work so often, for the primary effect of such ritual action is upon the doer. That action reaffirms first principles—destiny, strength, love, life, death; it recapitulates a man's relationship to his ancestors, his history, as well as his relationship to the contemporary community; it exercises and formalizes his own integrity and personality.... He emerges with a strengthened and refreshed sense of his relationship to cosmic, social and personal elements. A man so integrated is likely to function more effectively than one whose adjustment has begun to disintegrate, and this will be reflected in the relative success of his undertakings.

MAYA DEREN, *DIVINE HORSEMEN: THE LIVING GODS OF HAITI*

Michael Largey has developed the following definition of Vodou, which emphasizes the intimate communal healing and living traditions of the religion. His definition is useful for understanding "the process of 'surrogation'"[44] of Vodou ritual and the historical memory of Congo Square music derived from West African secret societies in Chief Montana's jazz funeral:

> Blending several West and Central African spiritual traditions with Roman Catholicism, Vodou is a religious practice focused on the spiritual and emotional well-being of its practitioners. Healing is effected through group worship and individual consultations with oungan and manbo (male and female Vodou priests, respectively). Practitioners believe that spirits, called lwa, travel from ancestral Africa, or Ginen, to help their followers in the material world. Through a series of prayers, songs, and dances, lwa are invited to possess the bodies of worshippers and to provide counsel— from friendly advice to stern admonition—through the mouths of their devotees. Iwa are anthropomorphic and have individual personalities; worshippers are drawn to those Iwa with whom they have a personal and spiritual affinity. Worshippers learn about lwa not only through Vodou ceremonies but also through the successive retelling of stories about lwa in which their personal attributes and extraordinary qualities are recounted. Such storytelling has both religious and political significance; worshippers use Vodou narrative to connect themselves with spiritual values and to make sense of political situations in the present.[45]

New Orleans jazz funerals synthesize spiritual and musical elements from Vodou, Christianity, and African American and Congo Square music to re-create, strengthen, and mend the relationships between the community of the living, the ancestors, and the dead. In doing so, these rituals draw on the power of the fanmi—the African-descended ancestral family over which the Gede spirits reign. The Gede are unique in Haitian and New Orleanian Vodou. According to Karen McCarthy Brown:

> They are neither Rada nor Petwo . . . Their aggregate is described by the intimate term fanmi (family) . . . Papa Gede sits at the center of the thick

weave of relationships that make up a family—an ideal place for a healer to be, because all Vodou healing is the healing of relationships.[46]

The Gede include numerous lwa who help human beings restore balance and "raise life energy"[47] through the healing strategies of humor and sensuality during the crisis of death. Chief among these lwa are Baron Samdi, the father and leader of the Gede. He is the judge of the dead who lives in the cemetery at the crossroads where his cross is located. He is an erotic trickster who adores children and wears a top hat and sunglasses that signify his wisdom to "see between the worlds of the dead and the living."[48] The Baron's wife is Manman Brijit, who also dwells in the cemetery and provides spiritual wisdom about regeneration, death, and judgment. She is known in New Orleanian Vodou as the "Mother of the Dead."[49]

At Chief Montana's funeral, thousands of New Orleanians waited for two hours in ninety-degree heat outside St. Augustine's Catholic Church where his funeral mass was conducted. The scene resembled an intimate extended family reunion, as people hugged, renewed family and friendship ties, and drank ice water provided by groups of women. Meanwhile, the members of the African diasporic secret societies— the Mardi Gras Indians, Vodouists, and second-line dancers—played their tambourines and drums, posed for pictures, and danced in the side streets around the church as we all awaited the end of the funeral mass and the ritual of transferring the casket from the church to a horse-drawn hearse. The jazz funeral procession began with a somber Black Protestant hymn, "Just a Closer Walk with Thee," performed by the Tremé Brass Band.[50] Black New Orleans brass bands trace their roots to West African secret societies and slave musicians in nineteenth-century Congo Square, and they are the key to re-creating both the Congo Square beat and the healing ethos of the African-descended communal family in jazz funeral processions.

Keeping the Congo Square Beat: Black Brass Bands and Black Secret Societies

Black brass bands have a long and venerable history in New Orleans that dates back to the 1860s and 1870s with the bands of Thomas Kelly, St. Bernard, Frank Dodson, Charlie Jaeger Richardson, Vinet, Wolf,

Louis Martin, and Sylvester Decker.[51] These early bands played popular music for concerts and dances, military music for parades, and "dignified sonorous dirges"[52] for funeral processions organized by black secret "societies of benevolence,"[53] during the Reconstruction era (1865–1877). Although William J. Schafer and Michael Burns trace these black bands to European and Euro-American brass bands, Samuel A. Floyd Jr. advances our understanding with his analysis of how their music is linked to the West African roots of the Gede spirits, how it maintains the healing wisdom of the Congo Square beat and "ring ceremonies," and how it encompasses the African diasporic rituals of jazz funerals. Floyd writes:

> In New Orleans, and in other cities, African Americans practiced ring ceremonies, accompanied funeral processions with marching bands, and organized secret societies. Some aspects of these activities merged to help create the environment for and the character of the music that would be called jazz. And in spite of the fact that the presence of marching bands and secret societies among African Americans is usually attributed by some scholars . . . to European influences, they are as much African as they are European, and the primary influences on black jazzmen were most likely the African antecedents. . . . As for the secret societies, I have already noted their presence in Africa before the slave trade, and the existence of African secret societies has long been known among some folklore scholars.[54]

Floyd cites the black musician Bunk Johnson's description of the interaction between music and ecstatic dance in the second line of an early-twentieth-century jazz funeral as a rich example of the West Africa roots of black brass bands and the influence of the Congo Square drum beat:

> On the way to the cemetery with an Odd Fellow or a Mason—they [were] always buried with music you see—we would always use slow, slow numbers such as "Nearer My God to Thee," "Flee as a Bird to the Mountains," "Come Thee Disconsolate." We would use almost any $\frac{4}{4}$, played very slow; they walked very slow behind the body.
>
> After we would get to the cemetery, and after that particular person were put away, the band would come to the front, out of the graveyard. . . . And then we'd march away from the cemetery by the snare drum only until we got about a block or two blocks from the cemetery. Then we'd go right into ragtime.
>
> We would play "Didn't He Ramble," or we'd take all of those spiri-

tual hymns and turned them into ragtime— $\frac{2}{4}$ movements, you know, step lively everybody . . . "When the Saints Go Marching In," . . . "Ain't Gonna Study War No More," and several others we would have and we'd play them just for that effect.

We would have a second line there that was the most equivalent to King Rex parade—Mardi Gras Carnival parade. The police were unable to keep the second line back—all in the street, all on the sidewalks, in front of the band, and behind the lodge, in front of the lodge. We'd have some immense crowds following.[55]

Finally, Floyd's commentary on the fragments of African historical memory in Johnson's aforementioned funeral narrative traces the origins of second lines and black brass band music in contemporary New Orleanian jazz funerals to "ring ceremonies" in West Africa and African American slave communities and "line dances" to the Congo Square beat:

> Cultural and "motor" memories of the mass, circle, and line dances of African societies and of slave culture were operative. The second-line . . . was not a new invention. . . . Akan children watch and imitate their elders in ring ceremonies, moving "along the fringes of the ring and behind it," . . . as do the children, youth, and adults in the second line of New Orleans jazz funerals.
>
> This mythic call to Dance, Drum, and Song in the form of parades goes back to the African processions . . . with trumpets and drums—and back to the burial rites of Africans and African-American slaves. . . . From these ceremonies, because of the necessity of the participants to move to a remote destination, the ring straightened to become the second-line Bunk Johnson described in his account; and the change from the slow dirge to the short spiritual on the return remarkably mimics the walk-to-shout, slow to quick progression of the ring shout. There can be no mistaking the fact that the beginnings of jazz in the ring—as partial as it may have been—was a direct result of the transference of the structure and character of the shout to funeral parades of black bands and community participants. . . .
>
> What I am saying is that the impetus for the development of this music was ritual, the ring ritual of transplanted Africans extended and elaborated through spirituals and folk rags. They converged in the ring— these spirituals and this ragtime—and awaited the blues, which joined them directly. In these early jazz funerals were found the trope of the ring, including the heterogenous sound ideal, which was creatively extended in the form of two rhythmic groups: the front line of cornet, clarinet, and trombone and a rhythm section of drums and tuba.[56]

The Tremé Brass Band that performed in Chief Montana's jazz funeral reinterpreted many of the fragments of West African ceremonial memory and "line dances" to the Congo Square beat that were performed by black brass bands in nineteenth- and early-twentieth-century jazz funerals. In Montana's funeral procession, performances by numerous African American secret societies including Mardi Gras Indian tribes, Vodouists, social and pleasure clubs, and Baby Dolls—a group of women who continue an early-twentieth-century Black Carnival tradition by dressing like dolls in short frilly dresses and baby hats—were rooted in the spirit of the Dahomean and Yoruba "social practices [for] a proper burial."[57] That spirit of West African community values, according to New Orleans musician Danny Barker, influenced the Crescent City's earliest jazz funerals. In the late nineteenth century the rapid growth of black secret societies in the Crescent City—benevolent and mutual aid associations to assist with health insurance and burial—paralleled the rapid growth of black brass bands and supported their music in funeral processions. These societies re-created the spirit of the African-descended fanmi and the Congo Square beat in New Orleans that had been cultivated in the city's complex Congo Square culture before the Civil War.[58]

Dorothy Rose Eagleson notes that black secret societies in New Orleans grew by leaps and bounds in the 1880s because legalized segregation "was not yet fixed by Louisiana law, although discrimination was everywhere evident."[59] Thus New Orleanians of African descent began to withdraw from white public life and "were forced to depend upon themselves for many of their social needs."[60] Benevolent and mutual aid associations that "gave pharmaceutical, medical, and financial assistance to the sick and provided burial service"[61] included L'Avenir, Francs Amis, Dames et Demoiselles de la Candor, Jeunes Amis, Young Men's Philanthropic, United Sons of America, Equal Justice and Marine, United Daughters of America, Ladies of Mercy, Pure Friendship, Young Friends of Hope, Pilgrim Aid, Rising Sons of Liberty, Perseverance, the Young Female Benevolent Association of Louisiana, No. 1, and La Concorde. More than one hundred of these societies and at least thirteen black fraternal orders existed in New Orleans during this period, and their members often participated in elaborate funeral processions and parades led by black brass bands.[62]

Although the early black brass bands also played for circuses, outdoor dances, minstrel shows, and church events, Schafer writes that from 1890 to 1915 their music had a profound influence on the emergence of New Orleans jazz as a new musical form:

> The main impact of band music on it was on strengthening its beat—providing a tension between the march's strong, striding 1- and 3-beat emphasis and the Afro-American penchant for 2- and 4-accents. . . . The multithematic structure of the march coupled with ragtime, gave early jazz a convenient formal basis. And the polyphonic formula of band scoring was crucial in conventionalizing instrumentation in early jazz.[63]

In jazz funerals, many important New Orleans musicians, such as Louis Armstrong, played in early-twentieth-century black brass bands that took the Eurocentric instrumental skills and "sight-reading" of downtown Afro-Creole musicians and combined them with the musical styles of uptown musicians derived from the improvisational music and the ecstatic behavior of Black Protestant churches.[64] The new music they created—jazz—expressed the healing wisdom of the Congo Square beat, the West African values of social interaction and improvisation in communal ritual music and black "masculine dignity"[65] and freedom in the streets of New Orleans. In the words of John Storm Roberts:

> [In the] repressive post Reconstruction period . . . Black musicians were then in the process of integrating what had been, on the one hand, definitely African survivals and, on the other, relatively undigested borrowings. The synthesis was being completed. A music that was truly Afro-American, in which African-derived musical techniques and concepts fundamentally made over elements from white America, was coming to maturity.[66]

After 1909 black social and pleasure clubs devoted to partying, social events, and second lining such as the Zulu Social Aid and Pleasure Club began to compete with the benevolent and mutual aid associations for membership. Meanwhile, the Tuxedo Brass Band led by trumpeter Oscar Celestin was re-creating the Congo Square beat and pioneering "the second-line beat"[67] that directed the improvisational performances of black secret societies in jazz funeral processions. This hypnotic beat is "a syncopated pattern on the brass drum that may be phonetically rendered as 'Dah, Dah, Dah, Didit, Dah!' Transfer this rhythmic feel to the horns, and the whole band swings—it makes you want to dance. . . . But it was the ability and inclination to depart from the written score that made New Orleans brass bands so special."[68]

The historical memory of the Congo Square beat, together with the ability of the black brass band's "second-line beat" to direct the performances of ritual dances and re-create fanmi power through communal dance in contemporary jazz funerals, connects its music to the Gede spirits in the danced religion of Vodou and in Big Chief Montana's public procession. Roberts sheds light on the nature of these interactions in African-derived music and ritual:

> Music is closely involved in religious practice. Whereas it is not essential to Christian rituals—however it may add to their impressiveness—many African ceremonies simply could not take place at all without appropriate music. To give just one example, the spirits are summoned by the drums in both Yoruba and Dahomeyan ceremonial, each by its own special rhythms. No drums, no spirits—and no ritual.[69]

Because of the high mortality and unhealthy housing conditions that black New Orleanians inherited from slavery, the early days of jazz funerals saw an acute demand for benevolent associations, which used black members' dues to provide health and burial insurance, and for the black brass bands that played at funerals. John W. Blassingame reports the following nineteenth-century statistics:

> Between 1860 and 1880 the annual death rate of Negroes fluctuated between 32 and 81 per thousand exceeding that of whites by from 5 to 39 per thousand. The infant mortality rate of Negroes was especially high: 450 per thousand in 1880. The differential in mortality is, of course, reflected in the lower life expectancy of blacks. While a white child at age one had a life expectancy of 46 years, a Negro child at age one had a life expectancy of only 36 years. . . . The most important cause of Negro family disorganization during Reconstruction, however, was the high rate of mortality among Negro males. In the age group 15 to 44, the death rate of Negro females was 15.93 per thousand in 1880; of Negro males, 26.66, or an excess of 10.73 deaths per thousand . . . the excess of deaths of Negro males over females increased at almost every age stratum. . . . Although the same pattern of increasing sex differentials in death rates at each age stratum prevailed among whites in New Orleans, it was not as serious as among blacks.[70]

Recently, the president of the National Urban League and former mayor of New Orleans Marc Morial reported contemporary national statistics with "devastating and far-reaching ramifications" for black mortality.[71] These statistics underline the interaction between systemic racism and high death rates in the Crescent City's black neighborhoods that produce the circumstances for jazz funerals and the healing wisdom of the Congo Square beat in the twenty-first century:

> African American men are more than twice as likely to be unemployed as white males and make only 75 percent as much a year. They're nearly seven times more likely to be incarcerated, and their average jail sentences are 10 months longer than those of white men. In addition, young black males between the ages of 15 and 34 years are nine times more likely to die of homicide than their white counterparts and nearly seven times as likely to suffer from AIDS.[72]

The power of jazz funerals and black brass band music to generate communal feelings of joy and triumph that trump the despair of death, in light of such constant and startling mortality for black New Orleanians from the nineteenth century to the present era, underlines these rituals' surrogation of key themes from Vodou and Congo Square culture, including strategies for healing, coping, resistance, and continuity. From this standpoint, the Congo Square beat, second lines, and jazz funerals present "a unified and formidable form of resistance to hostile authority, and over the years they have become closely associated with the idea of freedom and political advancement among blacks in New Orleans."[73] Although the themes of the African-descended communal fanmi, joy, triumph, freedom, and resistance have remained constant in the brass band performances of jazz funerals since the early days of Mahalia Jackson and Louis Armstrong in New Orleans, the music of black brass bands is nonetheless dynamic and has been significantly transformed and reinterpreted in twentieth- and twenty-first-century jazz funerals.[74]

The following sketch of the major transformations in twentieth-century black brass band music suggests that the jazz funeral tradition and the Congo Square beat change with the times and the social and political energy of the streets of the Crescent City.[75] In the 1880s and 1890s the most prominent black brass bands in New Orleans were the Excelsior, the Onward, the Pickwick, the Alliance, and the Pelican.[76]

Although the Onward Brass Band (1885–1930) and the Excelsior Brass Band (1880–1931) played marches and dirges for funeral processions and parades and were led by musicians who played "written music,"[77] these bands, along with the Eureka Brass Band and the Tuxedo Brass Band, employed some of New Orleans' most talented jazz musicians in the early twentieth century: Manuel Perez, Lee Collins, Kid Ory, Bunk Johnson, Johnny Dodds, King Oliver, and Louis Armstrong, who brought the improvisation and blues of the new music—jazz—to brass band performances.[78] The African communal spirit and the Congo Square beat of brass band music in jazz funerals was so irresistible to musicians in this era that, "on August 8, 1922, Armstrong finished playing for a funeral"[79] just before he boarded the train to leave New Orleans to move to Chicago.

In the early twentieth century new black clubs were organized such as the Merry-Go-Round Club (1914) and the Wolves Social and Pleasure Club (1915), and jazz funerals were somber and "dignified" processions dominated by mournful brass band renditions of gospel music, dirges, and blues, including "Nearer My God to Thee," "What a Friend We Have in Jesus," "Flee as a Bird," "In the Upper Garden," "Fallen Heroes," and "Weary Blues"—until the body was "cut away" at the cemetery. At that point the second line took over with joyful dancing to the Congo Square beat of such brass band numbers as "We're Glad You're Dead You Dirty Dog," "Oh, Didn't He Ramble," "Black Bottom," "Tell the Truth," and "Brown Skin, Who You For."[80] Danny Barker recalled a jazz funeral he attended in 1917:

> And the Masons turned out for him . . . Must have had 300 of 'em. They looked like an army with high plume hats like admirals wear. They had four brass bands. My grandfather (Isidore Barbarin) was playing alto horn in Onward (Brass Band).[81]

According to Schafer, black brass bands declined during the Great Depression and World War II, and began a long period of revival in 1945 and 1946, when Bunk's Brass Band and the Original Zenith Brass Band were recorded, respectively, on American Music and Circle Records. In the 1950s the Eureka Brass Band's sound was available on Folkways Records, and Atlantic Records produced albums for the Young Tuxedo

Brass Band in 1958 and the Eureka Brass Band in Preservation Hall in 1962. These records brought the music of black New Orleans' second lines and the Congo Square beat to a national audience.[82]

At the same time, as Gregg Stafford, a trumpeter with several contemporary black brass bands, notes, the music and traditions of jazz funerals and the Congo Square beat began to change in the period of commercialization and commodification of their music:

> I came up at a time when I was playing for Knights of Pythias, Oddfellows, all kinds of Masonic lodges. I saw the membership extend for five or six blocks. In later years, as the membership began to dwindle, I saw those blocks diminishing, lifestyles changed with the emergence of the insurance companies, so it was no longer necessary to belong to an organization. I loved that. I remember how proud I was, how good I felt about wearing a uniform and band cap . . .
>
> To see all those customs, and all these songs had structure, just thrown out of the window—you could hear the Onward band coming up the street sounding like a forty-piece band, all playing in harmony, nobody getting in anybody's way . . . Everybody still wants to ride on the coattails of Louis Armstrong, still claiming they're playing traditional jazz or brass band music. I guess they're using brass band instrumentation, but that's all.[83]

For others, by the 1960s era of civil rights activism the jazz funeral had become "a fading tradition" dominated by the music and respectability of aging jazz musicians. New bands, such as the Olympia Brass Band, organized by Harold Dejan in 1960, began to cater their performances to the tourist industry in New Orleans and abroad.[84] Nonetheless, contemporary jazz funerals with the Congo Square beat and the musical and spiritual vibrance of Big Chief Tootie Montana's procession may owe their existence to the Fairview Baptist Church Brass Band, organized in 1972 by the elder jazz guitarist Danny Barker, who had played with Jelly Roll Morton, Cab Calloway, and other jazz greats. This was a groundbreaking band that made brass bands, second-lining, and the Congo Square beat "cool"[85] for a new generation of talented young black jazz musicians in New Orleans. In the 1970s Barker's successful brass bands of teenage musicians evolved into the Hurricane Brass Band, the Younger Fairview Band, and the Charles Barbarin Sr. Memorial Band. In 1983 Danny Barker again organized the Roots of Jazz Brass Band

in the Tambourine and Fan Club community center for youth established in Hunter's Field by civil rights activist Jerome Smith. Some of
the New Orleans jazz musicians who played in these new brass bands included Michael White, Branford and Wynton Marsalis, James Andrews,
Nicholas Payton, Charles and Lucien Barbarin, Gregg Stafford, Joe Tor-
regano, Leroy Jones, William Smith, Revert Andrews, Gerry Anderson,
Anthony Lacen, Daryl Adams, Kevin Harris, Efrem Towns, Eddie Bo
Parish, and Charles Joseph.[86]

However, the Dirty Dozen Brass Band revived the Congo Square
beat and the African spirit of late-twentieth-century jazz funerals by
incorporating new musical influences from contemporary rhythm and
blues and New Orleans street and club dancing into the traditional brass
band repertoire.[87] The band was established in the Sixth Ward by trum-
peters Gregory Davis and Efrem Towns, saxophonists Roger Lewis and
Kevin Harris, sousaphonist Kirk Joseph, trombonist Charles Joseph,
and drummers Benny Jones and Jenell Marshall. Their innovations in
second-line music brought the Dirty Dozen record contracts and international fame. New Orleans music critic Kalamu ya Salaam evaluated
the influence of this band on a new generation of second-liners who re-
created the Congo Square beat in the 1980s:

> It is . . . the timeless "Africanoid celebration of life" spirit which lifts this
> band past anything you may have experienced before within the realm of
> twentieth century music. . . . The Dirty Dozen is dance music, procession/
> possessed music. Although you may find it hard to envision what kind of
> dancing is done to this furious accompaniment, just believe that the hu-
> man spirit can guide the feet of young men and women as they glide and
> hop through these familiar (to them) melodies and are buoyed by both an
> empathy with the music and an ability to move their bodies in time to the
> micro cross-rhythms that dart around between . . . the Dirty Dozen as they
> improvise new melodies over old rhythms.
>
> In New Orleans the Dirty Dozen makes its home in a tiny bar called
> the Glass House, located on Saratoga Street. Every Monday night that
> they are in town, the band blows as young dancers keep alive the "Bam-
> boula" movements of Congo Square where their slave ancestors danced on
> antebellum Sundays.[88]

Influenced by two 1970s bands that had begun to transform second-
line dancing and the Congo Square beat by introducing rhythm and

blues music—Dejan's Olympia Brass Band ("I Got a Woman," "No It Ain't My Fault," and "Mardi Gras in New Orleans") and The Majestic Brass Band ("Hey Pocky Way")—the Dirty Dozen, with their first album, *My Feet Can't Fail Me Now*, profoundly changed second-line dancing and shifted the mood of somber strutting at the beginning of jazz funerals to wild joyful dancing.[89] The title of that album became the anthem of a new generation of young second-liners at jazz funerals who demanded jubilant and up-tempo renditions of gospel hymns from the beginning to the end of a procession to accommodate "the faster urgency of modern dance rhythm . . . achieved by filling in the beat on both bass and snare drum and adding extra percussion in the form of cowbell and tambourine."[90]

Since the 1980s this innovative "funk" or "street" style of brass band music has generated new popularity and interest in the Congo Square beat, second-line culture, and jazz funerals, and has continued in the music of contemporary bands such as the Rebirth Band, the New Birth Brass Band, the Soul Rebels, and the Forgotten Souls Brass Band. Some bands such as the Dirty Dozen and the Forgotten Souls spent most of their time recording and giving concerts. Other groups—the Mahogany Brass Band and the Algiers Brass Band—continued to play the traditional repertoire of early-twentieth-century brass bands. Donna's Bar and Grill on Rampart Street and the Maple Leaf on Oak Street became known for brass band music and second-line dancing on specific nights every week.[91]

The Tremé Brass Band, formed in 1991, continued to play at jazz funerals and maintained its cultural and musical connections to its neighborhood and the Congo Square beat. It was also one of the first young brass bands to play regular gigs at local clubs such as Donna's.[92] The ascendancy and complexity of contemporary brass bands matched the popularity of contemporary social and pleasure clubs in black neighborhoods. At the time of Big Chief Montana's jazz funeral in 2005, black New Orleanians were members of the following clubs that sponsored annual second lines and jazz funerals for their members:

> 2nd Line Jammers Social and Pleasure Club, Avenue Steppers Social Club, Better Boy, Big 7, Big Nine, Black Men of Labor, Calliope High Steppers Social Club, Chosen Few, Devastating Ladies, Diamonte Ladies, Distinguished Gentlemen, Divine Ladies Social and Pleasure Club, Dumaine Gang, Extraordinary Gentlemen, Fazzio's First Ladies, Five Booster Club,

Golden Trumpets Social and Pleasure Club, Jolly Bunch Social Aid and Pleasure Club, Just Steppin', Keepin' It Real, Ladies of Dynasty, Ladies of Essence Social Aid and Pleasure Club, Ladies Prince of Wales, Lady Buck Jumpers Social Club, Lady Jet Setters, Lady Sequences Marching Club, Lady Zulus, Money Wasters Social and Pleasure Club, Nandi Exclusive Gentlemen and Ladies Social Aid and Pleasure Club, New Orleans Men Buck Jumpers, Nine Times Social and Pleasure Club, N'Krumah Better Boys Social Aid and Pleasure Club, N'Krumah Third Division Social Aid and Pleasure Club, No Limit Steppers, Old and New Style Fellas, Olympia Social Aid and Pleasure Club, Original 7 Social Aid and Pleasure Club, Original Black Magic Social Aid and Pleasure Club, Original Gentlemen, Original Lady Buck Jumpers, Original Men's Prince of Wales, Original New Orleans Lady, Original Step 'n' Style, Perfect Gentlemen Social and Pleasure Club, Pigeon Town Steppers Social Aid and Pleasure Club, Popular Ladies, Positive Ladies Social Aid and Pleasure Club, Prince of Wales, Real Men Social and Pleasure Club, Revolution Social Aid and Pleasure Club, The Rollers, Scene Boosters Social Aid and Pleasure Club, Single Ladies, Sophisticated Ladies Social Aid and Pleasure Club, Sudan Social Aid and Pleasure Club, Tambourine and Fan, Tremé Sidewalk Steppers, Unknown Steppers, The Untouchables, Valley of Silent Men Social Aid and Pleasure Club, VIP Ladies, West Bank Steppers Social Aid and Pleasure Club, Young and Old Men Legends Social Aid and Pleasure Club, Young Men's Olympian Social and Benevolent Club, Young Steppers Social and Pleasure Club, Zig Zag, Zulu Social Aid and Pleasure Club.[93]

By 2005 there were at least twenty-five black brass bands in New Orleans, with various musical and performance influences from traditional styles to rap, hip hop, and reggae (in the case of the Soul Rebels).[94] Yet the unifying musical and religious theme of brass bands in contemporary jazz funerals is how the musicians combine the gospel blues music of the Black Church with the African diasporic dance and music performances of the Congo Square beat and the second line. Roberts identifies New Orleans jazz funerals as the "best known of an array of New World funerary traditions with strong African elements—in this case not so much the music as the ways in which it is used. . . . The strongest elements of African music are retained when the music continues to serve the same purpose as it did in Africa."[95]

In the case of contemporary jazz funerals, such as Big Chief Montana's procession, gospel music played by the Tremé Brass Band involved several African elements of the Congo Square beat. Their wailing brass band instruments performed the function of "'talking' instruments" as they "imitated the human voice"[96] and interacted with talking drums in their rendition of the gospel hymn, "Just a Closer Walk with Thee." The connection of African music to speech is an important element of music derived from African sources, as is its relationship to dance and "bodily movements,"[97] of second-line dance performance. The Tremé Brass Band's performance of gospel music was an improvisational tapestry of call and response chanting and singing with the Mardi Gras Indians and the second-liners in Montana's jazz funeral. The call and response elements of gospel music are derived from African sources, according to Roberts.[98] As mentioned previously, African ceremonies that invoke the spirit world cannot occur "without the appropriate music."[99] In Dahomeyan and Yoruba rites, the "spirits are summoned"[100] by music and are returned to the supernatural realm by drum rhythms. As we return to the narrative account of Big Chief Montana's jazz funeral in the next section, we will see that one of the most striking African elements in that procession was how the brass band's performance of gospel music and the Congo Square beat interacted, through improvisations, with the appearance of the Vodou lwa of death and the cemetery Baron Samdi in the second line.[101]

Baron Samdi, Leader of the Gede: Healing and Life Energy

For the first few minutes of Chief Montana's jazz funeral, the twenty members of the Tremé Brass Band played a slow and sorrowful rendition of "Just a Closer Walk with Thee," as the grand marshall—"head erect, expression solemn, dressed in a black [suit] . . ., hat held respectfully in his hand while taking slow but measured steps"[102]—led the procession down St. Claude Avenue. The Vodou and Yoruba priestess Ava Kay Jones, wearing a white dress and head turban and shaking an ason—a sacred wood African rattle of Vodou ritual—also walked at the head of the procession. Then the energy of thousands of second-liners who crowded the streets and sidewalks shifted to joyful dancing, strutting, and hopping as the brass band began to play an upbeat version of the gospel hymn with a second-line Congo Square beat.

For the next four hours the ecstatic drumming, dancing, and chanting of the Mardi Gras Indians, Vodouists, and anonymous second-line dancers dominated the funeral procession as it wound through the steamy streets of the Tremé neighborhood of New Orleans. The powerful healing energies of Gede leader Baron Samdi switched the mood of the second line from somber mourning to joy and passion as people danced, partied, celebrated, and hugged one another while the procession traveled slowly to the cemetery. Bruce Barnes, the African American musician and folklorist who played the role of Baron Samdi in Chief Montana's second-line procession, described the significance of the Gede in New Orleans:

> The lwa Gede which is the guardian of the cemetery is very strongly present here. Early lwa that are revered here like Baron Samdi in New Orleans are the same in Haiti. . . . Gede is associated with death. He is very rambunctious, he's overly sexually active. . . . Gede controls the whole thing. The color of Gede is purple . . . the basic color of Mardi Gras. Gede is everywhere that has anything to do with Mardi Gras. . . . Part of their function is to remind us of our ancestors that have gone on.[103]

Gede's performances for death take second-liners "on a journey through their most out-of-control selves and, in so doing, prepare them to move back into the ordinary world where reserve and control must reign."[104] In this regard, fragments of historical memory about the healing arts of Vodou play an important role in contemporary jazz funerals. Baron Samdi's performance signals a linkage "between sexuality and life energy"[105] in the spiritual philosophy of the religion. According to Karen McCarthy Brown, the rituals of Vodou attempt to "heat things up"—"to raise luck, to raise life energy, to intensify sexuality."[106] The performances of Gede and the skeleton gangs at jazz funerals bring to the community "an extra, intense dose of the power needed to conquer life, to use it and enjoy it, rather than be conquered by it."[107]

The Skeleton Gangs: Introspection into the Mysteries of Life, Death, and the Ancestors

> These fragmentary remains stood for the dismembered bodies discarded on the ocean's floor—the residue, the "collateral damage" from the trade between three continents: Africa, the Americas, and Europe. The depth of the ocean is still the domain of Olokun, a Yoruba deity transmogrified by some in the Americas as the "patron

saint" of the black race. The bones were laid thick; they made a brittle carpet upon which slave ships glided and memories derailed.

PATRICK BELLEGARDE-SMITH, *FRAGMENTS OF BONE*

The skeleton gangs, also called the bone men, are an important manifestation of the Gede in New Orleanian funeral processions and Carnival. Their performances in jazz funerals "bring to the surface a connection between"[108] life, death, and the ancestors that is a central theme in Congo Square religion and music. I talked to a member of the skeleton gang outside St. Augustine's Church on the day of Chief Montana's funeral. He wore a large white skull-shaped mask with scary black eyes, a black nose, and large black and white teeth. He said:

> We are the oldest Indian gang. The skeleton gang goes back to the nineteenth century. We want to scare you and teach you that you never know when you're gonna go. Death can come at any time, so you better make the best of the life you have.[109]

Some members of the skeleton groups involved in Carnival and funerals also wear a body-length black costume on which the skeleton's white bones are painted, as well as a black apron depicting a white casket and a white cross on top of a cemetery headstone. According to Bruce Barnes:

> You see almost the exact same costume in terms of skeleton gang here in New Orleans and . . . in Haiti . . . Gede is a part of the spiritual pantheon of Haiti which was brought to New Orleans and incorporated into local Vodou beliefs. Gede is associated with death, the skeleton itself, and fertility.[110]

One member of the skeleton gang emphasized the aspect of Gede's "healing arts" that focus on children: "We go after kids . . . to stress to them a point about going to school. 'Are you going to school; are you being good? If not I'm gonna see you tonight.' We put fright into them to remind them of what they are supposed to be about."[111]

However, according to the above second-line participant, the most significant aspect of the skeleton's relationship to Gede "is to remind us to enjoy life while we can. You next! That's the main word. You are next!"[112] In the final section of this chapter, introspection into the mysteries of life, death, and the ancestors culminates in St. Louis Cemetery #2 and in the second line from the graveyard that expresses the communal love, healing, resistance, and life energy of Congo Square music and religion.

St. Louis Cemetery #2, City of the Dead: Crossroads for Congo Square Music and Religion

Go into the tombed cities along basin, canal boulevard, valence and esplanade . . . to honor the dead . . . live among your dead, whom you have every right to love.

BRENDA MARIE OSBEY, "PECULIAR FASCINATION WITH THE DEAD," IN *ALL SAINTS: NEW AND SELECTED POEMS*

New Orleans arguably has the most extensive above-ground tombs, crypts, and cemeteries in the United States because of its African-Latin heritage and the geology of the city, which is built below sea level and prone to floods. New Orleanians call their cemeteries "cities of the dead," an expression suggesting their significance as places where the ancestors live and as crossroads for the African diasporic funeral rituals of the living.[113] Here all the healing fragments of Congo Square music and religion come together in a final second line for a beloved member of the community. In Haiti the cemetery is the home of the Gede and also a crossroads for important Vodou rituals, as the Kwa Baron (the cross of Baron Samdi) is located there. The most important urban cemetery in Port-au-Prince is a city of the dead owned by the government. According to Karen McCarthy Brown, "it is not a point of acess to the most powerful of one's own family dead; instead it is the main shrine for Gede, representative of all the dead."[114] Because Vodou is a more powerful and popular religion and more of a competitor to Christianity in contemporary Haiti than in New Orleans, tensions have arisen between Vodou and the Catholic Church regarding the rituals at the Kwa Baron in the Port-au-Prince Cemetery.[115]

On the other hand, because contemporary New Orleanian Vodou is less openly practiced than its Haitian counterpart, there appears to be a more peaceful synthesis between Vodou and the Catholic Church in Crescent City cemeteries. All Saints' Day, the Catholic feast day on November 1 when New Orleans residents visit, decorate, clean, and celebrate the gravesites of their ancestors, is still a major holiday in New Orleans, and the two religions share significant thematic similarities in their death rituals. Robert Florence writes about these similarities and the West African roots of Congo Square religion and music:

> In a city whose largest cultural influences are Roman Catholic and West African—two traditions that involve an interplay with death—this spiritual disposition naturally imbues the cities of the dead. . . . Many people in New Orleans are conditioned by their environment and upbringing not to run from and shun death, but to embrace and celebrate it. New Orleans cemetery traditions are joyful; many paths leading there are paved by jazz funerals, and the popularity of New Orleans' All Saints Day is a definite American anomaly. . . . New Orleanians often go to the cemeteries not so much to mourn and lament but to pray for solace and to achieve communion with deceased friends and loved ones.[116]

The synthesis between Vodou and Christianity in Gulf Coast cemeteries is also highlighted by the arrangement of tombs in New Orleans' oldest city of the dead, St. Louis Cemetery #1. Established by the Archdiocese in 1789, it houses the tomb of Marie Laveau (1801–1881), which is an important crossroad for Vodou ritual and Congo Square music and religion, and is the most popular gravesite for tourists in the Crescent City. Yet many people of African descent who tap the spiritual wisdom of Laveau's resting place also revere the historically significant tombs of Black Catholic New Orleanians such as Homer Plessy (1862–1925), who, as noted, was the plaintiff in the famous Supreme Court case that established racial segregation in the United States, and Ernest "Dutch" Morial (1929–1989), the first African American mayor of New Orleans, whose tomb is next to Marie Laveau's.[117]

Big Chief Tootie Montana's final resting place is St. Louis Cemetery #2, New Orleans' "second oldest surviving city of the dead," founded in 1823.[118] The cemetery is situated beneath the Interstate 10 overpass, where the Black Mardi Gras parades led by the Zulu Social and Pleasure Club happen every year on Fat Tuesday. Square #3 of the cemetery houses some of New Orleans' most important African American citizens from the nineteenth century, including Oscar James Dunn (1821–

1871), Louisiana's first African American lieutenant governor; Henriette Delille (1813–1862), one of the co-founders of the Sisters of the Holy Family, the second order of African American nuns in the United States; Rodolphe Desdunes (1849–1928), early civil rights activist and author of *Nos Hommes et Notre Histoire,* which traces the history of the Afro-Creole community in New Orleans; Jean Baptiste Roudanez, who established the first African American daily newspaper in New Orleans; and, many believe, Marie Laveau's daughter, Marie Laveau II. There is also speculation that the remains of Marie Laveau might actually be in St. Louis Cemetery #2, not St. Louis Cemetery #1.[119]

Chief Montana's jazz funeral procession finally reached the gates of St. Louis Cemetery #2 at 3:30 PM, after many hours of joyous and sensuous dancing, drumming, and partying by the second-liners. In that "city of the dead" I experienced Gede's profound wisdom as "a transformation artist" and the healing power of Congo Square music and religion. According to Karen McCarthy Brown, "he raises life energy and redefines the most painful situation—even death—as one worth a good laugh."[120] When we entered the cemetery, several young men ran around the graveyard hugging the tombstones, greeting their ancestors. Other young people found a comfortable place to sit—on top of the tombstones of the city of the dead. Suddenly the thought came to me that this second line is not a party, it really is a funeral—and a man whom I have known, respected, and cared about is gone forever. And I began to shed tears that were hidden by my sunglasses.

Fifteen minutes later the second line sadly left the graveyard as we wound our way to the repast—the prepared meal awaiting us at the Tremé Community Center in Louis Armstrong Park. In a split second, the Tremé Brass Band began to play jubilant gospel music with the Congo Square beat, "When the Saints Go Marching In," that made the sad crowd begin to laugh, kick our legs up in the air, and swing our arms wildly. Hundreds of adventurous second-liners danced on parked cars and on the edge of high walls. Men, who ordinarily might fight one another after a drink or two, hugged instead. The healing power of the music coursed through our bodies, as we danced jubilantly from the graveyard to our repast of spicy red beans and rice and beer. I saw Baron Samdi with his large top hat and sunglasses mischievously heating up the positive energy and frenetic dancing in the midst of the final phase of the celebratory jazz funeral procession. Bruce Barnes's words shed light on the powerful interaction between Congo Square music and religion and the transformative energy of the Gede in New Orleans jazz funerals:

> Music is what makes the culture and it's the history and the story of the people . . . Music . . . is what everything is based off. It's a way of life. Not many things are done culturally without being based off the music whether it's a birth or a death.[121]

Jazz funerals are the culmination of second-line culture and Congo Square music and religion. They express some of the most profound innovations of jazz—"the notion of freedom, polyphony, spontaneity, and collective improvisation"[122]—in communal rites of passage exemplifying the African idea of musical traditions that encompass religious traditions and protect participants from the hardships of life and death. The musical and religious traditions of jazz funerals reinterpret fragments of African ancestral memory from Congo Square, Haiti, and West and Central Africa. According to Michael P. Smith:

> In African consciousness the sacred and the secular are inseparable. Just as jazz combines disparate elements into a harmonious whole, jazz funerals merge church life with street life. They are rites of passage with profound spiritual resonances: more than just burying the dead and celebrating eternal freedom, they serve as a ritual of community affirmation.[123]

I found the spiritual philosophy of resistance, continuity, and the healing and coping strategies in Congo Square music and religion to be personally meaningful at a crucial point in my life. My inclusion of personal material in this chapter and in the interlude "takes the reader to a deeper and broader understanding"[124] of African diasporic religions and follows a distinguished tradition of scholarship on these religions that was first established by Zora Neale Hurston and continues in the work of Maya Deren, Karen McCarthy Brown, Claudine Michel, and Patrick Bellegarde-Smith.

West and Central African spirituality, Vodou, Black Protestant and Catholic Christianity (and their synthesis in "jazz religion") are religions "of major stature, rare poetic vision, and artistic expression"[125] that deeply influence fragments of African diasporic religion, music, and dance performances in the second-line culture and jazz funerals of New Orleans. Second-line culture remembers the genius of African-descended ancestors from slavery and beyond who pieced together healing fragments of historical memory from Africa, the Caribbean, and Congo Square to re-create religion, music, and dance performances in the Crescent City—the most African city in the United States. Jazz religion continues to move New Orleans' black community into the sacred realm of introspection about the legacy of circum-Atlantic slavery and its ancestral culture in Congo Square, Haiti, and West and Central Africa in the twenty-first century.

A Jazz Funeral for "A City That Care Forgot": The New Orleans Diaspora after Hurricane Katrina

We were abandoned. City officials did nothing to protect us. We were told to go to the Superdome, the Convention Center, the Interstate Bridge for safety.... We tried them all for every day over a week. We saw buses, helicopters and FEMA [Federal Emergency Management Agency] trucks, but no one stopped to help us. We never felt so cut off in all our lives. When you feel like this you do one of two things, you either give up or go into survival mode. We chose the latter. This is how we made it. We slept next to dead bodies.... There was garbage everywhere in the city. Panic and fear had taken over.

PATRICIA THOMPSON, KATRINA SURVIVOR, 2005

Long before Hurricane Katrina, New Orleans, which was almost 70 percent African American, was known as "a city that care forgot" because of the mistreatment of its black citizens.[1] This phrase does not adequately express the contrast between the racial brutality experienced by black citizens and the pleasure enjoyed by tourists in the Crescent City. By 2000, 35 percent of the African American population lived in poverty and suffered the hardship of a failing public school system, high unemployment, racism, police brutality, and the highest imprisonment rate of any major U.S. city.[2] Hurricane Katrina, the deadliest natural disaster in American history, struck New Orleans on August 29, 2005, and, in the words of Xavier University professor and jazz musician Michael White "changed everything . . . for every resident of New Orleans."[3] From August 29 to September 1 the levees broke and water from Lake

Pontchartrain filled the city, resulting in deadly flooding that put 80 percent of New Orleans under water. City, state, and federal officials underestimated the severity of Katrina and its aftermath, and failed to evacuate many of the city's poorest and most vulnerable citizens, most of whom were black. The Superdome and the Convention Center, the shelters of "last resort" for the tens of thousands of people trapped in the floodwaters of New Orleans became, for all practical purposes, concentration camps. While President George W. Bush remained on vacation in the early days of the disaster,[4] citizens went for days without food, water, safety, medical care, or working toilet facilities. City, state, and federal officials did not make sensible plans to ensure for food, water, safety, and sanitary conditions in the facilities. As a result, thousands of Crescent City citizens went hungry or suffered major health crises, and some died in shelters, in the streets, in hospitals, and in their flooded homes as they waited in vain to be rescued by the New Orleans Police Department, FEMA, or the National Guard. In the words of Cleo Fisher, an elderly man who came to the Superdome without his heart medicine: "It's worse than being in prison in there. They don't have nothing for me."[5] Describing her experience in the Superdome, Tina Wilson said, "They have us living like not even pigs."[6]

Help for the citizens of New Orleans finally came on September 2, when President Bush toured the Gulf Coast and General Russel Honoré arrived to coordinate the National Guard's distribution of food, water, and medical help and the evacuation of the city.[7] During the evacuation in the following days, many black people were forced to leave the bodies of their dead relatives and neighbors on the streets, in the floodwaters, or in their abandoned homes. Lucrece Phillips will never forget the floating bodies and the face of death that she saw as she was rescued from the roof of her home in the Lower Ninth Ward:

> The rescuers in the boats that picked us up had to push the bodies back with sticks. And there was this little baby. She looked so perfect and so beautiful. I just wanted to scoop her up and breathe life back into her lungs. She wasn't bloated or anything, just perfect. . . . I know this storm killed so many people. There is no Ninth Ward no more. No Eighth or Seventh Ward or East New Orleans. All those people, all them black people drowned. . . . After all we had been through those damn guards at the Dome treated us like criminals.[8]

The National Guard treated Crescent City citizens like refugees from a foreign land; families were separated and people were forced to board buses and airplanes to destinations unknown across the United States. Michael Eric Dyson aptly described the evacuation as reminiscent of the Middle Passage of transatlantic slavery.[9]

At least 1,577 citizens in southern Louisiana died in Hurricane Katrina, and many of their names are still unknown.[10] According to Marc H. Morial, the former mayor of New Orleans and president of the National Urban League:

> One year later there are some signs of progress but also evidence that we have a long way still to go. Thousands remain dislocated. Employment is still far below pre-Katrina levels and many essential services—including public transportation, schools, and hospitals—haven't recovered fully.[11]

According to the National Urban League's "Katrina: One Year Later":

> In the first six months after Katrina, New Orleans lost nearly 280,000 residents—64 percent of its population. . . . The percentage of African-Americans in the city fell from 36% to 21%. Roughly 41% of Katrina evacuees are still displaced from their homes . . . 23% are unemployed. . . . Rent for 1-bedroom apartments is 39% higher than before the storm, and the number of households in trailers hit 114,000, 28% more than six months ago.[12]

What does all this portend for second-line culture and the healing arts of Congo Square music and religion two years after the storm? Although numerous second-line street parades and jazz funerals have taken place since Hurricane Katrina, the future of New Orleans' African diasporic culture has been profoundly affected by the city's African American diaspora after the storm,[13] the largest migration of black Americans in the U.S. since the Great Migration of the World War II era. One 2006 discussion of the demographics of the African American diaspora before Katrina pointed out that New Orleans "was predominantly black. Today there is parity between blacks and whites, or a slight advantage for whites, a first for New Orleans in decades."[14] As reported in the *Times-Picayune,* the U.S. Census Bureau estimated New Orleans' population as of July 2006 at 223,000.[15] In August 2007 the Brookings Institution's Metropolitan Policy Program reported that the Crescent City's population had reached "68 percent of its pre-hurricane level."[16]

Yet demographers and economists in Louisiana in January 2007 predicted that "New Orleans will top out at about half its pre-storm population of about 444,000. . . . At the moment, the population is well below half, and future gains are likely to be small."[17]

These estimates all suggest that the city has lost half its population since Hurricane Katrina. The federal government plans to destroy five thousand public housing units that were previously the homes of poor African American citizens of New Orleans.[18] In 2006 FEMA reported that 243,000 New Orleanians (many of whom are African American) had relocated to Houston, San Antonio, Baton Rouge, Atlanta, and Birmingham.[19] Recently the New Orleans City Council unveiled plans to rebuild forty-six storm-ravaged neighborhoods at a price of more than two billion dollars.[20] Yet little has been done to date to restore important African American neighborhoods such as the Ninth Ward, the Seventh Ward, Tremé, Gentilly, and New Orleans East, and a study of New Orleans by Brown University social scientist John Logan concludes that the city might lose "80 percent of its Black population."[21]

The Crescent City is now the "murder capital of the United States,"[22] and its current mayor, Ray Nagin, believes that "the slow pace of New Orleans' post-Katrina recovery is part of a plan to change the city's racial makeup."[23] At a March 2007 meeting of the National Newspaper Publishers Association, Nagin said, "What happened in New Orleans could happen anywhere. They [the white leaders?] are studying this model of natural disasters, dispersing the community and changing the electoral process in that community."[24]

Many New Orleans musicians who play in second-line brass bands and who are members of Mardi Gras Indian tribes moved to Houston, Austin, Atlanta, Nashville, and Lafayette, Louisiana, after the storm, and some have decided not to return to New Orleans. "Me and four of my kids lost our houses, and my brother Cyril lost his and my sister lost hers,"[25] said Aaron Neville, who was living in Nashville in 2006 and does not plan to move back to New Orleans because of his asthma. Some of the key performers have returned home to live. Greg Stafford, renowned trumpeter in the Young Tuxedo Brass Band, returned to reside in his Central City neighborhood in 2005 but worries that "the future depends on the leaders of the city and how they allow people to come back and not allow gouging by landlords."[26]

Terence Blanchard, who composed the music for Spike Lee's documentary, *When the Levees Broke,* says:

> My mom's house was destroyed and my wife had a house we used for an office. So we basically cleaned all that out to get a different place, a bigger place to accommodate all that. I wouldn't leave this city for anything in the world. This is one of the most significant periods in our history and I want to be here to be part of the rebuilding. . . . The product that is coming out of here is amazing, not only in terms of music, but in literature and everything else.[27]

"The music heals,"[28] says Cyril Neville, who is now living in Austin, Texas. Irvin Mayfield, director of the New Orleans Jazz Orchestra, lost his father in the flood after Hurricane Katrina but nonetheless is planning a foundation, named Music for Tomorrow, to help musicians return to New Orleans.[29] Darryl Montana, Chief of the Yellow Pocahontas Mardi Gras Indian tribe, lost everything during the disaster and evacuated to Texas, but he has returned to the city to rebuild his family home in New Orleans East. In June 2007 he estimated that 75 percent of the black people involved in second lines had returned home, but he did not know where they were living.[30] One of those, Michael White, the jazz clarinetist who lost thousands of New Orleans jazz materials of great historical significance when his Gentilly home was destroyed by the flood after the storm,[31] now "splits his time between New Orleans and an apartment in Houston."[32]

The jazz funeral procession continues to be an important ritual to express both grief and hope for "a city that care forgot" during and after Katrina. In late October 2005, a few days before All Saints' Day, the Young Tuxedo Brass Band led a jazz funeral procession in the streets of Gretna and New Orleans which was organized by the Crescent City Funeral Directors' Association to memorialize the deaths caused by Katrina.[33] In February 2006 the Zulu Social Aid and Pleasure Club, the oldest Black Mardi Gras krewe, sponsored a jazz funeral procession and second line from St. John Institutional Missionary Baptist Church on Jackson Avenue to their headquarters on Broad Street to remember the victims of the storm.[34] Two jazz funerals were noteworthy among the numerous memorial ceremonies that were held on August 29, 2006, the first anniversary of Hurricane Katrina. The Algiers Brass Band led a second-line funeral procession from the Superdome in the Central Business District, the site of so much suffering during the storm.[35] Second liners also participated in a ceremony performed by spiritual leaders at the location of the Lower Ninth Ward levee breach, and then followed a hearse and the Hot 8 Brass Band to Congo Square[36] in Louis Armstrong Park to "honor those who passed on [and to] fight for the right to return for those who are still displaced."[37] Clearly this was a healing ceremony, but the organizers of the ceremony were also issuing a call for social justice:

> Survivors of the Superdome, Convention Center and Gretna Bridge blockade—call to make an appointment with a lawyer to testify about witnessing crimes committed by agents of government. Nearly a hundred potential witnesses—still traumatized and seething with anger—have responded to a flyer announcing the arrival of representatives of the National Conference of Black Lawyers who are preparing for an International Tribunal. Some witnessed troopers holding guns to the heads of little girls, others speak of summary executions by agents of the government. They will march on August 29th demanding justice for the assault on the human rights of the people of New Orleans.[38]

Two years after Hurricane Katrina, prospects of most of New Orleans' African American residents to return to their city are uncertain, as is the reconstruction of their neighborhoods.[39] However, the musical and spiritual energy of jazz funerals, which are profoundly influenced by the synthesis of the healing and social justice values of Haitian and New Orleanian Vodou and African American Christianity, continues to provide solace and insight into the mysteries of life, death, and their ancestry for some black New Orleanians both at home and in the diaspora.[40] Sidney Bechet, in *Treat It Gentle*, expressed it well:

> All the beauty that there's ever been, it's moving inside that music . . . the voice the wind had in Africa, and the cries from Congo Square, and the fine shouting that came up from Free Day. The blues, and the spirituals, and the remembering, and the waiting, and the suffering, and the looking at the sky watching the dark come down—that's all inside the music.

NOTES

Preface

1. Sidney Bechet, *Treat It Gentle: An Autobiography* (New York: Da Capo, 2002 [1960]), 4, 5.

2. Ibid.

3. Ibid.

Introduction

The epigraph is from Sidney Bechet, *Treat It Gentle: An Autobiography* (New York: Da Capo, 2002), p. 202.

1. Walter Pitts Jr. discussed a similar personal spiritual transformation related to his fieldwork in Baptist churches in Texas. See his *Old Ship of Zion: The Afro-Baptist Ritual in the African Diaspora* (New York: Oxford University Press, 1993), pp. 3–4.

2. Several times I observed the physical manifestations of trance or spirit possession in second liners who were ritual dancers involved in the inner circle of the Mardi Gras Indian secret societies. See Daniel E. Walker, *No More, No More: Slavery and Cultural Resistance in Havana and New Orleans* (Minneapolis: University of Minnesota Press, 2004), p. vii.

3. I have benefited from Karen McCarthy Brown's sophisticated reflections about the "gains and risks of a scholar's 'personal involvement' in a religious tradition that is the subject of his or her fieldwork and academic analysis." My initial relationship to the community I am writing about was different from Brown's relationship to Haitian Vodou—I, like many other New Orleanians, began my involvement as a black New Orleanian experiencing religion, music, and performance as a natural part of my city's life. Like Brown, however, I have tried to make "the important distinction" in this book between the stories about my personal experiences and interactions with this culture and the historical narratives that document the interactions of New Orleans religion and music with the African diaspora over time. See Karen McCarthy Brown, *Mama Lola: A Vodou Priestess in Brooklyn* (Berkeley: University of California Press, 1991), p. 11.

4. For examples of African American communities ruled by British slavery in the United States that lost "the African religious heritage," see Albert J. Raboteau, *Slave Reli-*

gion: The "Invisible Institution" in the Antebellum South (New York: Oxford University Press, 1978), p. 47. In the afterword of the updated 2004 edition of *Slave Religion*, p. 330, he writes:

> Perhaps I should make it clear to those who have misinterpreted me as simply saying African religions disappeared in the United States that what I was attempting to say is that the distinctiveness of the slave's religious culture lay not in their preservation of "Africanisms" but in the African perspectives, habits, preferences, aesthetics, and styles with which Africans and their descendants shaped their religious choices in the very diverse situations and circumstances of slavery.

5. Katherine J. Hagedorn, *Divine Utterances: The Performance of Afro-Cuban Santeria* (Washington, D.C.: Smithsonian Institution Press, 2001), pp. 6, 116–117; and Walker, *No More, No More*, p. xii.

6. David Todd Lawrence, "Folkloric Representation and Extended Context in the Experimental Ethnography of Zora Neale Hurston," *Southern Folklore* 57:2 (2000): 125.

7. Donald J. Cosentino, ed., *Sacred Arts of Haitian Vodou* (Los Angeles: Fowler Museum of Culture History, University of California, 1995).

8. Joseph Roach, *Cities of the Dead: Circum-Atlantic Performance* (New York: Columbia University Press, 1996), pp. xi, xii, 4, 5. According to Walter Johnson, New Orleans housed the biggest slave market in North America in the nineteenth century, "where 100,000 men, women, and children were packaged, priced, and sold"; see his *Soul by Soul: Life inside the Antebellum Slave Market* (Cambridge, Mass.: Harvard University Press, 1999), front flap. Thus New Orleans was one of the major "cities of the dead" where "the unspeakable violence" and social death of slavery began for thousands of black people in the modern world (Roach, *Cities of the Dead*, pp. xi, 4). Roach's perspective overlaps with Paul Gilroy's ideas in *The Black Atlantic: Modernity and Double Consciousness* (Cambridge, Mass.: Harvard University Press, 1993); *Small Acts: Thoughts on the Politics of Black Cultures* (London: Serpent's Tail, 1993); and *"There Ain't No Black in the Union Jack": The Cultural Politics of Race and Nation* (Chicago: University of Chicago Press, 1987).

9. Michael A. Gomez, *Exchanging Our Country Marks: The Transformation of African Identities in the Colonial Antebellum South* (Chapel Hill: University of North Carolina Press, 1998), pp. 57–58.

10. Walker, *No More, No More*, pp. ix, xii.

11. John Storm Roberts, *Latin Jazz: The First of the Fusions, 1880s to Today* (New York: Schirmer Books, 1999), pp. 7–8.

12. David E. Estes, "The Neo-African Vatican: Zora Neale Hurston's New Orleans," in *Literary New Orleans in the Modern World*, ed. Richard S. Kennedy, pp. 67, 73 (Baton Rouge: Louisiana State University Press, 1998).

13. Pitts, *Old Ship of Zion*; Anthony B. Pinn, *Varieties of African-American Religious Experience* (Minneapolis: Fortress, 1998); and Robert A. Orsi, *The Madonna of 115th Street: Faith and Community in Italian Harlem, 1880–1950* (New Haven, Conn.: Yale University Press, 1985), idem, ed., *Gods of the City: Religion and the American Urban Landscape* (Bloomington: Indiana University Press, 1999), and *Between Heaven and Earth: The Religions People Make and the Scholars Who Study Them* (Princeton, N.J.: Princeton University Press, 2005). Also see Yvonne P. Chireau, *Black Magic: Religion and the African-American Conjuring Tradition* (Berkeley: University of California Press, 2003).

14. Vincent L. Wimbush, foreword to Pitts, *Old Ship of Zion*, p. xiv; Zora Neale Hurston, *Mules and Men* (New York: Harper Perennial, 1990); and Michael P. Smith, *Spirit World* (Gretna, La.: Pelican, 1992).

15. See the KOSANBA—The Congress of Santa Barbara Call for Papers for their International Colloquium VI—"2004 Onward/The Gede Family: Life and Death Struggles" at Universidad de Puerto Rico. See, too, Turner, *Remembering Song*, p. ix.

1. The Haiti–New Orleans Vodou Connection

The source of the epigraph is Zora Neale Hurston, *The Sanctified Church* (New York: Marlowe, 1998), p. 103.

1. "Hoodoo" is the term for the new, highly secretive magical practice in New Orleans Vodou that focused on spiritual work for clients and resistance to the religion's enemies.

2. Zora Neale Hurston, *Mules and Men* (New York: Harper Perennial, 1990); and idem, "Hoodoo in America," *Journal of American Folklore* 44, no. 174 (October–December 1931): 317–418.

3. David Todd Lawrence, "Folklore Representation and Extended Context in the Experimental Ethnography of Zora Neale Hurston," *Southern Folklore* 57, no. 2 (2000): 120, 125.

4. Katie C. Canon, *Black Womanist Ethics* (Atlanta, Ga.: Scholars, 1988), p. 15, back cover.

5. Donald H. Matthews, *Honoring the Ancestors: An African Cultural Interpretation of Black Religion and Literature* (New York: Oxford University Press, 1998), front flap.

6. Theophus H. Smith, *Conjuring Culture: Biblical Formations of Black America* (New York: Oxford University Press, 1994), p. 6.

7. Anthony H. Pinn, *Varieties of African-American Religious Experience* (Minneapolis, Minn.: Fortress, 1998), p. 1.

8. Ibid., p. 1, back cover.

9. Alan Wolfe, "Scholars Infuse Religion with Cultural Light," *Chronicle of Higher Education*, Section B (October 22, 2004): 86. Also, Walter F. Pitts, *Old Ship of Zion: The Afro-Baptist Ritual in the African Diaspora* (New York: Oxford University Press, 1993); Karen McCarthy Brown, *Mama Lola: A Vodou Priestess in Brooklyn* (Berkeley: University of California Press, 1991); and Robert A. Orsi, *Gods of the City* (Bloomington: Indiana University Press, 1999).

10. David C. Estes, "The Neo-African Vatican: Zora Neale Hurston's New Orleans," in *Literary New Orleans in the Modern World*, ed. Richard Kennedy (Baton Rouge: Louisiana State University Press, 1998), pp. 67–68.

11. Brown, *Mama Lola*, p. 384.

12. Milo Rigaud, *Secrets of Voodoo* (San Francisco: City Lights Books, 1985), p. 8.

13. Hurston, *Mules and Men*, p. 183.

14. André Pierre, "A World Created by Magic: Extracts from a Conversation with André Pierre," in *Sacred Arts of Haitian Vodou*, ed. Donald J. Cosentino (Los Angeles: Fowler Museum of Cultural History, University of California, 1995), p. xxii.

15. Smith, *Conjuring Culture*, p. 33.

16. Lawrence, "Folklore Representation and Extended Context," p. 125.

17. Ibid.

18. Ibid.

19. Based on fragmentary evidence from several Louisiana Writers' Project interviewees who interacted with Marie Laveau when she was Vodou queen of New Orleans, Carolyn Morrow Long claims that the spirits of Haitian Vodou were not "served and honored" during the Marie Laveau era. Long has constructed the following list of correspond-

ing spirits in Haitian and New Orleanian Vodou in the nineteenth century: Bondyé, the Supreme God in Haitian Vodou, was God in New Orleanian Vodou; Legba, spirit of the crossroads in Haiti, was Limba or LaBas in New Orleans; Dambala, sacred snake and rainbow in Haiti, was Daniel Blanc, Dambara, Danny in New Orleans; Agassu, spirit of the "Dahomean royal dynasty" in Haiti, was Yon Sue, Vert Agousou in New Orleans; and Ayizan Verikete, "patroness of the temple and marketplace" in Haiti, was Vériquite in New Orleans. See Carolyn Morrow Long, *A New Orleans Vodou Priestess: The Legend and Reality of Marie Laveau* (Gainesville: University Press of Florida, 2007), pp. 115–116.

20. Hurston, *Tell My Horse: Voodoo and Life in Haiti and Jamaica* (New York: Harper and Row, 1990), p. 120. According to Carolyn Morrow Long, among The Fon these spirits are called vodou; in the Yoruba religion they are called orisha; and the Kongo call them minkisi. See Long, *A New Orleans Voudou Priestess*, p. 94.

21. Patrick Bellegarde-Smith, ed., *Fragments of Bone: Neo-African Religions in a New World* (Champaign: University of Illinois Press, 2004); Gerdès Fleurant, *Dancing Spirits: Rhythms and Rituals of Haitian Vodun, the Rada Rite* (Westport, Conn.: Greenwood, 1996); Patrick Bellegarde-Smith and Claudine Michel, eds., *Haitian Vodou: Spirit, Myth, and Reality* (Bloomington: Indiana University Press, 2007).

22. Hurston, *Tell My Horse*, p. 114. Hurston incorrectly uses the word "gods," instead of "spirits," to describe the Iwa, who are intermediaries between God the creator and human beings.

23. Hurston, *Mules and Men*, p. 185.

24. Estes, "The Neo-African Vatican," p. 82.

25. Hurston, "Hoodoo in America," p. 318.

26. Paul F. Lachance, "The Foreign French," in *Creole New Orleans: Race and Americanization,* ed. Arnold R. Hirsch and Joseph Logsdon, pp. 103–105 (Baton Rouge: Louisiana State University Press, 1992); Gwendolyn Midlo Hall, "The Formation of Afro-Creole Culture," in Hirsch and Logsdon, *Creole New Orleans,* pp. 59–65; and idem, *Africans in Colonial Louisiana: The Development of Afro-Creole Culture in the Eighteenth Century* (Baton Rouge: Louisiana State University Press, 1992), pp. 158–159. Also see Michael A. Gomez, *Exchanging Our Country Marks: The Transformation of African Identities in the Colonial and Antebellum South* (Chapel Hill: University of North Carolina Press, 1998), chap. 3. Immigrants from St. Domingue arrived in New Orleans in two waves. The first and smaller group came to Louisiana in the 1790s. Most slave owners from St. Domingue who arrived in the United States in the first wave decided to settle in Charleston, Philadelphia, or Baltimore because the Spanish officials who ruled Louisiana in the late 1700s were concerned that slaves from St. Domingue (where a revolution was under way) might incite new slave rebellions in their midst. The second and most influential wave of 9,059 immigrants from Haiti came to New Orleans from Santiago de Cuba in 1809 and 1810. In 1796 new arrivals from St. Domingue were initially welcomed by the Cuban government. In 1809, however, warfare between France and Spain resulted in dangerous hostilities between the Spanish and French in Santiago de Cuba, and the immigrants from St. Domingue were forced to leave Cuba. Also in 1809, Louisiana governor William C. C. Claiborne allowed former planters from St. Domingue to bring their slaves to Louisiana and approved the emigration of free people of color from the island. All these developments made New Orleans a focal point for nineteenth-century Haitians and former residents of St. Domingue. See Laurent Dubois, "The Revolutionary Period in Haiti, 1791–1804," The Historic New Orleans Collection, *Common Routes: St. Domingue. Louisiana* (Paris: Somogy Art Publishers; ADAGP and New Orleans: The Historic New Orleans Collection, March 14–June 30, 2006), p. 70; and Alfred E. Lemmon and John H. Lawrence, "Common Routes: St. Domingue and Loui-

siana," The Historic New Orleans Collection, *Common Routes*, pp. 87, 89. The January 27, 1810, issue of *Le Moniteur de la Louisiane* reported that the immigrants from Cuba were comprised of "2,731 whites . . . 3,102 free people of color . . . and 3, 226 slaves," and the majority of slaves and free people of color were women. See Long, *A New Orleans Vodou Priestess*, p. 29.

27. Jerah Johnson, *Congo Square in New Orleans* (New Orleans: Louisiana Landmarks Society, 1995), pp. 9–11; Carolyn Morrow Long, *Spiritual Merchants: Religion, Magic, and Commerce* (Knoxville: University of Tennessee Press, 2001), p. 21; George Washington Cable, "The Dance in Place Congo," *Century Magazine* 31 (February 1986): 517–532; Michel S. Laguerre, "Voodoo as Religious and Revolutionary Ideology," *Freeing the Spirit* 4 (1971): 24; Robert Farris Thompson, *Face of the Gods: Art and Altars of Africa and the African Americas* (New York: Museum for African Art, 1993), p. 56; Donald J. Cosentino, "From The Isle Beneath the Sea: Haiti's Africanizing Vodou Art," in idem, *Sacred Arts of Haitian Vodou*, p. 108; and Gomez, *Exchanging Our Country Marks*, p. 137. According to Long, the square was known as the Place Publique right after the Louisiana Purchase and was also the location for Gaetano Mariatini's "Congo Circus from Havana" until 1817. See Long, *A New Orleans Vodou Priestess*, p. 40.

28. Roach, *Cities of the Dead: Circum-Atlantic Performance*, pp. 56–57. Long, in *A New Orleans Vodou Priestess*, provides evidence that Spanish law on slavery in Louisiana was more liberal than the *Code Noir*. *Codigo Negro* allowed slaves to "accumulate wealth" by keeping their wages from outside labor.

> Over eight hundred slaves were freed between 1769 when the Spanish arrived to govern the colony and 1803, the date of the Louisiana Purchase. The number of free people of African descent increased from 7.1 percent of the non-white population of New Orleans in 1769 to 33.5 percent in 1805, when the first census was taken after the transfer of Louisiana to the United States. (pp. 14–15)

29. Long, *A New Orleans Vodou Priestess*, pp. 56–58, 63–64.

30. Bobby Joe Neeley, "Contemporary Afro-American Voodooism (Black Religion): The Retention and Adaptation of the Ancient African-Egyptian Mystery System," Ph.D. diss., University of California, Berkeley, 1998, p. 449.

31. Johnson, *Congo Square in New Orleans*, pp. 25–26, 31.

32. Michael Ventura, *Shadow Dancing in the U.S.A.* (New York: St. Martin's, 1985), pp. 123–124.

33. Long, *Spiritual Merchants*, p. 30. Gail Feigenbaum, "Jefferson's America and Napoleon's France," *Louisiana Cultural Vistas* 13, no. 4 (winter 2002–2003): 12–25. The 1805 U.S. Census showed that the majority of New Orleans' residents were of African descent. See Matthew Flannery, *A Directory and Census Together with Resolutions Authorizing Same* (1805). When the "territory of New Orleans" became the state of Louisiana in 1812, some representatives were alarmed because a "large proportion" of its residents were of African descent (Long, *A New Orleans Vodou Priestess*, p. 29).

34. See Claudine Michel, "Of Worlds Seen and Unseen: The Educational Character of Haitian Vodou," *Comparative Education Review* 40, no. 3 (August 1996): 280–294.

35. Katherine J. Hagedorn, *Divine Utterances: The Performance of Afro-Cuban Santeria* (Washington, D.C.: Smithsonian Institution Press, 2001), p. 6.

36. Ibid.

37. Ibid., pp. 5–6.

38. Ibid., p. 6.

39. James C. Scott, *Domination and the Arts of Resistance: Hidden Transcripts* (New

Haven, Conn.: Yale University Press, 1990); Ranajit Guha, *Elementary Aspects of Peasant Insurgency* (Delhi: Oxford University Press, 1983); Antonio Gramsci, *Selections from the Prism Notebooks* (London: Wishart, 1971); and Barrington Moore Jr., *Injustice: The Social Bases of Obedience and Revolt* (White Plains, N.Y.: M. E. Sharpe, 1987).

40. Daniel E. Walker, *No More, No More: Slavery and Cultural Resistance in Havana and New Orleans* (Minneapolis: University of Minnesota Press, 2004), p. xi.

41. Ibid. Also see John W. Nunley and Judith Bettelheim, eds., *Caribbean Festival Arts: Each and Every Bit of Difference* (Seattle and St. Louis: University of Washington Press and St. Louis Art Museum, 1988).

42. Walker, *No More, No More*, p. viii.

43. Ibid., p. xii.

44. Ibid., p. viii. On June 27, 1850, the Third Municipality Guards began to persecute Vodouists in New Orleans and arrested an assemblage of women "for being in contravention of the law, being slaves, free colored persons, and white persons assembled and dancing Vodou all together in St. Bernard Street near the woods at eight o'clock PM." See *Third Municipality Guards Mayor's Book, 1838–1850*, June 27, 1850, vol. 7, p. 495, microfilm, New Orleans Public Library; cited in Long, *A New Orleans Vodou Priestess*, p. 103, p. 247 n. 21. In July the *Picayune* newspaper stated that "Marie Laveau, otherwise Widow Paris, f.w.c., the head of the Voudou women, yesterday appeared before Recorder Seuzeneau and charged Watchman Abreo of the Third Municipality Guards with having by fraud come into possession of a statue of a virgin worth fifty dollars" ("Curious Charge of Swindling," *Daily Picayune*, July 3, 1850, p. 21, col. 2; cited in Long, *A New Orleans Vodou Priestess*, pp. 105–106, p. 248 n. 30. The persecution of New Orleans' Vodouists continued into the late 1850s; the *Crescent* reported that Marie Laveau "the Queen of the Voudous was complained of by her neighbor, Bernardo Rodriguez, residing on Love Street between Union and Bagatelle" for "singing and yelling" in a Vodou ceremony ("Local Intelligence—Recorder Long's Court," *Daily Crescent*, July 12, 1859, p. 1, col. 7; cited in Long, *A New Orleans Vodou Priestess*, pp. 107–108, 248 n. 35).

45. Walker reports that the New Orleans slave market included the following sites: "Exchange Alley, extending over six blocks along both Royal and Chartres streets from St. Peter to Canal. . . . Maspero's Exchange in the Corner of Chartres and St. Louis streets . . . and The Rotunda of the St. Louis Hotel" (*No More, No More*, p. 36).

46. Ibid., p. 128; Monique Guillory, "Under One Roof: The Sins and Sanctity of the New Orleans Quadroon Balls," in *Race Consciousness: African American Studies for the New Century*, ed. Judith Jackson Fossett and Jeffrey Tucker (New York: New York University Press, 1997), p. 70. The quadroon balls are discussed in Henry A. Kmen, *Music in New Orleans: The Formative Years, 1791–1841* (Baton Rouge: Louisiana State University Press, 1999), chap. 2. See, too, Tracy Fessenden, "The Sisters of the Holy Family and the Veil of Race," *Religion and American Culture: A Journal of Interpretation* 10, no. 2 (summer 2000): 205. Long believes that plaçage "often resembled true marriages" but led to Governor Esteban Miró's "tignon law" in Louisiana in 1786 to humiliate and distinguish placée free women of color from white women (*A New Orleans Vodou Priestess*, pp. 19–21). Also see Don Esteban Miró, *Banda de Buen Gobierno, Deliberations of the Cabildo*, June 1, 1786, vol. 3, no. 1 (1784–87); and *Records of the Cabildo Proceeding*, English trans., pp. 106–107, microfilm, New Orleans Public Library; and Long, *A New Orleans Vodou Priestess*, p. 229.

47. Walker, *No More, No More*, p. 28.

48. Ibid., pp. 88–89, 64. Walker writes that the numerical dominance of women in both slave and free colored communities in nineteenth-century New Orleans reflected the Crescent City's "demands for female domestic workers" and the demands of Louisi-

ana's rural cotton and sugar plantations for black males "above age ten" (*No More, No More,* pp. 61, 63).

49. Ibid., pp. 89, 98–99. For a discussion of circular dances, such as the ring shout, and their connection to Pan African identities in American slave communities, see Sterling Stuckey, *Slave Culture: Nationalist Theory and the Foundations of Black America* (New York: Oxford University Press, 1987). Also see Lynne Fauley Emery, *Black Dance from 1619 to Today,* 2nd rev. ed. (Princeton, N.J.: Princeton Book Company Publishers, 1988).

50. Walker, *No More, No More,* p. 100.

51. Ibid., p. 1.

52. Sallie Ann Glassman, *Vodou Visions: An Encounter with Divine Mystery* (New York: Villard, 2000), p. 99; Walker, *No More, No More,* p. 101.

53. Ibid.

54. Ibid., p. 8; Dele Jegede, "'Art for Life's Sake': African Art as a Reflection of Afrocentric Cosmology," in *The African Aesthetic: Keeper of Traditions,* ed. Kariamu Welsh-Asante (Westport, Conn.: Greenwood, 1993), p. 224.

55. Walker, *No More, No More,* pp. 9–13, 45.

56. Ibid., p. 46.

57. Lachance, "The Foreign French," p. 101. According to Carolyn Morrow Long, in antebellum Louisiana civil and religious documents, a "black or negro (nègre/nègresse in French) was a person of pure African descent and was assumed to be a slave. A free black or free negro (nègre/nègresse libre) was a free person of unmixed African blood. A free man/woman of color (homme/femme de couleur libre) meant a free person of mixed race. . . . These men and women were further classified as free mulatto (mulâtre/mulâtresse libre), of half African and half European ancestry, or free quadroon (quarteron/quarteronne libre), of one-quarter African and three-quarters European blood. . . . The word griffe could refer to an individual of mixed African and Native American ancestry or could mean yet another gradation between black and mulatto. Métis/métisse also indicated Indian ancestry and was applied to mixtures with both blacks and whites" (Long, *A New Orleans Vodou Priestess,* p. xxi).

58. Long, *A New Orleans Vodou Priestess,* pp. 108–109. Marie Laveau's baptismal record does not include her surname. See "Baptism of Maria, St. Louis Cathedral Baptisms of Slaves and Free Persons of Color, September 16, 1801, vol. 7, part 1, p. 41 verso, act 320"; also in Long, *A New Orleans Vodou Priestess,* p. 230.

59. Hurston, "Hoodoo in America," p. 317.

60. Ina Johanna Fandrich, "The Mysterious Voodoo Queen Marie Laveaux: A Study of Female Leadership in Nineteenth-Century New Orleans," Ph.D. diss., Temple University 1994, p. 44. The Vodou Queen's name is spelled both "Laveaux" and "Laveau" in historical record and scholarship. The spelling the author uses, "Laveau," is popular in contemporary black New Orleans communities. Long believes that Sanité Dédé was "possibly a fictitious character from nineteenth-century literature" (*A New Orleans Vodou Priestess,* p. 100). Long places the Vodou priesthood in New Orleans in the context of other important organized South American and Caribbean religions in Portuguese, Spanish, and French colonies such as Santeria in Cuba, Vodou in Haiti, and Candomblé in Brazil. These religions were the result of complex syntheses of African traditional religions with Catholicism, and New Orleanian Vodou "is the only Afro-Catholic religion to emerge in North America." See Long, *A New Orleans Vodou Priestess,* p. 93. According to Alexander Augustin, "Marie Saloppé . . . lived on St. Phillip St. She preceded Marie Laveau in . . . Voudouism" (Henriette Michinard interview of Alexander Augustin, May 16, 1940, Louisiana Writers' Project folder 25, Cammie G. Henry Research Center, Federal Writers' Collec-

tion, Watson Memorial Library, Northwestern State University of Louisiana at Natchitoches; also in Long, *A New Orleans Vodou Priestess*, p. 100). Betsy Toledano, who lived on Bienville Street, was arrested at Vodou ceremonies on June 27 and July 30, 1850, for illegal assemblies of slaves, free people of color, and whites. See *Third Municipality Guards Mayor's Book, 1838–1850*, June 27, 1850, vol. 7, p. 495, microfilm, New Orleans Public Library, cited by Long, *A New Orleans Vodou Priestess*, p. 247 n. 21; and "The Rites of Voudou," *Daily Crescent*, July 31, 1850, p. 3, col. 1, cited in Long, *A New Orleans Vodou Priestess*, p. 248 n. 28. Doctor Jim Alexander's (1836?–1890) home and Vodou temple was on 319 Orleans Street (Long, *A New Orleans Vodou Priestess*, p. 111). Doctor John (Jean Montanée) (d. 1885), a conjurer from Africa and a slave in Cuba, was well known in New Orleans as a Vodouist and a fortune teller. Long reports that the U.S. Census from 1850 to 1880 identifies him as a property owner in the Bayou Road area of New Orleans and as a "physician" (*A New Orleans Vodou Priestess*, pp. 146, 254). Also see his death certificate for August 23, 1885, in New Orleans Public Library microfilm, vol. 87, p. 914.

61. "Marriage of Santiago Paris and Marie Labeau, St. Louis Cathedral Marriages of Slaves and Free People of Color, August 4, 1819, vol. 1, p. 59, act 256, Archives of the Archdiocese of New Orleans"; also cited in Long, *A New Orleans Vodou Priestess*, p. 235. After Paris's disappearance, Marie Laveau had a long-term relationship and several children with Louis Glapion. The *Sacramental Records* of St. Louis Cathedral demonstrate that Catholic priests regarded the new Anglo-Protestants in New Orleans as foreigners from "the United States" (Long, *A New Orleans Vodou Priestess*, p. 38; and Charles E. Nolan, ed., *Sacramental Records of the Roman Catholic Church of the Archdiocese of New Orleans*, vol. 15 [New Orleans: Archives of the Archdiocese of New Orleans, 1987–2004], p. xx).

62. Fandrich, "The Mysterious Voodoo Queen Marie Laveux," pp. 166–167. Tracy Fessenden has discussed the possibility of a spiritual connection between Marie Laveau and Henriette Delille, one of the founders of the Sisters of the Holy Family—New Orleans' first Catholic religious order of African-descended sisters in the nineteenth century. See her "Sisters of the Holy Family and the Veil of Race," *Religion and American Culture: A Journal of Interpretation* 10, no. 2 (summer 2000): 187–224. Long believes that Laveau and Delille "may have been second cousins" (*A New Orleans Vodou Priestess*, p. 234).

63. Fandrich, "The Mysterious Voodoo Queen Marie Laveux."

64. Ibid., p. 82.

65. *Daily Picayune*, June 16, 1881. Although Long's research provides convincing evidence that Laveau and her white, second (common-law) husband Christophe Glapion "between 1828 and 1854 . . . bought and sold eight slaves," there is also strong evidence that Laveau's work exemplified the "humanistic values" central to Vodou. See Carolyn Morrow Long, "Marie Laveau: A Nineteenth-Century Voudou Priestess," *Louisiana History* 46, no. 3 (summer 2005): 273. Fandrich's dissertation and Martha Ward's *Voodoo Queen: The Spirited Lives of Marie Laveau* (Jackson: University Press of Mississippi, 2004) present Laveau as an activist against slavery. I disagree with their assessment of Laveau on this issue, as no evidence supports it. See "Sale of Slave Irma by Widow L. Paris to Demoiselle C. Pyroux, Acts of Louis T. Caire, October 21, 1839, act 676, Notarial Archives Research Center, New Orleans" and "Sale of Slave Juliette by Marie Laveau to Sanité Couvreure F.W.C., Acts of Jean Aguisse, April 27, 1848, vol. 6, pp. 79–80, act 42, Notarial Archives Research Center, New Orleans"; also cited in Long, *A New Orleans Vodou Priestess*, pp. 242–243 (see, too, page 67 for information on Laveau's connection to the Choctaw).

66. Hurston, "Hoodoo in America," p. 359.

67. Ibid., p. 237.

68. Ibid., pp. 358, 360.

69. Long, *Spiritual Merchants*, p. 52. According to Long, Laveau had seven children with Christophe Glapion: "Marie Heloise Euchariste, Marie Louise Caroline, Christophe, Jean Baptiste, François Maurice Christophe, Marie Philomène, and Archange Edouard." (*A New Orleans Vodou Priestess*, p. 53).

70. Arnold R. Hirsch and Joseph Logsdon, "Franco-Africans and African-Americans," in idem, *Creole New Orleans*, p. 190. See "Free Black Emigration," *Daily Picayune*, June 23, 1859, p. 5, col. 5; and Long, *A New Orleans Vodou Priestess*, pp. 86, 245. Reconstruction in New Orleans, from 1863 to 1877, gave black men the right to vote and interracial couples the right to marry and many blacks were elected to the Louisiana Senate and House of Representatives. A violent backlash from the Ku Klux Klan and other white racist terrorist organizations from the mid-1870s into the twentieth century reversed the progress toward full citizenship that black New Orleanians had made during the Reconstruction era. See Long, *A New Orleans Vodou Priestess*, p. 165.

71. Fandrich, "The Mysterious Voodoo Queen Marie Laveaux," p. 257.

72. Hurston, "Hoodoo in America," p. 358.

73. Long, *Spiritual Merchants*, p. 53; Hurston, *Hoodoo in America*, p. 319.

74. Laennec Hurbon, "American Fantasy and Haitian Vodou," in Cosentino, *Sacred Arts of Haitian Vodou*, pp. 182–187; Boyd, *Wrapped in Rainbows*, p. 178. In this period stereotypes of Marie Laveau were published in George William Nott, "Marie Laveau, Long High Priestess of Voudouism in New Orleans," *Times-Picayune* Sunday Magazine, November 19, 1922; Lyle Saxon, *Fabulous New Orleans*, repr. (Gretna, La.: Pelican, 1988 [1928]); and Herbert Asbury, *The French Quarter: An Informal History of the New Orleans Underground*, repr. (Emeryville, Calif.: Thunder's Mouth, 2003 [1936]).

75. Long, *Spiritual Merchants*, p. 53.

76. Ibid., p. 54. Hurston, "Hoodoo in America," p. 319.

77. Claude F. Jacobs and Andrew J. Kaslow, *The Spiritual Churches of New Orleans: Origins, Beliefs, and Rituals of an African-American Religion* (Knoxville: University of Tennessee Press, 1991); Jason Berry, *The Spirit of Black Hawk: A Mystery of Africans and Indians* (Jackson: University Press of Mississippi, 1995); and Marcus Bruce Christian, "Manuscript for a Black History of Louisiana," in *The Marcus Bruce Christian Collection*, Earl K. Long Library, University of New Orleans, and *René Grandjean Collection*, Earl K. Long Library, University of New Orleans.

78. Hurston, "Hoodoo in America," pp. 358–359.

79. Long, *Spiritual Merchants*, p. 55.

80. Hurston, *Mules and Men*, p. 191.

81. Hurston, "Hoodoo in America," p. 317.

82. Hurston, *Mules and Men*, pp. 192–193.

83. Hurston, "Hoodoo in America," p. 357.

84. Tina Girouard, *Sequin Artists of Haiti* (Port-au-Prince: Haiti Arts, 1994); Thompson, *Face of the Gods*, p. 28.

85. Donald J. Cosentino, "Bizango Altar," in idem, *Sacred Arts of Haitian Vodou*, p. 302.

86. Rachel Beauvoir-Dominque, "Underground Realms of Being: Vodou Magic," in Cosentino, *Sacred Arts of Haitian Vodou*, p. 166. Yvonne P. Chireau discusses the dichotomy between religion and magic in scholarship on European and Euro-American religions in *Black Magic: Religion and the African American Conjuring Tradition* (Berkeley: University of California Press, 2003). She writes:

> In contemporary scholarship . . . magic is generally characterized as the an-
> tithesis of religion. . . . Magic is used for specific personal ends. It operates
> mechanically—as opposed to prayer, which is communal, devotional, and non-
> coercive. . . . Religion is . . . a public and social activity; magic is private, mani-
> fested in solitary, focused events, and has no church or sustained collective.
> (p. 3)

The above dichotomy between religion and magic is not useful for understanding magic in New Orleans Vodou, which Long describes as "an organized religion with a complex theology, a pantheon of deities and spirits, a priesthood and a congregation of believers . . . the only Afro-Catholic religion to emerge in North America" (*A New Orleans Vodou Priestess*, p. 93). Finally, Chireau argues that "historically many black Americans have not separated magical beliefs from religion, seeing that the two exist as necessary counterparts" (*Black Magic*, p. 151).

87. Thompson, *Face of the Gods*, p. 21.

88. Hurston, "Hoodoo in America," pp. 358–360. See also the provocative analysis of Hurston's initiation and spiritual work in Robert E. Hemenway, *Zora Neale Hurston: A Literary Biography* (Urbana: University of Illinois Press, 1977); Alice Walker, ed., *I Love Myself When I Am Laughing . . . And Then Again When I Am Looking Mean and Impressive: A Zora Neale Hurston Reader* (New York: Feminist Press at the City University of New York, 1979); Houston A. Baker Jr., *Workings of the Spirit: The Poetic of Afro-American Women's Writing* (Chicago: University of Chicago Press, 1991); and Cheryl A. Wall, "Mules and Men and Women: Zora Neale Hurston's Strategies of Narration and Visions of Female Empowerment," in *Critical Essays on Zora Neale Hurston*, ed. Gloria L. Cronin (New York: C.K. Hall, 1998).

89. Arnold van Gennep, *The Rites of Passage* (Chicago: University of Chicago Press, 1966), p. 11.

90. Victor Turner, *The Forest of Symbols: Aspects of Ndembu Ritual* (Ithaca, N.Y.: Cornell University Press, 1957), pp. 93, 94.

91. Bobby C. Alexander, *Victor Turner Revisited: Ritual as Social Change* (Atlanta, Ga.: Scholars, 1991), p. 1.

92. Turner, *The Ritual Process: Structure and Anti-Structure* (Chicago: Aldine, 1969), p. viii.

93. Beauvoir-Dominque, "Underground Realms of Being," p. 166.

94. Hurston, "Hoodoo in America," p. 360.

95. Beauvoir-Dominque, "Underground Realms of Being," p. 166.

96. Hurston, "Hoodoo in America," p. 360.

97. Hurston, *Tell My Horse*.

98. Author's interview with Ava Kay Jones, December 1997, New Orleans. Long, *Spiritual Merchants*, p. 69. F & F Co. Spiritual and Church Supply on 801 North Broad Avenue was the largest botanica in New Orleans before Hurricane Katrina struck the city in August 2005.

99. Linda Bays Powers, "Haiti: Waves of Sound and Rhythm," in *The 1996 Official New Orleans Jazz and Heritage Festival Program Guide Book*, p. 36.

2. Mardi Gras Indians and Second Lines, Sequin Artists and Rara Bands

The epigraph is from Irvin Mayfield, liner notes, *Los Hombres Calientes: Bill Summers, Irvin Mayfield, Jason Marsalis, Vol. 2* (Basin Street Records, 2000).

1. Important sources on Rara and sequin artists include Elizabeth McAlister, *Rara!: Vodou, Power, and Performance in Haiti and Its Diaspora* (Berkeley: University of California Press, 2002); and Tina Girouard, *Sequin Artists of Haiti*, 2nd ed. (Port-au-Prince, Haiti, and Cecilia, Louisiana: Haiti Arts, and Girouard Art Projects, 1994). The author's perspective on the Mardi Gras Indian tribes and second lines is informed by his intensive community and fieldwork in New Orleans from 1996 to 1999.

2. Rockefeller Fellowships at the Center for Black Music Research, Columbia College Chicago, 2003–2004, p. 1.

3. Samuel Floyd Jr., *The Power of Black Music* (New York: Oxford University Press, 1995); Robert Farris Thompson, *The Four Moments of the Sun* (New Haven, Conn.: Eastern Press, 1981); idem, *Flash of the Spirit* (New York: Vintage, 1984); idem, *Face of the Gods: Art and Altars of Africa and the African Americans* (New York: Museum for African Art, 1993); and idem, "From the Isle Beneath the Sea: Haiti's Africanizing Vodou Art," in Donald J. Cosentino, ed., *Sacred Arts of Haitian Vodou* (Los Angeles: Fowler Museum of Cultural History, University of California, 1993).

4. Abstract for the Rockefeller Fellowship Program, Stone Center for Latin American Studies and Deep South Regional Humanities Center, Tulane University, New Orleans.

5. Joseph Roach, *Cities of the Dead: Circum-Atlantic Performance* (New York: Columbia University Press, 1996).

6. Ibid., pp. xi, 4.

7. Ibid., p. xii

8. Craig Steven Wilder, *In the Company of Black Men: The African Influence on African American Culture in New York City* (New York: New York University Press, 2000), p. 9.

9. Ibid. Melville J. Herskovits, *Myth of the Negro Past* (Boston: Beacon, 1941). J. Lorand Matory discusses Herskovits's Africanisms legacy in the context of New World African religions in the introduction to his book, *Black Atlantic Religion: Tradition, Transnationalism, and Matriarchy in the Afro-Brazilian Candomblé* (Princeton, N.J.: Princeton University Press, 2005).

10. Wilder, *In the Company of Black Men*, p. 9.

11. Roach, *Cities of the Dead*, back flap.

12. Ibid.

13. Wilder, *In the Company of Black Men*, p. 12, back flap.

14. Ibid., p. 20.

15. Ibid., pp. 20–21.

16. Roach, *Cities of the Dead*, p. 10.

17. Michael Ventura, *Shadow Dancing in the U.S.A.* (New York: St. Martin's, 1985), p. 130.

18. See Carolyn Morrow Long, *Spiritual Merchants: Religion, Magic, and Commerce* (Knoxville: University of Tennessee Press, 2001), for details of this period in New Orleans' history. See Reid Mitchell, *All on a Mardi Gras Day: Episodes in New Orleans Carnival* (Cambridge, Mass.: Harvard University Press, 1995), p. 126, for information about "a small size race riot" on Mardi Gras Day, 1908, "between the Mardi Gras Indians and the white boys and men."

19. Geraldine Wyckoff, "Big Bad Voodoo Daddies, Los Hombres Calientes Trekked Through Trinidad, Haiti, Cuba, Brazil, Jamaica, and New Orleans to Make Congo Square Music," *Jazz Times*, May 2003, p. 165.

20. David Yih, "The Diversity of Vodou Music," liner notes, p. 4, *Rhythms of Rapture:*

Sacred Music of Haitian Vodou, comp. Elizabeth McAlister (Smithsonian Folkways Records, 1995).

21. Gerdes Fleurant, "The Music of Vodou: Rada, Kongo-Petwo, and Bizanago Rites," liner notes, p. 6, *Rhythms of Rapture: Sacred Music of Haitian Vodou.*

22. Elizabeth McAlister, "Introduction: Vodou Music and Ritual Work," liner notes, p. 3, *Rhythms of Rapture: Sacred Music of Haitian Vodou.*

23. Gage Averill, "Vodou and Pop Music: The Roots Connection," liner notes, p. 7, *Rhythms of Rapture: Sacred Music of Haitian Vodou.*

24. Gage Averill, liner notes, Boukman Eksperyans, *Vodou Adjae* (Island Records, 1991). Also see Sue Steward, "Ram: Vodou Dancehall," *Straight No Chaser* 2, no. 17 (fall 2001): 50-53, and John Storm Roberts, *Black Music of Two Worlds: African, Caribbean, Latin, and African-American Traditions,* 2nd rev. ed. (New York: Schirmer Books, 1998), pp. 146-150.

25. McAlister, *Rara!,* pp. 3-4.

26. Ibid., p. 31.

27. See Robert Orsi, *Gods of the City: Religion and the American Urban Landscape* (Bloomington: Indiana University Press, 1999); and *The Madonna of 115th Street: Faith and Community in Italian Harlem* (New Haven, Conn.: Yale University Press, 1985), for the concept of "mapping" sacred space in urban contexts.

28. McAlister, *Rara!,* p. 89.

29. Ibid., p. 87.

30. Bobby C. Alexander, *Victor Turner Revisited: Ritual as Social Change* (Atlanta: Scholars, 1991), p. 1; and Victor Turner, *The Ritual Process: Structure and Anti-Structure* (Chicago: Aldine, 1969), p. viii.

31. Thompson, "From the Isle Beneath the Sea," p. 107.

32. Roberts, *Black Music of Two Worlds,* p. 67.

33. Thompson, *Face of the Gods,* p. 28. Karl Edward Laman, *Dictionnaire Kikongo-Français: M–Z,* repr. (Hants: Gregg, 1964 [1936]), p. 574.

34. McAlister, *Rara!,* p. 85.

35. Averill, *Vodou Adjae,* liner notes.

36. Averill, *Vodou and Pop Music,* p. 7.

37. Boukman Eksperyans, *Vodou Adjae.*

38. McAlister, *Rara!,* pp. 209-212.

39. Ibid., p. 44.

40. The description is based on the author's fieldwork and participation in New Orleans' second lines from 1996 to 1999.

41. McAlister, *Rara!,* p. 44.

42. Author's fieldwork and participation in New Orleans' second lines from 1996 to 1999.

43. McAlister, *Rara!,* p. 44.

44. Author's fieldwork and participation in Chicken Man's jazz funeral in New Orleans in 1998.

45. McAlister, *Rara!,* pp. 44-47, 52, 55.

46. Jason Berry, Jonathan Foose, and Tad Jones, *Up from the Cradle of Jazz: New Orleans Music since World War II* (New York: Da Capo, 1992), pp. 4, 5. John Edward Hasse lists six conditions that created jazz in New Orleans: "fluid cultural boundaries; active Afro-Caribbean culture; vital music life; strong dance tradition; pervasive 'good times' atmosphere; prevalence of brass bands" (Hasse, ed., *Jazz: The First Century* [New York: William Morrow, 2000], pp. 6-8).

47. Berry, Foose, and Jones, *Up from the Cradle of Jazz*, p. 10.

48. Ibid., pp. 5, 10.

49. Ibid., p. 9.

50. Ibid., pp. 10–11, 13.

51. Ibid., pp. xii–xiii.

52. Loyce Arthur, "Captivated by Carnival: Cuban Carnival Conveys Fascinating Blend of Old, New Cultural Elements," *International Accents* 5, no. 1 (spring/summer 2005): 1.

53. Claudine Michel, "Of Worlds Seen and Unseen: The Educational Character of Haitian Vodou," *Comparative Education Review* 40, no. 3 (August 1996): 280–294.

54. Berry, Foose, and Jones, *Up from the Cradle of Jazz*, pp. 11–12.

55. Frederick Turner, *Remembering Song: Encounters with the New Orleans Jazz Tradition*, exp. ed. (New York: Da Capo, 1994), pp. ix, 14, 18. Sidney Bechet, *Treat It Gentle: An Autobiography* (New York: Da Capo, 2002), chaps. 1–4.

56. Douglas Henry Daniels, "Vodun and Jazz: Jelly Roll Morton and Lester 'Pres' Young—Substance and Shadow," *Journal of Haitian Studies* 9, no. 1 (spring 2003): 115, 116. See, too, Allan Lomax, *Mister Jelly Roll: The Fortunes of Jelly Roll Morton, New Orleans Creole and "Inventor of Jazz"* (New York: Pantheon Books, 1993); Howard Reich and William Gaines, *Jelly's Blues: The Life, Music, and Redemption of Jelly Roll Morton* (New York: Da Capo, 2003); and Phil Pastras, *Dead Man Blues: Jelly Roll Morton Way Out West* (Berkeley and Chicago: University of California Press and Center for Black Music Research, Columbia College, 2001).

57. Floyd Levin, *Classic Jazz: A Personal View of the Music and the Musicians* (Berkeley: University of California Press, 2000), pp. 187, 188.

58. Eric Porter, *What Is This Thing Called Jazz? African American Musicians as Artists, Critics, and Activists* (Berkeley: University of California Press, 2002), pp. xiii, xvii, xviii.

59. Ibid., back flap, Farah Jasmine Griffin blurb.

60. David Ake, *Jazz Cultures* (Berkeley: University of California Press, 2002), p. 7. See Donald M. Marquis, *In Search of Buddy Bolden First Man of Jazz* (Baton Rouge: Louisiana State University Press, 1978).

61. Turner, *Remembering Song*, pp. 14, 18; Bechet, *Treat It Gentle*.

62. Jonathan Tbak, liner notes, *Los Hombres Calientes: Irvin Mayfield and Bill Summers*, Vol. 3, *New Congo Square* (Basin Street Records, 2001).

63. Turner, *Remembering Song*, pp. 18–23; Wynton Marsalis, "Jazz Education in the New Millennium," *Jazz Educators Journal* 33 (September 2000): p. 46; David Ake, *Jazz Cultures* (Berkeley: University of California Press, 2002), chap. 1.

64. See Dorothy Rose Eagleson, "Some Aspects of the Social Life of the New Orleans Negro in the 1880s," M.A. thesis, History Department, Tulane University, New Orleans, May 1961; John W. Blassingame, *Black New Orleans, 1860–1880* (Chicago: University of Chicago Press, 1973); William J. Schafer, *Brass Bands and New Orleans Jazz* (Baton Rouge: Louisiana State University Press, 1997).

65. Reid Mitchell, *All on a Mardi Gras Day: Episodes in the History of New Orleans Carnival* (Cambridge, Mass.: Harvard University Press, 1995), p. 114. Jason Berry, "African Cultural Memory in New Orleans," *Black Music Research Journal*, p. 8, paper, National Conference on Black Music Research New Orleans, Louisiana, October 15–17, 1987.

66. Cherice Harrison-Nelson, "Sewing behind the Scenes: Indian Wives," lecture, Louisiana State Museum, New Orleans, June 29, 1999. The oral histories do not support Michael P. Smith's thesis on the origins of the Black Indian tribes in the New Orleans Buf-

falo Bill Wild West shows in the 1880s. See Michael P. Smith, "New Orleans' Carnival Culture from the Underside," *Plantation Society in the Americas* (1990): 11–32.

67. *Times-Democrat*, February 12, 1902. Also see *Times-Democrat*, February 15, 1899, for an earlier description of a Mardi Gras Indian gang. The origins of the Mardi Gras Indians are also discussed in Mitchell, *All in a Mardi Gras Day*, p. 115; Samuel Kinser, *Carnival American Style: Mardi Gras at New Orleans and Mobile* (Chicago: University of Chicago Press, 1990); and David Elliott Draper, "The Mardi Gras Indians: The Ethnomusicology of Black Associations in New Orleans," Ph.D. diss., Tulane University, New Orleans, 1973.

68. Berry, "African Cultural Memory in New Orleans Music," p. 8. See also Florence E. Borders, "Researching Creole and Cajun Musics in New Orleans," *Black Music Research Journal*, pp. 18–20, National Conference on Black Music Research, New Orleans, Louisiana, October 15–17, 1987, paper.

69. Sec Allan Lomax, *Mister Jelly Roll: The Fortunes of Jelly Roll Morton, New Orleans Creole and "Inventor of Jazz"* (New York: Pantheon Books, 1950), pp. 17–19; Mitchell, *All on a Mardi Gras Day*, pp. 17–18; Anna Maria Alonso, "Men in 'Rags' and the Devil on the Throne: A Study of Protest and Inversion in the Carnival of Post-Emancipation Trinidad," *Plantation Society in the Americas* (1990): 73–120; Errol Hill, *The Trinidad Carnival: Mandate for a National Theatre* (Austin: University of Texas Press, 1972); and Maurice M. Martinez Jr., "Two Islands: The Black Indians of Haiti and New Orleans," *Arts Quarterly* (July/August/September 1979): 5–17, 18.

70. Berry, "African Cultural Memory in New Orleans Music," pp. 4–8.

71. Roach, *Cities of the Dead*, pp. 192–194.

72. The Spiritual churches of New Orleans began in the 1920s with Mother Leafy Anderson, a black migrant from Chicago. Her spiritual work was inspired by Black Hawk, an Indian spirit guide. See Jason Berry, *The Spirit of Black Hawk: A Mystery of Africans and Indians* (Jackson: University Press of Mississippi, 1995); and Claude F. Jacobs and Andrew J. Kaslow, *The Spiritual Churches of New Orleans: Origins, Beliefs, and Rituals of an African-American Religion* (Knoxville: University of Tennessee Press, 1991). Based, too, on the author's conversations with Elaine Brown, Spiritual church member and Vodou princess, New Orleans, Louisiana, 1997–2001.

73. Roach, *Cities of the Dead*, p. 14.

74. "Thompson, *Face of the Gods: Art and Altars of Africa and the African Americas*, p. 28; and idem, "From the Isle beneath the Sea," p. 107.

75. Tina Girouard, *Sequin Artists of Haiti*; and Patrick Polk, "Sacred Banners and the Divine Charge," in Cosentino, *The Sacred Arts of Haitian Vodou*, pp. 325–326, 329.

76. James Hinton and Maurice M. Martinez Jr., "The Black Indians of New Orleans," video, Chalmalma Media Institute, 1976; Larry Bannock, "Mardi Gras Indians, Spy Boy, Flag Boy, and Big Chiefs!" pp. 1, 2; Mardi Gras New Orleans Web site, www.mardigrasindians.com/indirank.html (accessed 2008).

77. Polk, "Sacred Banners and the Divine Charge," pp. 326, 327, 329.

78. Ibid., p. 331.

79. Ibid., p. 330.

80. Maya Deren, *Divine Horsemen: The Living Gods of Haiti* (New York: Chelsea House, 1953), p. 177.

81. Polk, "Sacred Banners and the Divine Charge," p. 331.

82. "Mardi Gras Indians Spy Boy Flag Boy, and Big Chiefs!" Mardi Gras New Orleans Web site, www.mardigrasindians.com/indirank.html (accessed 2008).

83. Hinton and Martinez, "The Black Indians of New Orleans."

84. "Mardi Gras Indians Spy Boy, Flag Boy, and Big Chiefs!" Mardi Gras New Orleans Web site, www.mardigrasindians.com/indirank.html (accessed 2008).

85. Hinton and Martinez, "The Black Indians of New Orleans."

86. Maurice M. Martinez, "Delight in Repetition: the Black Indians," *Wavelength* (February 1982): 23.

87. Girourd, *Sequin Artists of Haiti,* p. 23.

88. Ibid.

89. Sallie Ann Glassman, *Vodou Visions: An Encounter with Divine Mystery* (New York: Villard, 2000), p. 127.

90. Marie-José Alicide St.-Lot, "Wisdom and Beauty in Haitian Vodou," paper, "Across the Waters: The Haitian Religious Diaspora," Congress of Santa Barbara Colloquium V, Nova Southeastern University, Fort Lauderdale, Florida, June 7, 2003.

91. Thompson, "From the Isle Beneath the Sea," p. 92.

92. Ibid.

93. Hinton and Martinez, "The Black Indians of New Orleans."

94. Keith Weldon Medley, *We as Freemen: Plessy v. Ferguson* (Gretna, La.: Pelican, 2003), dustcover notes.

95. Roach, *Cities of the Dead,* p. 207.

96. Girouard, *Sequin Artists of Haiti,* pp. 33, 36, 37, 42.

97. From the author's telephone conversation with Darryl Montana, Big Chief of the Yellow Pocahontas tribe, May 2003.

98. Maurice M. Martinez Jr., "Two Islands: The Black Indians of Haiti and New Orleans," *Arts Quarterly* 1, no. 7 (July/August/September, 1979): 6. For information on the African–Native American connection in other locations, see Jack D. Forbes, *Africans and Native Americans,* 2nd ed. (Urbana: University of Illinois Press, 1993); William Loren Katz, *Black Indians: A Hidden Heritage* (New York: Atheneum, 1986); David Littlefield, *Africans and Seminoles* (Westport, Conn.: Greenwood, 1977); and Richard Price, ed., *Maroon Societies: Rebel Slave Communities in the Americas* (Baltimore, Md.: Johns Hopkins University Press, 1979).

99. Michael Smith, *Mardi Gras Indians* (Gretna, La.: Pelican, 1994), p. 96.

100. Roach, *Cities of the Dead,* p. 194.

101. From the author's interview with Big Chief Tootie Montana on Good Friday, 1997.

102. Ibid.

103. "Martinez, "Two Islands," p. 6.

104. From the author's interview with Big Chief Tootie Montana on Good Friday, 1997.

105. Ibid.

106. Ibid.

107. Panel discussion on the History of the Mardi Gras Indians, Xavier University, New Orleans, Louisiana, March 17, 1997.

108. Ibid.

109. From the author's interview with Big Chief Tootie Montana on Good Friday 1997. See Robert A. Hall with Suzanne Comhaire-Sylvain, H. Ormonde McConnell, and Alfred Métraux, "Haitian Creole Grammar, Texts, Vocabulary," *American Anthropologist* 55, no. 2 (April–June 1953): 7–309.

110. Alan Lomax, *Mister Jelly Roll,* pp. 17, 18. Also see Howard Reich and William Gaines, *Jelly's Blues: The Life, Music, and Redemption of Jelly Roll Morton* (New York:

Da Capo, 2003); and Phil Pastras, *Dead Man Blues: Jelly Roll Morton Way Out West* (Berkeley: University of California Press, 2001).

111. Maurice M. Martinez Jr., "Delight in Repetition: The Black Indians," *Wavelength* (February 1982): 23.

112. Ibid.

113. George Landry, "Indian Red," *The Wild Tchoupitoulas* (New York: Mango Island Records, 1976).

114. Ibid.

115. Donald Harrison Jr., *Young Guardians of the Flame . . . For Generations Yet to Come* (New Orleans: Junebug Productions, 1999).

116. Ibid.

117. From the author's interview with Darryl Montana, June 23, 2003.

118. "Sewing Behind the Scenes: Indian Wives," Louisiana State Museum, New Orleans, June 29, 1999.

119. The author's interview with Sylvester Francis, Backstreet Cultural Museum, New Orleans, June 23, 2003. Sylvester Francis is Darryl Montana's uncle.

120. St. Joseph is also the patron saint for Italians in New Orleans; see Anna Maria Chupa, "St. Joseph's Day Altars," *Cultural Crossroads,* Houston Institute for Culture, www.cultural-crossroads.com, p. 1; and Ethelyn Orso, *The St. Joseph Altar Traditions of South Louisiana* (Lafayette: Center for Louisiana Studies, University of Southwestern Louisiana, 1990).

121. J. B. Borders, "Changing the Changing Same: Halting Arrested Development in the Crescent City: A New Study Points the Way Out of Economic Inequity for Afro-Orleanians," *New Orleans Tribune,* May/June 2003, p. 13; Beverly Hendrix Wright, "New Orleans a City That Care Forgot," in *In Search of the New South: The Black Urban Experience in The 1970s and 1980s,* ed. Robert D. Bullard (Tuscaloosa: University of Alabama Press, 1991).

122. Kalamu ya Salaam, liner notes, "You Ain't Heard Nothin' Yet," *The Dirty Dozen Brass Band Live: Mardi Gras in Montreaux* (Cambridge, Mass.: Rounder Records, 1986).

123. Ibid. The Wild Magnolias, *The Wild Magnolias: They Call Us Wild* (Germany: Polydor, 1994 [1975]).

124. The Neville Brothers, *The Wild Tchoupitoulas.* See also Art, Aaron, Charles, and Cyrill Neville, and David Ritz, *The Brothers Neville* (Boston: Little, Brown, 2000).

125. The Neville Brothers, *Live on Planet Earth.*

126. Ibid.

127. The Meters, *The Essentials* (New York: Warner Brothers Records, 2002); B. R. Hunter, "The Meters," *Vibe* 4, no. 1 (February 1996): 104.

128. Michael P. Smith, *New Orleans Jazz Fest: A Pictoral History* (Gretna, La.: Pelican, 1991); Brian Federico, *The Origins of New Orleans' Greatest Music Festival* (New Orleans: New Orleans Scriptorum, 2001). The 2005 New Orleans Jazz and Heritage Festival showcased the music of the Mardi Gras Indian tribes, the brass bands, and the social aid and pleasure clubs of black New Orleans.

129. The Dirty Dozen Brass Band, *Voodoo* (New York: Columbia Records, 1989); *Buck Jump* (Carrboro, N.C.: Mammoth Records, 1999), and *Medicated Magic* (New York: The Ropeadope Music Company LLC, 2002). Rebirth Brass Band, *The Main Event: Live at the Maple Leaf* (New Orleans: Louisiana Red Hot Records, 1999).

130. From the author's interview with Sylvester Francis, New Orleans, June 23, 2003. The current brass bands include Olympia, Dirty Dozen, Rebirth, Chosen Few, Tremé, Li'l

Rascals, Soul Rebels, Hot Eight, Algiers, Storyville, Pinstripe, Majestic, Pinettes, Trombone Shorty, Bone Tone, and Li'l Stooges.

131. Leslie Gourse, *Wynton Marsalis: Skain's Domain, a Biography* (New York: Schirmer Books, 1999).

132. Anthony Fox and Bill Summers, liner notes, *Los Hombres Calientes, Vol. 4: Vodou Dance* (New Orleans: Basin Street Records, 2003).

133. Gwendolyn Midlo Hall, *Africans in Colonial Louisiana: The Development of Afro-Creole Culture in the Eighteenth Century* (Baton Rouge: Louisiana State University Press, 1992), p. 157.

Interlude

The epigraph is from Patrick Bellegarde-Smith, ed., *Fragments of Bone: Neo-African Religions in a New World* (Urbana and Chicago: University of Illinois Press, 2005), p. 4.

1. Karen McCarthy Brown, *Mama Lola: A Vodou Priestess in Brooklyn* (Berkeley: University of California Press, 1991), back flap.

2. Ibid., p. 10.

3. Robert A. Orsi, *Between Heaven and Earth: The Religious Worlds People Make and the Scholars Who Study Them* (Princeton, N.J.: Princeton University Press, 2005), front flap.

4. Elaine Pagels, *Beyond Belief: The Secret Gospel of Thomas* (New York: Vintage Books, 2003), p. 4.

5. Helen A. Regis analyzes how the use of memorial T-shirts in contemporary jazz funerals not only reconstructs the memory of young black New Orleanians who have died in violent circumstances but also expresses a moral and political critique of the conditions of marginalization in local black neighborhoods. See her "Keeping Jazz Funerals Alive: Blackness and the Politics of Memory in New Orleans," in *Southern Heritage on Display: Public Ritual and Ethnic Diversity within Southern Regionalism*, ed. Celeste Ray (Tuscaloosa: University of Alabama Press, 2003).

6. John W. Blassingame, *Black New Orleans, 1860–1880* (Chicago and London: University of Chicago Press, 1973), back flap. Blassingame traces the complex patterns of black community life in New Orleans back to the Reconstruction period.

3. In Rhythm with the Spirit

The epigraph is from Jack V. Buerkle and Danny Barker, *Bourbon Street Black: The New Orleans Black Jazzman* (New York: Oxford University Press, 1973), p. 188.

1. From http://www.gede.org/lwas/gede.html (accessed 2008).

2. Patrick Bellegarde-Smith, ed., *Fragments of Bone: Neo-African Religions in a New World* (Urbana and Chicago: University of Illinois Press, 2005), p. 1.

3. Ibid., p. 2.

4. I attended several jazz funerals in New Orleans from 1998 to 2005, including the famous jazz funerals of Donald Harrison Sr., Big Chief of the Guardians of the Flame Tribe, which began at St. Augustine Church in Tremé on December 5, 1998, and the "Farewell Service" for the King of Vodou, Chicken Man, on January 30, 1999, in the French Quarter and on Rampart Street.

5. Katy Rechdahl, "Chief of Chiefs," *Gambit Weekly* 26, no. 27 (July 5, 2005): 17, 19. In the Caribbean St. Joseph's feast is the day for Legba, the Vodou Iwa of the crossroads.

6. "Chief 'Tootie' Montana Dies of a Heart Attack at City Council Meeting," *New*

Orleans Independent Media Center, June 28, 2005, http://neworleans.indymedia.org/news/2005/06/3515.php (accessed 2008).

7. Anthropologist Helen A. Regis correctly notes that jazz funerals are not homogeneous but are dynamic neighborhood and community rituals in black New Orleans. Some jazz funerals, particularly those for young black men who die in violent circumstances, do not highlight or feature African diasporic elements but instead focus on the identities and experiences of blackness in a post-industrial urban environment, as represented on memorial T-shirts of the deceased. In her analysis, photographic studies of jazz funerals, such as *Rejoice When You Die* by Leo Touchet and Vernel Bagneris, focus on the dignified funeral processions for black community elders from 1968 to 1970 and commodify the "traditional jazz funeral" as a static and "dying tradition." Allison "Tootie" Montana's funeral, however, provides strong evidence that the traditional jazz funeral is still a dynamic, living ritual in New Orleans that often uses powerful African diasporic elements. Regis's analysis of African diasporic elements in New Orleans jazz funerals is based on a fictional depiction of a jazz funeral in the James Bond movie, *Live and Let Die* (1973). She critiques the stereotypical images of black New Orleans in the film to move beyond what she terms a "bizarre, exotic, or even perverse" connection between jazz funerals and Vodou by focusing on the ways in which jazz funerals have evolved into youth-oriented contemporary jazz funerals that balk at tradition and African diasporic connections. See Helen A. Regis, "Blackness and the Politics of Memory in the New Orleans Second-line," pp. 754, 767, 768, 770.

8. Margaret Thompson Drewal, *Yoruba Ritual: Performers, Play, Agency* (Bloomington: Indiana University Press), p. xiii.

9. Joseph Roach, *Cities of the Dead: Circum-Atlantic Performance* (New York: Columbia University Press, 1996), p. 2. Sometime in the winter months in 1823 Timothy Flint was the first white person to see and document a procession of African-descended people traveling through the streets of New Orleans. He called the procession the "great Congo-dance" and described "some hundred of Negroes, male and female, follow the king of the wake, who is conspicuous for his youth, size, the whiteness of his eyes, and the blackness of his visage." The king has "oblong, gilt-paper boxes on his head, tapering upwards like a pyramid. . . . From the ends of these boxes hang two huge tassels, like those on epaulets." He "wags his head and . . . grimaces." Those who follow him "have their own peculiar dress and their own contortions" (Reid Mitchell, *All on a Mardi Gras Day: Episodes in the History of New Orleans Carnival* [Cambridge, Mass.: Harvard University Press, 1995], pp. 29–30). Also see Timothy Flint, *Recollections of the Last Ten Years, Passed in Occasional Residence and Journeyings in the Valley of the Mississippi* (New York, 1968 [1826]), p. 140; and Jason Berry, "When Slaves Die," *Louisiana Endowment for the Humanities* (spring 1999): 54–62.

10. Drewal, *Yoruba Ritual,* p. 7.

11. "A Celebration Honoring the Life of Allison Marcel Montana, Big Chief Tootie, Chief of Chiefs, December 16, 1922–June 27, 2005," pp. 2–3.

12. Lolis Eric Elie, "Big Chief Gets Spirited Sendoff," *Times-Picayune,* July 11, 2005, p. B1. Also see Marta Moreno Vega, *The Altar of My Soul: The Living Traditions of Santeria* (New York: One World/Ballantine, 2000), pp. 107–108; and Miguel Barnet, *Afro-Cuban Religions,* trans. Christine Renata Ayorinde (Princeton, N.J.: Markus Wiener, 2001), pp. 47–48.

13. Ibid.

14. Ibid., p. 8.

15. Ibid., pp. 90, 90, 33, 92.

16. The author was a second-liner in Chicken Man's jazz funeral on January 31, 1999.

Also see Rick Bragg, "Jazzy Final Sendoff for Chicken Man," *New York Times,* February 1, 1999, national section, p. 1.

17. Yvonne Daniel, *Dancing Wisdom: Embodied Knowledge in Haitian Vodou, Cuban Yoruba, and Bahian Candomblé* (Urbana: University of Illinois Press, 2005), p. 63.

18. Ibid., p. 59.

19. Ibid., pp. 59, 61.

20. Jason Berry, "Churches the Missing Link in Jazz History," *Louisiana Endowment for the Humanities* (Fall 1998): 54.

21. Jackson, with Wylie, *Movin' On Up,* p. 33.

22. Ibid., p. 30.

23. Democracy Now, a daily radio and TV news program heard on more than five hundred stations, pioneering the largest community media collaboration in the U.S., "Historic African-American New Orleans Church Reopened after Weeks of Protests and Rectory Sit-In," Monday, April 10, 2006.

24. Ibid.

25. Robert Florence and Mason Florence, *New Orleans Cemeteries: Life in the Cities of the Dead* (New Orleans: Batture, 1997), p. 57.

26. Mike Burns, *Keeping the Beat on the Street: The New Orleans Brass Band Renaissance* (Baton Rouge: Louisiana State University Press, 2006), p. 65.

27. Ibid.

28. Ibid.

29. Jerry Block, "The Culture Collector, In his Backstreet Cultural Museum, Sylvester Francis Documents the Living Arts of Black New Orleans," *Gambit Weekly,* August 7, 2001; Sylvester Francis, "Keeping Jazz Funerals Alive," unpublished manuscript. Also see Karla F.C. Holloway, *Passed On: African American Mourning Stories* (Durham, N.C.: Duke University Press, 2002), for an analysis of African American funeral homes.

30. Michael Largey, *Vodou Nation: Haitian Art Music and Cultural Nationalism* (Chicago: University of Chicago Press, 2006), p. 17.

31. Robert Anthony Orsi uses the provocative term "theology of the streets" to describe the annual Italian American street "festa of the Madonna of 115th Street" in New York City in his book, *The Madonna of 115th Street: Faith and Community in Italian Harlem, 1880–1950* (New Haven, Conn.: Yale University Press, 1985), p. 219. See James B. Bennett, *Religion and the Rise of Jim Crow in New Orleans* (Princeton, N.J.: Princeton University Press, 2005), for the early-twentieth-century history of other black Catholic churches in New Orleans such as Corpus Christi Church and St. Dominic Church. Bobby Joe Neeley analyzes African-derived sacred music styles in the masses of contemporary black Catholic churches in New Orleans, such as St. Peter Claver Church and St. Francis de Sales Church, in his Ph.D. dissertation, "Contemporary Afro-American Voodooism (Black Religion): The Retention and Adaptation of the Ancient African-Egyptian Mystery System," University of California, Berkeley, 1988.

32. Jackson, with Wylie, *Movin' On Up,* pp. 32–33.

33. Thomas Brothers, *Louis Armstrong's New Orleans* (W.W. Norton, 2006), p. 86.

34. Ibid., p. 4.

35. Ibid.

36. Ibid., 31.

37. Ibid., pp. 38, 51.

38. Ibid., p. 21.

39. Ibid.

40. Ibid., p. 86.

41. Claude F. Jacobs and Andrew J. Kaslow, *The Spiritual Churches of New Orleans: Origins, Beliefs, and Rituals of an African-American Religion* (Knoxville: University of Tennessee Press, 1991), front flap.

42. Jason Berry, *The Spirit of Black Hawk: A Mystery of Africans and Indians* (Jackson: University Press of Mississippi, 1995), front flap.

43. Ibid., pp. 73–75 and photos between pp. 98 and 99. Also see Zora Neale Hurston, *The Sanctified Church* (Berkeley: Turtle Island, 1983); and "Hoodoo in America," *Journal of American Folklore* 44 (1931): 317–417.

44. Largey, *Vodou Nation*, p. 17.

45. Ibid., p. 3.

46. Karen McCarthy Brown, *Mama Lola: A Vodou Priestess in Brooklyn* (Berkeley: University of California Press, 1991), pp. 330–331.

47. Ibid., p. 374.

48. Ibid., p. 362; Donald J. Cosentino, ed., *Sacred Arts of Haitian Vodou* (Los Angeles: Fowler Museum of Cultural History, University of California, 1995), p. 408.

49. Sallie Ann Glassman, *Vodou Visions: An Encounter with Divine Mystery* (New York: Villard, 2000), p. 113.

50. Leo Touchet and Vernal Bagneris, *Rejoice When You Die: The New Orleans Jazz Funeral* (Baton Rouge: Louisiana State University Press, 1998), p. 2.

51. William J. Schafer, *Black Brass Bands and New Orleans Jazz* (Baton Rouge: Louisiana State University Press, 1977), pp. 9, 12; John W. Blassingame, *Black New Orleans, 1860–1880* (Chicago: University of Chicago Press, 1973), p. 140.

52. Mark Burns, *Keeping the Beat on the Street: The New Orleans Brass Band Renaissance* (Baton Rouge: Louisiana State University Press, 2006), p. 1.

53. Schafer, *Black Brass Bands and New Orleans Jazz*, p. 12.

54. Samuel J. Floyd Jr., *The Power of Black Music: Interpreting Its History from Africa to the United States* (New York: Oxford University Press, 1995), pp. 81, 82.

55. Ibid., pp. 82, 83.

56. Ibid., pp. 83, 84.

57. Jack V. Buerkle and Danny Barker, *Bourbon Street Black: The New Orleans Black Jazzman* (New York: Oxford University Press, 1973), p. 88.

58. Dorothy Rose Eagleson, "Some Aspects of the Social Life of the New Orleans Negro in the 1880s," M.A. thesis, Department of History, Tulane University, New Orleans, May 1961.

59. Ibid., p. 4.

60. Ibid.

61. Ibid., pp. 69–71.

62. Ibid., 77.

63. Ibid.

64. Brothers, *Louis Armstrong's New Orleans*, p. 174.

65. Ibid., pp. 209, 214.

66. John Storm Roberts, *Black Music of Two Worlds: African, Caribbean, Latin, and African-American Traditions*, 2nd rev. ed. (New York: Schirmer Books, 1998), p. 174.

67. Burns, *Keeping the Beat on the Street*, p. 2. Marjorie Thomas Zander's research on jazz funerals demonstrates that musicians in black brass bands differentiate between the two groups that employ them for funerals. The organizations established for benevolent works, such as the Young Men Olympians Benevolent Association, are known as societies and groups seeking pleasure such as the Jolly Band are clubs. See Marjorie Thomas Zander, "The Brass Band Funeral and Related Negro Burial Customs," M.A. thesis in Folk-

lore, University of North Carolina, Chapel Hill, 1962, p. 80. According to Burns, the first recording of the New Orleans brass band sound was in a 1929 film newsreel.

68. Burns, *Keeping the Beat in the Street*, p. 2.

69. Roberts, *Black Music of Two Worlds*, p. xxiv.

70. Blassingame, *Black New Orleans*, pp. 103, 163.

71. Hazel Trice Edney, "Future of Black Men Critical to 'American Family,'" *Louisiana Weekly*, April 23, 2007, p. 4.

72. Ibid. National Urban League, *The State of Black America 2007, Executive Summary: Portrait of a Black Male* (Washington, D.C.: National Urban League, 2007).

73. Michael P. Smith, *Mardi Gras Indians* (Gretna, La.: Pelican, 1994), p. 51.

74. Regis, "Blackness and Politics of Memory in the New Orleans Second-line," pp. 754–755.

75. Ibid., p. 754.

76. Schafer, *Brass Bands and New Orleans Jazz*, p. 28.

77. Ibid., pp. 32, 60.

78. Ibid., p. 33. Lee Collins, *Oh Didn't He Rumble: The Life Story of Lee Collins as Told to Mary Collins*, ed. Frank J. Gillis and John W. Miner (Urbana: University of Illinois Press, 1989).

79. Brothers, *Louis Armstrong's New Orleans*, p. 272

80. Zander, "The Brass Band Funeral and Related Negro Burial Customs," pp. 99–100. Michael P. Smith, "Jazz Funerals: Joie de Vivre, Joie de Morte," *Louisiana Cultural Vistas* (spring 1996): 38–39

81. Jason Berry, "Jazz Funerals: Second-line through Time," *Lagniappe: The States-Item/New Orleans*, October 28, 1988.

82. Schafer, *Brass Bands and New Orleans Jazz*, pp. 60–61. See J. Mark Souther, *New Orleans on Parade: Tourism and the Transformation of the Crescent City* (Baton Rouge: Louisiana State University Press, 2006), chap. 4.

83. Burns, *Keeping the Beat on the Street*, pp. 46–47. Also see Chris Gray and John McCusker, "Tradition-bound Mourn Loss of Dignity at Funerals," *Times-Picayune*, August 24, 1997; Lolis Eric Elie, "Funerals Not for Tourists," *Times-Picayune*, May 11, 1998; Don Lee Keith, "Second-line Blues: The Untimely Passing of Another Tradition," *The Courier: The Weekly Newspaper of New Orleans* (May 13–19, 1976): 4–6; Don Lee Keith, "Are We Witnessing the Death of the Jazz Funeral?" *Lagniappe: The States-Item/New Orleans*, August 25, 1979; Jim Amos, "The Day They Buried Big Jim Robinson," *Lagniappe: The States-Item/New Orleans*, May 8, 1976, pp. 3, 9; Pen Wilson, "Thousands View Celestine Rites: Dirges Sound for Noted Musician, but No Jazz," *Times-Picayune*, December 19, 1954; Arana Sonnier, "A Final Note," *Times-Picayune*, February 27, 1992; Robin von Breton Davis and Jim Pitts, "Traditional Funeral for a Jazzman," *The States-Item/New Orleans Lagniappe*, December 1, 1973; Jim Amos, "Everybody's a Big Mama, A Dirge for Miss Currie," *The States-Item/New Orleans Lagniappe*, July 18, 1974; Frank Trippett, "In Louisiana: Jazzman's Last Ride," *Time*, April 20, 1981; "Incidents Mar Jazz Funeral," *Times-Picayune*, October, 4, 1974; Valerie Faciane, "Dead Boy's Classmates Say Goodbye with Music," *Times-Picayune/The States Item*, July 23, 1981, sec. 1, p. 11; Vicki Ferstel, "Brass Band Leads Musician, Inventor Leonard Julian Sr. to his Final Rest," *Advocate Baton Rouge*, March 2, 1994; Susan Poag, "Jazz Funeral," *Times-Picayune*, May 8, 1993; and Joan Treadway, "Jazz Is Played at Rites Here: Black Berets Leader Is Laid to Rest," *Times-Picayune*, January 29, 1995.

84. Souther, *New Orleans on Parade*, pp. 123–124.

85. Burns, *Keeping the Beat on the Street*, p. 6.

86. Ibid., pp. 15–16.

87. Ibid., p. 70.

88. Dirty Dozen Brass Band, *The Dirty Dozen Brass Band: Mardi Gras in Montreux* (Cambridge, Mass.: Rounder Records, 1986), liner notes.

89. Burns, *Keeping the Beat on the Street*, p. 7.

90. Ibid.

91. Ibid., pp. 7, 11.

92. Ibid., p. 147.

93. David Kunian, "Social Aid and Pleasure Clubs Continue a Centuries-Old Tradition of 'Second-line' Parades—All Year Long, Their Strong Neighborhood Ties Have Helped Them Withstand Many Challenges," *Gambit Weekly*, February 6, 2007.

94. Burns, *Keeping the Beat on the Street*, pp. 4, 7, 11.

95. Roberts, *Black Music of Two Worlds*, pp. 158, 227.

96. Ibid., p. xxv.

97. Ibid.

98. Ibid., p. 185.

99. Ibid., p. xxiv.

100. Ibid.

101. One of the signature hymns of gospel music, "Precious Lord, Take My Hand," originated in Thomas Dorsey's experience of religious conversion when his wife and baby died in childbirth in 1932. Dorsey, the former blues pianist from Georgia, began to institutionalize gospel music at National Baptist Conventions and the Ebenezer Baptist Church in Chicago in the early 1930s. This new urban black sacred music combined the "intimate wail of the blues" with spirituals and Protestant hymns. New Orleans native Mahalia Jackson was one of the greatest twentieth-century performers of gospel music. See Robert Darden, *People Get Ready! A New History of Black Gospel Music* (New York: Continuum, 2004), pp. 169–171. Also see Walter F. Pitts Jr., *Old Ship of Zion: The Afro-Baptist Ritual in the African Diaspora* (New York: Oxford University Press, 1993), for a fascinating analysis of parallels between the performance of gospel music in Black Baptist churches in Texas and the religious ceremonies of African and African diasporic religions such as Vodou, Santeria, and Candomble.

102. Touchet and Bagneris, *Rejoice When You Die*, p. 3.

103. *All on a Mardi Gras Day*, Louisiana Endowment for the Humanities, The Arts Council of New Orleans, and PBS, 2003.

104. Brown, *Mama Lola*, pp. 361–362.

105. Ibid., p. 362.

106. Ibid.

107. Ibid.

108. Brown, *Mama Lola*, p. 362.

109. Author's fieldwork, Chief Allison Tootie Montana's jazz funeral, July 9, 2005.

110. *All on a Mardi Gras Day*.

111. Ibid.

112. Ibid.

113. Florence and Florence, *New Orleans Cemeteries*, pp. 53, 60.

114. Brown, *Mama Lola*, p. 330.

115. Ibid., pp. 369–370.

116. Florence and Florence, *New Orleans Cemeteries*, p. 21.

117. Ibid., pp. 53, 55, 57, 59. Tourists mark Xs on Marie Laveau's tomb to invoke her spirit.

118. Ibid., pp. 53, 60.

119. Ibid., pp. 68, 69, 73.

120. Brown, *Mama Lola*, p. 330.

121. *All on a Mardi Gras Day.*

122. Smith, "Jazz Funeral," p. 37.

123. Smith, *Mardi Gras Indians*, p. 30.

124. Karen McCarthy Brown's comments quoted in Patrick Bellegarde-Smith, *Fragments of Bone*, back flap.

125. Deren, *Divine Horsemen*, p. 15.

Epilogue

The epigraph is from Patricia Thompson, Select Committee Hearing, December 6, 2005, Select Bipartisan Committee to Investigate the Preparation and Response to Hurricane Katrina, *A Failure of Initiative: Final Report of the Select Bipartisan Committee to Investigate the Preparation for and Response to Hurricane Katrina, U.S. House of Representatives* (Washington, D.C.: U.S. Government Printing Office, 2006), p. 6.

1. Beverly Hendrix Wright, "New Orleans: A City That Care Forgot," in *In Search of the New South: The Black Urban Experience in the 1970s and 1980s*, ed. Robert D. Bullard (Tuscaloosa: University of Alabama Press, 1989), p. 45.

2. Ibid., pp. 73–74; American Civil Liberties Union's National Prison Project, "Abandoned and Abused: Orleans Parish Prisoners in the Wake of Hurricane Katrina," August 10, 2006; Avis A. Jones-DeWeever and Heidi Hartmann, "Abandoned before the Storms: The Glaring Disaster of Gender, Race, and Class Disparities in the Gulf," in *There Is No Such Thing as a Natural Disaster: Race, Class, and Hurricane Katrina*, ed. Chester Hartman and Gregory D. Squires (New York: Routledge, 2006), pp. 85–101; Chester Hartman and Gregory D. Squires, "Pre-Katrina, Post-Katrina," in idem, *There Is No Such Thing as a Natural Disaster*, p. 3.

3. American Library Association, "Newsmaker: Straight Answers from Michael White," *American Libraries Online,* http://www.ala.org/ala/alonline/selectedarticles/michaelwhite.htm (p. 1).

4. See Michael Eric Dyson, *Come Hell or High Water: Hurricane Katrina and the Color of Disaster* (New York: Basic Civitas Books, 2006); Douglas Brinkley, *The Great Deluge: Hurricane Katrina, New Orleans, and the Mississippi Gulf Coast* (New York: William Morrow, 2006); Jed Horne, *Breach of Faith: Hurricane Katrina and the Near Death of a Great American City* (New York: Random House, 2006); Christopher Cooper and Robert Block, *Disaster: Hurricane Katrina and the Failure of Homeland Security* (New York: Holt Paperbacks, 2007); Ivor van Heerden, *The Storm: What Went Wrong and Why during Hurricane Katrina—The Inside Story from One Louisiana Scientist* (New York: Viking Adult, 2006); John McQuaid and Mark Schleifstein, *Path of Destruction: The Devastation of New Orleans and the Coming Age of Superstorms* (New York: Little, Brown, 2006); *The Times-Picayune, Katrina: The Ruin and Recovery of New Orleans* (New Orleans: Spotlight Press, 2006); Editors of *Time* magazine, *Time: Hurricane Katrina: The Storm That Changed America* (New York: Time, 2005); CNN News, *Hurricane Katrina: CNN Reports: State of Emergency* (New York: Andrews McNeel, 2005); Jason David Rivera and DeMond Shondell Miller, "Continually Neglected: Situating Natural Disasters in the African-American Experience," *Journal of Black Studies* 37, no. 4. (March 2007): 502–522; Patricia Spence, Kenneth A. Lachlan, and Donyale R. Griffin, "Crisis Communication, Race, and Natural Disasters," *Journal of Black Studies* 37, no. 4 (March 2007): 539–554; and Gordon Russell, "Hurricane Katrina Ground Zero: Superdome Becomes Last Resort for

Thousands Unable to Leave. New Orleans Braces for Nightmare of The Big One," *Times-Picayune*, August 29, 2005, p. A1.

5. Russell, "Refugees Find Dome an Intolerable Refuge," Thursday, September 1, 2005, nola.com, http://www.nola.com/weblogs/pring.ssf?/mtlogs/nola_tporleans/arch (accessed 2008).

6. Ibid.

7. Brinkley, *The Great Deluge*, p. 543.

8. Trymaine D. Lee, "Rescuers 'had to push the bodies back with sticks,'" Thursday, September 1, 2005, nola.com, http://www.nola.com/weblogs/print.ssf?/mtlogs/nola_tporleans/arch.

9. Dyson, *Come Hell or High Water*. See, too, Pamela Denise Reed, "From the Freedman's Bureau to FEMA: A Post-Katrina Historical, Journalistic, and Literary Analysis," *Journal of Black Studies* 37, no. 4 (March 2007): 561; Adeline Masquelier, "Why Katrina's Victims Aren't Refugees: Musings on a 'Dirty' Word," *American Anthropologist* 108, no. 4 (December 2006): 735–743; and Spike Lee, "When the Levees Broke: A Requiem in Four Acts," HBO documentary, August 21 and 22, 2006.

10. Patrick Sharkey, "Survival and Death in New Orleans: An Empirical Look at the Human Impact of Katrina," *Journal of Black Studies* 37, no. 4 (March 2007): 484; Michele Krupa, "Remembering Katrina: In Memory 1,464 People Perished as a Result of Katrina. To Date, a Complete List Does Not Exist. Here, 817 Names Are Listed," *Times-Picayune*, August 30, 2006, p. A17; Gwen Filosa, "Remembering Ethel Freeman: She's Known Worldwide by the Picture of her Body at the Convention Center, and Her Son Won't Rest until Her Dignity Is Returned," *Times-Picayune*, September 3, 2006, www.nola.com (accessed 2008).

11. Ricky Clemons, "Recovery Less Than Impressive One Year after Katrina, Urban League Report Shows," National Urban League, 2006 Press Releases, p. 2.

12. Ibid. National Urban League Policy Institute, "Katrina: One Year Later, A Policy and Research Report on the National Urban League's Katrina Bill of Rights," August 24, 2006, Washington, D.C. Also see NAACP, Gulf Coast Advocacy Center, Opportunity Agenda, Kirwan Institute for the Study of Race and Ethnicity, "The State of Housing in New Orleans One Year after Katrina: A Plan for Equitable Rebuilding," 2006; and Center for Social Inclusion: A Project of the Tides Center, "The Race to Rebuild: The Color of Opportunity and the Future of New Orleans," August 2006.

13. "Jazz Funeral Tradition Returns to New Orleans," October 10, 2005, *taphophilia.com*, http://www.taphophilia.com (accessed 2007); "Music Returns to New Orleans," *Online News Hour*, MacNeil/Lehrer Productions, http://www.pbs.org/newshour/bb/entertainment/July-dec05/Orleans-music (accessed 2008); "Trumpeter Irvin Mayfield commissioned to write and conduct Katrina," 2005, *Dolan Media Newswires*, http://findarticles.com/p/articles/mi_qn4200/is_/ai_n15809826 (accessed 2008); Gwen Filosa, "Funeral Group Sponsors Service, Parade," *Times-Picayune*, October 30, 2005, p. B1; Jazz Journalists Association, "New Orleans Jazz Funeral Procession," September 9, 2005, http://www.jazzhouse.org/bulletin/viewtopic (accessed 2008); "New Orleans Bayou Steppers Pleasure Club," January 15, 2006, *New Orleans Bayou Steppers Social Aid and Pleasure Club* Web site, http://www.neworleansbayousteppers.com/bayousteppers/index.html (accessed 2008); Deborah Cotton, "From the Ground Up: Zulus Hold City's First Memorial for Katrina's Lost Lives," Week of March 2, 2006, *The Beehive*, http://www.thebeehive.org/Templates/HurricaneKatrina/Leve13noFrills (accessed 2008); Jason Berry, "Tremé's Cultural Heartbeat: The Backstreet Cultural Museum, like its battered Creole neighborhood, Struggles to hang on in post-Katrina." *Gambit Weekly*, March 7, 2006, http://www

.bestofneworleans.com/dispatch/2006-03-07/news_feat2PhP (accessed 2008); Sharon Keating, "Wynton Marsalis and the Second Line," April 26, 2006, *About.com: New Orleans Travel,* http://goneworleans.about.com/b/2006/04/21 (accessed 2008); "New Orleans Second Line Parade," *Coffee-and-Pie,* June 2006, http://coffeeandpie.planetchicken .com/pages/25e/new-orleans-second-line-parade (accessed 2008); Anya Kamenety, "Sweet Sounds of Home: Bringing Musicians Back to New Orleans," May 2, 2006, http://www .villagevoice.com/2006-05-02 (accessed 2008); "Kufaru Aaron Mouton, Second Line," June 26, 2006, http://www.kufaru.com/secondline.html (accessed 2008); "New Orleans Remembers," *New York Times,* Tuesday, May 30, 2006, p. A17; "One Year Later—Life in N.O. is Like Listening to Donny Hathaway," *Second Line II: Prelude,* August 17, 2006, http://journals.aol.com/secondlineno/thesecondline/entries/2006 (accessed 2008); Chris Rose, "Rebirth at the Maple Leaf: If it is late on Tuesday night, the brass band is rocking uptown, just like before the thing," *Times-Picayune,* August 25, 2006, http://www.nola .com; Mira Oberman, "New Orleans Remembers Katrina with Jazz Funerals," *Middle East Times,* August 30, 2006, http://www.metimes.com/international/2006/08/30 (accessed 2008); Larry Gabriel, "How I Learned the Second Line, Connecting Congo Square to the Detroit Jazz Fest," *Metrotimes, Detroit's Weekly Alternative,* August 30, 2006, http://www .metrotimes.com/editorial/story (accessed 2008); Mark Silva, "Bush: 'New Orleans is going to rise again': President Urges Residents to return 1 year after Hurricane Katrina," *Chicago Tribune,* Wednesday, August 30, 2006, Section 1; "Mardi Gras Drew More Locals, Study Says," *Times-Picayune,* September 5, 2006, http://www.nola.com; Offbeat Stuff, "Keith Keller, 1952–2006," *Offbeat.com,* http://offbeat.com; "The Algiers Brass Band Marks the Katrina Anniversary with a Jazz Funeral Procession in New Orleans Aug. 25, 2006," *NPR: Katrina: One Year Later,* October 1, 2006, http://www.npr .org/news/specials/Katrina/oneyearlater (accessed 2008); "200 Join March from Levee to Congo Square," *Second Line, Newsletter of Peoples' Hurricane Relief Fund* 1, no. 2 (September–October 2006): 1; Rukmini Callimachi, "City Dances, Mourns a Year after Katrina," August 30, 2006, http://www.cbsnews.com/stories/2006/08/30/ap/national/ maind8jqleego.shtml (accessed 2008); "Night Vision: Drums Beat in the Treme this Sunday," Monday, *Times-Picayune,* September 18, 2006, http://www.nola.com; "Black Men of Labor Parade 2006," *WWOZ Street Talk,* Friday, September 22, 2006, http:// wwozstreettalk.blogspot.com (accessed 2008); "Treme Brass Band Named a National Treasure," *Louisiana Weekly,* September 25, 2006, http://www.louisianaweekly.com; Katy Reckdahl, "Feeling His Spirit: Hot 8 Brass Band Serenades School Still Grieving for Slain Band Director," *Times-Picayune,* January 10, 2007, http://www.nola.com; David Kunian, "A Positive Cultural Thing: Social Aid and Pleasure Clubs continue a centuries-old tradition of 'second-line' parades—all year long. Their strong neighborhood ties have helped them withstand many challenges," *Gambit Weekly,* February 6, 2007, http://www .bestofneworleans.com/dispatch/2007-02-06/cover_story.php (accessed 2008); John Pope, "Optimism Reigns over Carnival 2007: Signs of Recovery Build as Krewes Get Ready," *Times-Picayune,* February 9, 2007, http://www.nola.com; Bruce Nolan, "Back in the Swing: Black, Middle-Class Social Clubs Ready to Revel Again," *Times-Picayune,* February 16, 2007, http://www.nola.com; Gwen Filosa, "Zulu King Sees Club as Beacon of Recovery," *Times-Picayune,* February 20, 2007, http://www.nola.com; Katy Reckdahl, "Bead-Dazzling Bonanza: Mardi Gras Indian Gangs Hit the Street in Full Force on Super Sunday," *Times-Picayune,* March 19, 2007, http://www.nola.com; "Fest Resurgent: Overall Attendance of 375,000 Is Highest since 2003," *Times-Picayune,* May 7, 2007, http://www.nola.com; Keith Spera, "New Orleans Mourns the Loss of Clarinestist Alvin Batiste," *Times-Picayune,* May 6, 2007, http://blog.nola.com/times-picayune; David

Walker, "CBS Newsman Ed Bradley Gets a Proper Jazzfest Send-Off," *Times-Picayune*, Living/Lagniappe, April 30, 2007, http://blog.nola.com/living2007/04/cbs_newsman _ed_bradley_gets (accessed 2008); Lisa Katzman, "Tootie's Last Suit," http://www .tootieslastsuit.com/film/hmtl (accessed 2008); Keith Spera, "Fats Back? Fats Domino is slated to perform on Saturday at Tipitina's—the first time since Hurricane Katrina," *Times-Picayune*, May 18, 2007, http://www.nola.com; Keith I. Marszalek, "Tambourine and Fan Will Celebrate Super Sunday Today," *Nola Entertainment*, May 27, 2007, http:// blog.nola.com/entertainment/2007/05/tambourine_and_fan (accessed 2008); Darran Simon, "Super Sunday on the Bayou: Indian Tribes Strut their Gorgeous Stuff," *Times-Picayune*, May 28, 2007, http://www.nola.com; Keith Spera, "Essence Homecoming: The Music and Empowerment Festival Returns to New Orleans," *Times-Picayune*, June 29, 2007, http://www.nola.com; "Funeral Arrangements Final for Oliver Morgan," Living/ Lagniappe, *Times-Picayune*, August 1, 2007, http://blog.nola.com (accessed 2008); "Protesters, Mourners Return to Ninth Ward," August 30, 2007, *Photo Galleries*, http://www .nola.com/katrinaphotos/tp/gallery (accessed 2008); "Massive Demonstration to Mark Katrina Observance," *Louisiana Weekly*, August 27, 2007, http://stayinthecenter.com/ massive-demonstrations-to-mark-katrina-observance (accessed 2008); Adam Nossiter, "Commemorations for a City That Needs No Reminders," *New York Times*, Monday, August 30, 2007, p. A12; Keith I Marszalek, "Brass Band Series Taking It to the Streets," September 6, 2007, *Nola Entertainment*, http://blog.nola.com/2007/09/french_quarter _brass_b (accessed 2008); and Katy Reckdahl, "Culture, Change Collide in Treme," *Times-Picayune*, October 2, 2007, http://blog.nola.com/updates2007/10/culture _change_collide_in_tr (accessed 2008).

14. Michael Collins, "The Disenfranchisement of Katrina's Survivors," *Scoop Independent News*, March 1, 2006, http://www.scoop.co.nz/stories/HL0603/s00016.htm (accessed 2008).

15. Matt Scallan, "N.O. at 223,000 in Census Estimates," *Times-Picayune*, March 22, 2007, http://www.nola.com.

16. Amy Liu and Nigel Holmes, "The State of New Orleans: An Update," *New York Times*, August 28, 2007, p. A23.

17. Adam Nossiter, "As New Orleans Shrinks, Some See an Upside," *New York Times*, January 21, 2007, p. A1.

18. Bill Quigly, "New Orleans a Year after Katrina: New Orleans Is Still in Intensive Care," *Black Commentator*, no. 195, August 31, 2006, http://www.blackcommentator.com (accessed 2008); Adam Nossiter, "In New Orleans, Some Hopes of Taking Back the Projects: Homes Sit Empty as Razing Is Planned," *New York Times*, December 26, 2006, p. A19; Susan Saulny, "New Orleans Hurt by Acute Rental Shortage: After FEMA Trailers Many Are Facing Homelessness," *New York Times*, December 3, 2007, pp. A1, A21; Leslie Eaton, "In New Orleans, Plan to Raze Low-Income Housing Draws Protest," *New York Times*, December 14, 2007, p. A22; Adam Nossiter and Leslie Eaton, "New Orleans Council Votes for Demolition of Housing," *New York Times*, December 21, 2007, p. A27.

19. Maria Godoy, "Katrina One Year Later, Tracking the Katrina Diaspora: A Tricky Task," NPR.org, August 2006, pp. 1–2.

20. Gwen Filosa, "N.O. Neighborhood Plans Unveiled but Total Price Tag Exceeds $2 Billion," *Times-Picayune*, September 24, 2006.

21. Zenitha Prince, "Black Culture Washed Away by Hurricane Katrina," *Louisiana Weekly*, March 6, 2006, p. 2.

22. Adam Nossiter, "Storm Left New Orleans Ripe for Violence," *New York Times*, January 11, 2007, p. A22; Bill Sothern, "Taken by the Tide," *New York Times*, January 10,

2007, op-ed page; Brendan McCarthy, "Study: Murder Rate Is Even Higher, Figures Make N.O. the Deadliest City," *Times-Picayune*, March 12, 2007, http://www.nola.com.

23. Dennis Persica, "Nagin Calls Diaspora a Racial Plot: City's Makeup Altered Intentionally, he says," *Times-Picayune*, March 19, 2007, http://www.nola.com.

24. Ibid.

25. Alex Rawls, "Back Talk with Aaron Neville," *Offbeat* (2006) http://offbeat.com.

26. Allen Johnson Jr., "Central City: Street Sense," *Gambit Weekly*, November 8, 2005, http://www.bestofneworleans.com.

27. Chris Rose, "The 60-Second Interview, Terence Blanchard," *Times-Picayune*, April 29, 2006, http://www.nola.com.

28. "New Orleans Social Club Musicians Band Together," *Associated Press MSN Music* (2006), http://music.msn.com (accessed 2006).

29. "Jude Law, Irvin Mayfield Headline Benefit," Photo Galleries, September 20, 2006, http://www.nola.com.

30. Author's telephone conversation with Darryl Montana, June 2007, New Orleans.

31. Howard Reich, "Crisis of Culture in New Orleans: Treasures of music lovers now just so much debris: Even as the city rebuilds, it is clear 'a whole universe' of jazz history is lost," *Chicago Tribune*, November 27, 2006, pp. 1, 9.

32. Keith Spera, "Bringing It All Back Home: Clarinetist/Collector Michael White lost everything with Katrina, but he's channeling those emotions in his music," *Times-Picayune*, June 15, 2007, http://www.nola.com.

The blatant disrespect shown by the New Orleans Police Department and the city government for Congo Square culture and the harassment of second-line performances in the streets of New Orleans will affect the future of jazz religion in the Crescent City. See Cain Burdeau, "ACLU Sues New Orleans over Parade Fees," *Associated Press*, November 16, 2006, http://www.washingtonpost.com (accessed 2008); Ann Simmons, "New Orleans' Fee Will Kill Jazz Funerals, Suit Says," *Los Angeles Times*, November 17, 2006, p. A20; Adam Nossiter, "Another Social Conflict Confronts New Orleans," *New York Times*, November 26, 2006, http://www.nytimes.com; Eve Troeh, "Transcript–Second Line Fee Increase," May 2, 2006, *WWOZ Street Talk*, http://wwozstreettalk.blogspot.com (accessed 2008); "'Cultural Disconnect' Citing Violence in Some Crowds, NOPD has drastically hiked some fees for second-line parades. Are cops protecting or proscribing street culture?" *Gambit Weekly*, June 27, 2006, http://www.bestofneworleans.com (accessed 2008); Katy Reckdahl, "Permit Fees Raining on Second-Line Parades: ACLU Seeking Temporary Order Halting 'Unreasonable' Charges," *Times-Picayune*, Thursday, March 29, 2007, http://www.nola.com; "Slashed Fee Let Second-Line Roll: NOPD, Club Agree on Temporary Deal," *Times-Picayune*, April 5, 2007, http://nola.com; Jason Berry, "Culture, a Saving Grace," *Gambit Weekly*, May 29, 2007, http://www.bestofneworleans.com; and Katy Reckdahl, "Culture, Change Collide in Treme," *Times-Picayune*, October 2, 2007, http://nola.com.

33. Gwen Filosa, "Funeral Group Sponsors Service Parade," *Times-Picayune*, October 30, 2005, p. B1.

34. Deborah Cotton, "From the Ground Up: Zulus Hold City's First Memorial for Katrina's Lost Lives," *Katrina Help Center*, March 2, 2006, http://www.thebeehive.org, p. 1.

35. Mira Oberman, "New Orleans Remembers Katrina with Jazz Funerals," *Middle East Times*, August 30, 2006, p. 1, http://www.metimes.com (accessed 2008).

36. WWOZ 90.9 FM New Orleans Jazz and Heritage Station, "Katrina Memorial Ceremony at 9th Ward Levee Breach," Press Release, August 20, 2006.

37. United Front to Commemorate the Great Flood, "Final Program for August 29th

Community-Based Commemoration of the Great Flood Announced," Press Release, August 20, 2006.

38. Ibid. Kevin Fox Gotham posits "three contrasting scenarios" for rebuilding New Orleans after Hurricane Katrina: (1) New Orleans reduced to "a cultural wasteland" stripped of its distinctive culture and communities; (2) a "Disneyized New Orleans," a by-product of ethnic cleansing with flashes of pre-Katrina culture contrived for the tourist industry; and (3) "a cultural renaissance" in which post-Katrina New Orleans will be rebuilt with sensitivity to local culture, diverse neighborhoods, and social justice. See Gotham's *Authentic New Orleans: Tourism, Culture, and Race in the Big Easy* (New York: New York University Press, 2007), pp. 2, 199, 201, 208. Despite the negative predictions about the future of New Orleans' black community after Hurricane Katrina, a major study of African American churches in the Crescent City after the disaster provides evidence from thirty-six interviews that churches and, one hopes, other black institutions are now rebuilding and providing resilience as well as economic, social, and spiritual support to black communities in New Orleans and in the Katrina diaspora in Houston, Memphis, and Columbia, South Carolina. See Patricia Stone Motes, Andrew Billingsley, Arlene Bowers Andrews, Kenneth Campbell, and Beverly Mason, "Role of the African American Church in Promoting Post-Catastrophe Resilience," an article not yet published.

39. Seven members of the Parker family migrated from New Orleans to the San Francisco Bay area in the aftermath of Hurricane Katrina. The Parkers' extensive family network in Monterey, San Francisco, and Sacramento, California, traces its roots to 1963, when Bettie Ruth Maxie Parker Johnson, the family matriarch, migrated from New Orleans to San Francisco with the freedom ride from Louisiana. Bettie's sister Patricia Maxie, whose apartment and possessions in the Bywater neighborhood of New Orleans were destroyed in the floodwaters of the levee break, had previously lived in San Francisco in the 1980s and 1990s. Patricia and her three daughters now have a beautiful new townhouse in San Francisco and do not plan to reside in New Orleans again. Ceola has rebuilt her single-family home in New Orleans East "better," she says, "than it was before Katrina," adding that "the majority of her neighbors have rebuilt their homes" on Craigie Road, a black, middle-class neighborhood in New Orleans East. Still, Ceola was not unscathed by the crisis of Hurricane Katrina. Initially her home and all her possessions were submerged in the floodwaters after the storm, and Ceola evacuated to live in San Antonio, Texas, for several months. By the fall of 2006 she had returned to live in a trailer in her yard during the reconstruction of her house. In September 2006 her daughter, Lynn, a premedical student at Xavier University, died in a car that crashed while the father of her child was driving it. Ceola, who raised four children to adulthood, is now raising Lynn's child by herself; her husband, Shawn, died in 2000, in his early fifties. Ceola's sister, Elaine Brown, and her mother, Delphine, survived Hurricane Katrina. They were rescued from the rooftop of the St. Bernard housing project in August 2005 and now live in an uptown apartment in New Orleans. From author's interview with Ceola Burks in San Francisco, December 24, 2007.

40. CDs by New Orleans musicians that discuss Hurricane Katrina include the Dirty Dozen Brass Band, *What's Going On* (Los Angeles: Shout! Factory LLC, 2006); Juvenile, *Reality Check* (New York: Atlantic Recording, 2006); Jazz at Lincoln Center Orchestra with Wynton Marsalis, Odadaa! With Yacub Addy, *Congo Square: Love. Libation. Liberation.* (New York: Jazz at Lincoln Center, 2006); and Irma Thomas, *After the Rain* (Cambridge, Mass.: Rounder Records, 2006).

BIBLIOGRAPHY

The *Times-Picayune,* the *New York Times,* and the *Chicago Tribune* provided excellent coverage of the post-Katrina crisis in New Orleans in 2005 and 2006. I also recommend black New Orleans newspapers such as the *New Orleans Tribune,* the *Louisiana Weekly,* and *Gambit Weekly* for important stories on the impact of Hurricane Katrina on the local communities.

Ake, David. *Jazz Cultures.* Berkeley: University of California Press, 2002.

Alter, Jonathan. "How to Save the Big Easy." *Newsweek,* September 12, 2005, 53.

Ancelet, Barry J., et al. *Cajun Country.* Jackson: University Press of Mississippi, 1991.

Anderson, Brett. "Surveying Eastern New Orleans." *Times-Picayune,* September 8, 2005.

Andrade, Mary J. *Day of the Dead in Mexico: Through the Eyes of the Soul: Oaxaca.* San Jose, Calif.: La Oferta Review Newspaper, 1999.

———. *Day of the Dead through the Eyes of the Soul: Puebla, Tlaxcala, San Luis Potosi, Hadalgo.* San Jose, Calif.: La Oferta Review, 2002.

Armstrong, Louis. *Satchmo: My Life in New Orleans.* New York: Da Capo, 1986 [1954].

———. *Swing That Music.* New York: Da Capo, 1993 [1936].

Aschenbrenner, Joyce. *Katherine Dunham: Dancing a Life.* Urbana: University of Illinois Press, 2002.

Averill, Gage. *A Day for the Hunter, a Day for the Prey: Popular Music and Power in Haiti.* Chicago: University of Chicago Press, 1997.

Barnes, Sandra T., ed. *Africa's Ogun: Old World and New.* Bloomington: Indiana University Press, 1989.

Barnet, Miguel. *Afro-Cuban Religions.* Translated by Christine Renata Ayorinde. Princeton, N.J.: Marcus Wiener, 2001 [1995].

Barringer, Felicity. "Long after the Storm, Shortages Overwhelm New Orleans's Few Hospitals." *New York Times,* January 23, 2006, p. A12.

Barry, Dan. "Texas Way Station Offers a First Serving of Hope." *New York Times,* September 5, 2005, p. A9.

———. "Away from Mardi Gras, Glints of Life as the Hopeful Trickle Home." *New York Times,* February 22, 2006, p. A10.

Barry, Ellen. "A Child in Charge of 'Six Babies.'" *Chicago Tribune,* September 6, 2005, p. 3.

———. "Giving the Bereaved 'Some Sense of Self.'" *Chicago Tribune,* September 18, 2005, p. 10.

Barry, John M. "The Prologue, and Maybe the Coda." *New York Times,* September 4, 2005, sec. 4, p. 1.

Bartels, Paul, and Richard Boyd. "Want Red Cross Aid? Get in Line." *Times-Picayune,* September 29, 2005.

Barthelme, Frederick. "Mississippi's Morning After." *New York Times,* September 2, 2005, p. A23.

Bastide, Roger. *African Civilizations in the New World.* Translated by Peter Green. New York: Harper and Row, 1971.

Bechet, Sidney. *Treat It Gentle: An Autobiography.* New York: Da Capo, 2002 [1960].

Bell, Caryn Cossé. *Revolution, Romanticsm, and the Afro-Creole Protest Tradition in Louisiana, 1718–1768.* Baton Rouge: Louisiana State University Press, 1997.

Bellegarde-Smith, Patrick. *Haiti: The Breached Citadel.* Boulder, Colo.: Westview, 1990.

———, ed. *Fragments of Bone: Neo-African Religions in a New World.* Urbana: University of Illinois Press, 2005.

Bellegarde-Smith, Patrick, and Claudine Michel, eds. *Haitian Vodou: Spirit, Myth, and Reality.* Bloomington: Indiana University Press, 2006.

Bennet, James. "In Search of a Family Treasure." *New York Times,* September 16, 2005, p. A18.

———. *Religion and the Rise of Jim Crow in New Orleans.* Princeton, N.J.: Princeton University Press, 2005.

Berger, Susan. "Displaced College Students Scramble to Find New Schools." *Chicago Tribune,* September 5, 2005, p. 5.

Bergner, Daniel. *God of the Rodeo: The Quest for Redemption in Louisiana's Angola Prison.* New York: Ballantine Books, 1988.

Berry, Jason. *The Spirit of Black Hawk: The Mystery of Africans and Indians.* Jackson: University Press of Mississippi, 1995.

Berry, Jason, Jonathan Foose, and Tad Jones. *Up from the Cradle of Jazz: New Orleans Music since World War II.* New York: Da Capo, 1992.

Black Hawk and Milo Milton Quarfe, eds. *Black Hawk.* New York: Dover, 1994 [1916].

Blassingame, John W. *Black New Orleans, 1860–1880.* Chicago: University of Chicago Press, 1973.

Blier, Suzanne Preston. *African Vodun: Art, Psychology, and Power.* Chicago: University of Chicago Press, 1995.

Bockie, Simon. *Death and the Invisible Powers: The World of Kongo Belief.* Bloomington: Indiana University Press, 1993.

Bodin, Ron. *Voodoo: Past and Present.* Lafayette: University of Southwestern Louisiana, 1990.

Bordelon, Pamela, ed. *Go Gator and Muddy the Water: Writings by Zora Neale Hurston from the Federal Writers' Project.* New York: W. W. Norton, 1999.

Boyd, Valerie. *Wrapped in Rainbows: The Life of Zora Neale Hurston.* New York: Scribner, 2003.

Bramly, Serge. *Macumba: The Teachings of Maria-José, Mother of the Gods.* San Francisco: City Lights Books, 1994 [1975].

Brandon, George. *Santeria from Africa to the New World: The Dead Sell Memories.* Bloomington: Indiana University Press, 1993.

Brasseaux, Carl A. *Creoles of Color in the Bayou Country.* Jackson: University Press of Mississippi, 1994.

Brick, Michael. "The Preservation Hall Band, Far from Preservation Hall." *New York Times,* September 10, 2005, p. A17.

Bridges, Flora Wilson. *Resurrection Song: African-American Spirtituality.* Maryknoll, N.Y.: Orbis Books, 2001.

Broder, John M. "Amid Criticism of Federal Efforts, Charges of Racism Are Lodged." *New York Times,* September 5, 2005, p. A9.

Brothers, Thomas, ed. *Louis Armstrong in His Own Words: Selected Writings.* New York: Oxford University Press, 1999.

———. *Louis Armstrong's New Orleans.* New York: W. W. Norton, 2006.

Brown, Diana De G. *Umbanda: Religion and Politics in Urban Brazil.* New York: Columbia University Press, 1994 [1986].

Brown, Karen McCarthy. *Mama Lola: A Vodou Priestess in Brooklyn.* Berkeley: University of California Press, 1991.

Browning, Barbara. *Samba: Resistance in Motion.* Bloomington: Indiana University Press, 1995.

Buerkle, Jack V., and Danny Barker. *Bourbon Street Black: The New Orleans Black Jazzman.* New York: Oxford University Press, 1973.

Bullard, Robert D., ed. *In Search of the New South: The Black Urban Experience in the 1970s and 1980s.* Tuscaloosa: University of Alabama Press, 1991.

Bumiller, Elisabeth. "Democrats and Others Criticize White House's Response to Disaster." *New York Times,* September 2, 2005, p. A14.

———. "In New Orleans, Bush Speaks with Optimism but Sees Little of Ruin." *New York Times,* January 13, 2006, p. A12.

Burton, Richard D. E. *Afro-Creole: Power, Opposition, and Play in the Caribbean.* Ithaca, N.Y.: Cornell University Press, 1997.

Canizares, Raul. *Walking with the Night: The Afro-Cuban World of Santeria.* Rochester, Vt.: Destiny Books, 1993.

Carey, Benedict. "Storm Will Have a Long-Term Emotional Effect on Some Survivors, Experts Say." *New York Times,* September 4, 2005, p. 21.

Carter, William. *Preservation Hall: Music from the Heart.* New York: W.W. Norton, 1991.

Chernoff, John Miller. *African Rhythm and African Sensibility: Aesthetics and Social Action in African Musical Idioms.* Chicago: University of Chicago Press, 1979.

Childress, Mark. "What It Means to Miss New Orleans." *New York Times,* September 4, 2005, sec. 9, p. 1.

Chilton, John, and Max Jones. *Louis: The Louis Armstrong Story, 1990–1971.* New York: Da Capo, 1988 [1971].

Chireau, Yvonne P. *Black Magic: Religion and the African American Conjuring Tradition.* Berkeley: University of California Press, 2003.

Clifford, Jan, and Leslie Blackshear Smith. *The Incomplete Year by Year Selectively Quirky, Prime Facts Edition of the History of the New Orleans Jazz and Heritage Festival.* New Orleans: e/Prime, 2005.

Collins, Mary. *Oh, Didn't He Ramble: The Life Story of Lee Collins.* Urbana: University of Illinois Press, 1989.

Cosentino, Donald J., ed. *Sacred Arts of Haitian Vodou.* Los Angeles: UCLA Fowler Museum of Cultural History, 1995.

Cowan, Walter G., Charles L. Dufour, and John Wilds. *Louisiana Yesterday and Today: A Historical Guide to the State.* Baton Rouge: Louisiana State University Press, 1996.

Creel, Margaret Washington. *"A Peculiar People": Slave Religion and Community—Culture among the Gullahs.* New York: New York University Press, 1988.

Crosley, Reginald. *The Vodou Quantum Leap: Alternate Realities, Power, and Mysticism.* St. Paul, Minn.: Llewellyn, 2000.

Da Matta, Roberto. *Carnivals, Rogues, and Heroes: An Interpretation of the Brazilian Dilemma.* Notre Dame: University of Notre Dame Press, 1991.

Daniel, Yvonne. *Dancing Wisdom: Embodied Knowledge in Haitian Vodou, Cuban Yoruba, and Bahian Candomble.* Urbana: University of Illinois Press, 2005.

Daniels, Douglas Henry. "Vodun and Jazz: 'Jelly Roll' Morton and Lester 'Press' Young—Substance and Shadow." *Journal of Haitian Studies* 9, no. 1 (spring 2003): 109–122.

Dankner, Laura, and Grace Lichtenstein. *Musical Gumbo: The Music of New Orleans.* New York: W.W. Norton, 1993.

Davies, Carole Boyce, Ali A. Mazrui, and Isidore Okpewho, eds. *African Diaspora: African Origins and New World Identities.* Bloomington: Indiana University Press, 2001.

Davis, Rod. *American Voudou: Journey into a Hidden World.* Denton: University of North Texas Press, 1998.

Davis, Wade. *The Serpent and the Rainbow.* New York: Warner Books, 1985.

Dayan, Joan. *Haiti, History, and the Gods.* Berkeley: University of California Press, 1995.

Deggs, Mary Bernard, Virgina Meecham Gould, and Charles E. Nolan, eds. *No Cross, No Crown: Black Nuns in Nineteenth-Century New Orleans.* Bloomington: Indiana University Press, 2000.

Deren, Maya. *Divine Horsemen: The Living Gods of Haiti.* Kingston, N.Y.: Documentext, 1970 [1953].

Desmangles, Leslie G. *The Faces of the Gods: Vodou and Roman Catholicism in Haiti.* Chapel Hill: University of North Carolina Press, 1992.

DeVore, Donald E. "Water in Sacred Places: Rebuilding New Orleans Black Churches as Sites of Community Empowerment." *Journal of American History* 94 (December 2007): 762–769.

Dewan, Shaila. "With Its First Jazz Funeral, New Orleans Reclaims Its Spirit." *New York Times,* October 10, 2005, p. A15.

Dje Dje, Jacqueline Coydell, ed. *Turn up the Volume! A Celebration of African Music.* Los Angeles: Fowler Museum of Cultural History, University of California, 1999.

Domínguez, Virgina. *White by Definition: Social Classification in Creole Louisiana.* New Brunswick, N.J.: Rutgers University Press, 1986.

Dorman, James H., eds. *Creoles of Color of the Gulf South.* Knoxville: University of Tennessee Press, 1996.

Draper, David Elliott. "The Mardi Gras Indians: The Ethnomusicology of Black Associations in New Orleans." Ph.D. diss., Tulane University, New Orleans, 1973.

Drewal, Henry, and John Mason. *Beads Body and Soul: Art and Light in the Yoruba Universe.* Los Angeles: Fowler Museum of Cultural History, University of California, 1998.

Drewal, Margaret Thompson. *Yoruba Ritual: Performers, Play, Agency.* Bloomington: Indiana University Press, 1992.

Dunham, Katherine. *Dances of Haiti.* Los Angeles: Center for Afro-American Studies, University of California, 1983.

———. *Island Possessed.* Chicago: University of Chicago Press, 1994 [1969].

Dunlap, David W. "Future Face of New Orleans Has an Uncertain Look for Now." *New York Times,* September 1, 2005, p. A17.

Dyson, Michael Eric. *Come Hell or High Water: Hurricane Katrina and the Color of Disaster.* New York: Basic Civitas, 2006.

Eagleson, Dorothy Rose. "Some Aspects of the Social Life of the New Orleans Negro in the 1880s." Master's thesis, Tulane University, New Orleans, 1961.

Eckstein, Barbara. *Sustaining New Orleans: Literature, Local Memory, and the Fate of a City.* New York: Routledge, 2006.

Egan, Timothy. "Uprooted and Scattered Far from the Familiar." *New York Times,* September 11, 2005, p. A1.

Elie, Lolis Eric. "Big Chief Gets Spirited Sendoff." *Times-Picayune,* July 11, 2005, p. B1.

Emery, Lynne Fauley. *Black Dance from 1619 to Today.* Pennington, N.J.: Princeton Book Company, 1988.

Ephirim-Donkor, Anthony. *African Spirituality: On Becoming Ancestors.* Trenton, N.J.: Africa World Press, 1997.

Epstein, Dena J. *Sinful Times and Spirituals: Black Folk Music to the Civil War.* Urbana: University of Illinois Press, 1977.

Fabre, Genevieve, and Ramon A. Gutierrez, eds. *Feasts and Celebrations in American Ethnic Communities.* Albuquerque: University of New Mexico Press, 1995.

Fandrich, Ina Johanna. "The Mysterious Voodoo Queen Marie Laveau: A Study of Power and Female Leadership in Nineteenth-Century New Orleans." Ph.D. diss., Temple University, Philadelphia, 1994.

———. *The Mysterious Voodoo Queen Marie Laveaux.* New York: Routledge, 2005.

Feinstein, Sascha, and Yusef Komunyakaa, eds. *The Jazz Poetry Anthology.* Bloomington: Indiana University Press, 1991.

Fernandez-Olmos, Margarite, and Lizabeth Paravisini-Gebert, eds. *Sacred Possessions: Vodou, Santeria, Obeah, and the Caribbean.* New Brunswick, N.J.: Rutgers University Press, 1977.

Fleurant, Gerdès. *Dancing Spirits: Rhythms and Rituals of Haitian Vodou, The Rada Rite.* Westport, Conn.: Greenwood, 1996.

Florence, Robert, and Mason Florence. *New Orleans Cemeteries: Life in the Cities of the Dead.* New Orleans: Batture, 1997.

Floyd, Samuel A., Jr. *The Power of Black Music: Interpreting Its History from Africa to the United States.* New York: Oxford University Press, 1995.

Foner, Laura. "The Free People of Color in Louisiana and St. Domingue: A Comparative Portrait of Two Three-Caste Slave Societies." *Journal of Social History* 3–4 (summer 1970): 406–430.

Forbes, Jack D. *Africans and Native Americans: The Language of Race and the Evolution of Red-Black Peoples.* Urbana: University of Illinois Press, 1993.

Gaillard, Frye. "After the Storms: Tradition and Change in Bayou La Batre." *Journal of American History* 94 (December 2007): 856–862.

Gaines, Ernest J. *A Lesson before Dying.* New York: Vintage Books, 1993.

Gaines, William, and Howard Reich. *Jelly's Blues: The Life, Music, and Redemption of Jelly Roll Morton.* New York: Da Capo, 2003.

Garciagodoy, Juanita. *Digging the Days of the Dead: A Reading of Mexico's Dias de Muertos.* Niwot: University Press of Colorado, 1998.

Gebhardt, Nicholas. *Going for Jazz: Musical Practices and American Ideology.* Chicago: University of Chicago Press, 2001.

Gehman, Mary. *The Free People of Color of New Orleans: An Introduction.* New Orleans: Margaret Media, 1994.

Gerard, Charley. *Jazz in Black and White: Race, Culture, and Identity in the Jazz Community.* Westport, Conn.: Praeger, 2001.

Germany, Kent B. "The Politics of Poverty and History: Racial Inequality and the Long Prelude to Katrina." *Journal of American History* 94 (December 2007): 743–751.

Gibbs, Nancy. "An American Tragedy." *Time,* September 12, 2005, 28–49.

Gillespie, Dizzy, with Al Fraser. *To Be, or Not ... To Bop: Memoirs.* Garden City, N.Y.: Doubleday, 1979.

Gilroy, Paul. *The Black Atlantic: Modernity and Double Consciousness.* Cambridge, Mass.: Harvard University Press, 1993.

Girourd, Tina. *Sequin Artists of Haiti.* Cecilia, La.: Girourd Art Projects, 1994.

Glassman, Sallie Ann. *Vodou Visions: An Encounter with Divine Mystery.* New York: Villard Books, 2000.

Gomez, Michael A. *Exchanging Our Country Marks: The Transformation of African Identities in the Colonial and Antebellum South.* Chapel Hill: University of North Carolina Press, 1998.

Gould, Philip. *Louisiana Faces: Images from a Renaissance.* Baton Rouge: Louisiana State University Press, 2000.

Gourse, Leslie. *Wynton Marsalis: Skain's Domain: A Biography.* New York: Schirmer Books, 1999.

Gray, Steven, and Evan Perez. "A City That Made an Art of Funerals Now Just Makes Do." *Wall Street Journal,* September 9, 2005, p. A1.

Guterman, Lila. "Decades of Research Destroyed by Katrina." *Chronicle of Higher Education,* September 30, 2005, p. A14.

Guthrie, Ramsey, Jr. *Race Music: Black Music from Bebop to Hip-Hop.* Berkeley: University of California Press, 2003.

Hagedorn, Katherine J. *Divine Utterances: The Performance of Afro-Cuban Santeria.* Washington, D.C.: Smithsonian Institution Press, 2001.

Hair, William Ivy. *Carnival of Fury: Robert Charles and the New Orleans Race Riot of 1900.* Baton Rouge: Louisiana State University Press, 1976.

Hale, Thomas A. *Griot and Griottes: Masters of Words and Music.* Bloomington: Indiana University Press, 1998.

Haley, Shawn D., and Fukuda, Curt. *Day of the Dead: When Two Worlds Meet in Oaxaca.* New York: Berghahn Books, 2004.

Hall, Gwendolyn Midlo. *Africans in Colonial Louisiana: The Development of Afro-Creole Culture in the Eighteenth Century.* Baton Rouge: Louisiana State University Press, 1992.

Handy, D. Antoinette. *Jazz Man's Journey: A Biography of Ellis Louis Marsalis, Jr.* Lanham, Md.: Scarecrow, 1999.

Harding, Rachael E. *A Refuge in Thunder: Candomblé and Alternative Spaces of Blackness.* Bloomington: Indiana University Press, 2000.

Harrison, Robert Pogue. *The Dominion of the Dead.* Chicago: University of Chicago Press, 2003.

Hasse, John Edward, ed. *Jazz: The First Century.* New York: William Morrow, 2000.

Hauser, Christine. "On Bourbon Street, the Good Times Roll a Little Later as the Curfew Is Extended." *New York Times,* October 16, 2005, p. 22.

———. "Mayor of New Orleans Vows to Rebuild Two Devastated Areas." *New York Times,* October 21, 2005, p. A20.

Hauser, Christine, and Christopher Drew. "Three Police Officers Deny Battery Charges after Videotaped Beating in New Orleans." *New York Times,* October 11, 2005, p. A16.

Hernandez, Daisy. "The Future of the Ninth Ward." *ColorLines,* spring 2006, p. 29.

Hirsch, Arnold R. "Fade to Black: Hurricane Katrina and the Disappearance of Creole New Orleans." *Journal of American History* 94 (December 2007): 752–761.

Hirsch, Arnold R., and Joseph Logsdon, eds. *Creole New Orleans: Race and Americanization.* Baton Rouge: Louisiana State University Press, 1992.

Hobson, Katherine. "Keeping Jazz Alive, Post-Katrina." *Princeton Alumni Weekly,* April 5, 2006, p. 50.

Holloway, Joseph E., ed. *Africanisms in American Culture.* Bloomington: Indiana University Press, 1990.

Holloway, Karla F. C. *Passed On: African American Mourning Stories.* Durham, N.C.: Duke University Press, 2002.

Huber, Leonard B. *Our Lady of Guadalupe Church the International Shrine of St. Jude, New Orleans, La. 150th Anniversary Edition, 1826–1973.* Hackensack, N.J.: Custombook, 1976.

Hunter, B. R. "The Meters." *Vibe* 4, no. 1 (February 1996): 104.

Hurston, Zora Neale. *Mules and Men.* New York: Harper Perennial, 1990 [1935].

———. *Tell My Horse: Voodoo and Life in Haiti and Jamaica.* New York: Harper and Row, 1990 [1938].

———. *Dust Tracks on a Road.* New York: Harper Perennial, 1991 [1942].

———. *Every Tongue Got to Confess: Negro Folk-Tales from the Gulf State.* New York: Harper Collins, 2001.

Isaacson, Walter. "How to Bring the Magic Back." *Time,* September 12, 2005, 71.

Ivey, Steve, and Ray Quintanilla. "Reuniting Families Could Take 'Months.'" *Chicago Tribune,* September 24, 2005, p. 5.

Jackson, Derrick Z. "Health Care Is Swept away with Katrina." *Chicago Tribune,* September 26, 2005, p. 17.

Jackson, Mahalia, and Evan McLeod Wylie. *Movin' On Up.* New York: Hawthorn Books, 1966.

Jacobs, Claude F., and Andrew J. Kaslow. *The Spiritual Churches of New Orleans: Origins, Beliefs, and Rituals of an African-American Religion.* Knoxville: University of Tennessee Press, 1991.

James, Frank, and Andrew Martin. "Ex-Officials Say Weakened FEMA Botched Response." *Chicago Tribune,* September 3, 2005, p. 1.

Johnson, Jerah. "New Orleans Congo Square: An Urban Setting for Early American Culture Formation." *Louisana History* 32, no. 2 (spring 1991): 117–157.

———. *Congo Square in New Orleans.* New Orleans: Louisiana Landmark Society, 1995.

Johnson, Kirk. "For Storm Survivors, a Mosaic of Impressions Rather Than a Crystalline Moment." *New York Times,* September 11, 2005, p. 25.

———. "45 Bodies Found in a New Orleans Hospital." *New York Times,* September 13, 2005, p. A1.

———. "Where Musical Refugees Can Thicken the Gumbo." *New York Times,* September 15, 2005, p. B1.

Johnson, Walter. *Soul by Soul: Life Inside the Antebellum Slave Market.* Cambridge, Mass.: Harvard University Press, 1999.

Jones, Leroi. *Blues People: The Negro Experience in White America and the Music That Developed from It.* New York: Morrow Quill Paperbacks, 1963.

Jones, Tim. "Scattered by the Storm." *Chicago Tribune,* September 11, 2005, p 1.

———. "Town Defends Closing Bridge to Safety." *Chicago Tribune,* October 10, 2005, p. 7.

Jurgensen, John. "A Jazz Diaspora Redraws the Musical Map." *Wall Street Journal,* April 8, 2005, p. P1.

Kahn, Ashley. *A Love Supreme: The Story of John Coltrane's Signature Album.* New York: Viking, 2002.

Kaplan, Carla, ed. *Zora Neale Hurston: A Life in Letters.* New York: Doubleday, 2002.

Kashef, Ziba. "Newsflash: Race and Class Matter." *ColorLines,* spring 2006, p. 5.

Katz, William Loren. *Black Indians: A Hidden Heritage.* New York: Atheneum, 1986.

Kaufman, Leslie. "An Uprooted Underclass, Under the Microscope." *New York Times,* September 25, 2005, sec. 4, p. 4.

Keil, Charles. *Urban Blues.* Chicago: University of Chicago Press, 1966.

Kein, Sybil. *An American South.* East Lansing: Michigan State University Press, 1996.

———. *Gumbo People.* New Orleans: Margaret Media, 1999 [1981].

———, ed. *Creole: The History and Legacy of Louisiana's Free People of Color.* Baton Rouge: Louisiana State University Press, 2000.

Kelman, Ari. "Boundary Issues: Clarifying New Orleans's Murky Edges." *Journal of American History* 94 (December 2007): 695–703.

Kennedy, Richard S., ed. *Literary New Orleans in the Modern World.* Baton Rouge: Louisiana State University Press, 1998.

Kerr, Drew. "Soul Patrol Led the Way." *Daily Iowan,* September 27, 2005, p. A1.

Kinser, Samuel. *Carnival American Style: Mardi Gras at New Orleans and Mobile.* Chicago: University of Chicago Press, 1990.

Klein, Herbert S. *African Slavery in Latin America and the Caribbean.* New York: Oxford University Press, 1986.

Kmen, Henry A. *Music in New Orleans.* Baton Rouge: Louisiana State University Press, 1966.

Kot, Greg. "Storm-Driven Musicians Band Together." *Chicago Tribune,* September 16, 2005, sec. 2, p. 1.

Laderman, Gary. *The Sacred Remains: American Attitudes toward Death, 1799–1883.* New Haven, Conn.: Yale University Press, 1996.

Laguerre, Michel S. *Voodoo and Politics in Haiti.* New York: St. Martin's, 1989.

Landphair, Juliette. "'The Forgotten People of New Orleans': Community, Vulnerability, and the Lower Ninth Ward." *Journal of American History* 94 (December 2007): 837–845.

Leathem, Karen Trahan. "Women on Display: The Gendered Meanings of Carnival in New Orleans." *Locus* 5, no. 1 (fall 1992): 1–18.

Levin, Floyd. *Classic Jazz: A Personal View of the Music and the Musicians.* Berkeley: University of California Press, 2000.

Levine, Lawrence W. *Black Culture and Black Consciousness: Afro-American Folk Thought from Slavery to Freedom.* New York: Oxford University Press, 1977.

Levy, Nathan. "In a Hub of Music, Playing the Relief Refrain." *New York Times,* October 11, 2005, p. A16.

Lewis, Rudolph, and Amin Sharif, eds. *I Am New Orleans and Other Poems by Marcus B. Christian.* New Orleans: Xavier Review, 1999.

Lichtblau, Eric. "Chertoff Draws Fire on Briefing." *New York Times,* September 8, 2005, p. A20.

Lipsitz, George. *Dangerous Crossroads: Popular Music, Postmodernism, and the Focus of Peace.* London: Verso, 1994.

———. *Footsteps in the Dark: The Hidden Histories of Popular Music.* Minneapolis: University of Minnesota Press, 2007.

Lock, Graham. *Blutopia: Visions of the Future and Revisions of the Past in the Work of Sun Ra, Duke Ellington, and Anthony Braxton.* Durham, N.C.: Duke University Press, 2000.

Lomax, Allan. *Mister Jelly Roll: The Fortunes of Jelly Roll Morton, New Orleans Creole and "Inventor of Jazz."* New York: Pantheon Books, 1993 [1950].

Long, Alecia P. "Poverty Is the New Prostitution: Race, Poverty, and Public Housing in Post-Katrina New Orleans." *Journal of American History* 94 (December 2007): 795–803.

Long, Carolyn Morrow. *Spiritual Merchants: Religion, Magic, and Commerce.* Knoxville: University of Tennessee Press, 2001.

———. *A New Orleans Voudou Priestess: The Legend and Reality of Marie Laveau.* Gainesville: University Press of Florida, 2006.

Long, Richard A. *The Black Tradition in American Dance.* London: Prion, 1989.

Lyons, Mary E., ed. *Talking with Tebe: Clementine Hunter, Memory Artist.* Boston: Houghton Mifflin, 1998.

Malone, Jacqui. *Steppin' on the Blues: The Visible Rhythms of African American Dance.* Urbane: University of Illinois Press, 1996.

Marquis, Donald M. *In Search of Buddy Bolden: First Man of Jazz.* Baton Rouge: Louisiana State University Press, 1978.

Marsalis, Wynton. "After Katrina: 'It's Time Somebody Woke Us Up.'" *Louisiana Cultural Vistas* 16, no. 4 (winter 2005/2006): 12.

———. "Jazz Education in the New Millennium." *Jazz Educators Journal* (September 2000): 46–52.

———. "Saving America's Soul Kitchen." *Louisiana Cultural Vistas* 16, no. 3 (fall 2005): 18.

———. "Shaken but Not Broken." *U.S. News & World Report,* February 27, 2006, p. 60.

Martinez, Maurice M., Jr. "Two Islands: The Black Indians of Haiti and New Orleans." *Arts Quarterly* 1, no. 7 (July/August/September 1979).

Mason, Beverly J. "AND I AM PART OF THE GREATNESS: Twelve Black Elderly Women and Men Decry Their Urban Community's Reality." *Journal of Black Studies* (September 2005): 97.

Mbiti, John S. *African Religions and Philosophy,* 2nd ed. Portsmouth, N.H.: Heinemann, 1997 [1969].

McAlister, Elizabeth. *Rara! Vodou, Power, and Performance in Haiti, and Its Diaspora.* Berkeley: University of California Press, 2002.

———. "The Madonna of 115th Street Revisited: Vodou and Haitian Catholicism in the Age of Transnationalism." In *Gatherings in Diaspora: Religious Communities and the New Immigration,* ed. R. Stephen Warner and Judith G. Wittner. Philadelphia: Temple University Press, 1998.

Medley, Keith Weldon. *We as Freemen: Plessy v. Ferguson.* Gretna, La.: Pelican, 2003.

Métraux, Alfred. *Voodoo in Haiti.* New York: Schocken Books, 1972 [1959].

Michel, Claudine. *Aspects éducatifs et moraux du Vodou Haïtien.* Port-au-Prince: Imprimerie le Natal, 1995.

———. "The Educational Character of Haitian Vodou." *Comparative Education Review* 40, no. 3 (August 1996): 280–294.

Mills, Gary B. *The Forgotten People: Cane River's Creoles of Color.* Baton Rouge: Louisiana State University Press, 1977.

Mitchell, Reid. *All on a Mardi Gras Day: Episodes in the History of New Orleans Carnival.* Cambridge, Mass.: Harvard University Press, 1995.

Mitchell, Reid. "Carnival and Katrina." *Journal of American History* 94 (December 2007): 789–794.

Mohr, Clarence L., and Lawrence N. Powell. "Through the Eye of Katrina: The Past as Prologue? An Introduction." *Journal of American History* 94 (December 2007): 693–694.

Murphy, Joseph M. *Santeria: An African Religion in America.* Boston: Beacon, 1988.

National Urban League Policy Institute. *Katrina: One Year Later: A Policy and Research Report on the National Urban League's Katrina Bill of Rights.* Washington, D.C.: National Urban League, 2006.

Neeley, Bobby Joe. "Contemporary Afro-American Voodooism (black religion): The Retention and Adaptation of the Ancient African-Egyptian Mystery System." Ph.D. diss., University of California, Berkeley, 1988.

Neville, Art, Aaron Neville, Charles Neville, Cyril Neville, and David Ritz. *The Brothers Neville.* Boston: Little, Brown, 2000.

Newman, Elve Louise. "The Ramifications of Voodoo and Gris-Gris in Some New Orleans' Drug Stores." Bachelor of Science thesis, Loyola University of the South, New Orleans, 1943.

O'Brien, Rosary Hartel. "The New Orleans Carnival Organizations: Theatre of Prestige." Ph.D. diss., University of California, Los Angeles, 1973.

Ochs, Stephen J. *Desegregating the Altar: The Josephites and the Struggle for Black Priests, 1871–1960.* Baton Rouge: Louisiana State University Press, 1993.

Ogren, Kathy J. *The Jazz Revolution: Twenties America and the Meaning of Jazz.* New York: Oxford University Press, 1989.

Oliver, Paul. *The Story of the Blues.* Boston: Northeastern University Press, 1997 [1969].

Olupona, Jacob K., ed. *African Traditional Religions in Contemporary Society.* St. Paul, Minn.: Paragon House, 1991.

Orsi, Robert A. *Between Heaven and Earth: The Religious Worlds People Make and the Scholars Who Study Them.* Princeton, N.J.: Princeton University Press, 2004.

———, ed. *Gods of the City: Religion and the American Urban Landscape.* Bloomington: Indiana University Press, 1999.

———. *The Madonna of 115th Street: Faith and Community in Italian Harlem, 1880–1950.* New Haven, Conn.: Yale University Press, 1985.

Orso, Ethelyn. *The St. Joseph Altar Traditions of South Louisiana.* Lafayette: University of Southern Louisiana Press, 1990.

Osbey, Brenda Marie. *All Saints.* Baton Rouge: Louisiana State University Press, 1997.

Owusu-Frempong, Yaw. "Afrocentricity, the Adae Festival of the Akan, African American Festivals, and Intergenerational Communication." *Journal of Black Studies* 35, no. 6 (July 2005): 730–750.

Pareles, Jon. "Marsalis Leads a Charge for the Cradle of Jazz." *New York Times,* September 19, 2005, p. B7.

———. "Rolling Rhythms to Beat the Bayou Blues." *New York Times,* September 22, 2005, p. B5.

———. "In the Music of New Orleans, Katrina Leaves Angry Edge." *New York Times,* February 27, 2006, p. A1.

———. "Mardi Gras Dawns with Some Traditions in Jeopardy." *New York Times,* February 28, 2006, p. E1.

———. "Many Friends Help Open New Orleans Fest." *New York Times,* April 29, 2006, p. A13.

———. "Continuity at Jazzfest: The Party Must Go On." *The New York Times,* May 1, 2006, p. B5.

Pastras, Phil. *Dead Man Blues: Jelly Roll Morton Way Out West.* Berkeley: University of California Press, 2001.

Peretti, Burton W. *The Creation of Jazz: Music, Race, and Culture in Urban America.* Urbana: University of Illinois Press, 1992.

Piazza, Tom. *The Guide to Classic Recorded Jazz.* Iowa City: University of Iowa Press, 1995.

Pinn, Anthony B. *Varieties of African-American Religious Experience.* Minneapolis: Fortress, 1998.

Pitts, Walter F., Jr. *Old Ship of Zion: The Afro-Baptist Ritual in the African Diaspora.* New York: Oxford University Press, 1993.

Plummer, Brenda Gayle. *Haiti and the Great Powers, 1902–1915.* Baton Rouge: Louisiana State University Press, 1988.

Polk, Patrick A. *Haitian Vodou Flags.* Jackson: University Press of Mississippi, 1997.

Pongracz, Patricia C., ed. *Threads of Faith: Recent Works from the Women of Color Quilters Network.* New York: Gallery at the American Bible Society, 2004.

Pope, John, and Matt Scallan. "Black Precincts Buttress Nagin Victory." *Times-Picayune,* April 24, 2006.

Porter, Horace A. *Jazz Country: Ralph Ellison in America.* Iowa City: University of Iowa Press, 2001.

Porter, Lewis. *Jazz: A Century of Change.* New York: Schirmer Books, 1997.

———. *What Is This Thing Called Jazz? African-American Musicians as Artists, Critics, and Activists.* Berkeley: University of California Press, 2002.

Potts, Bobby. *Jazz New Orleans Style.* Harahan, La.: Express, 1998.

Powell, Lawrence N. "What Does American History Tell Us about Katrina and Vice Versa?" *Journal of American History* 94 (December 2007): 863–876.

Price, Richard, ed. *Maroon Societies: Rebel Slave Communities in the Americas.* Baltimore, Md.: John Hopkins University Press, 1979.

Raabe, Phyllis Hutton. "Status and Its Impact: New Orleans Carnival, the Social Upper Class, and Upper Class Power." Ph.D. diss., Penn State University, 1973.

Raeburn, Bruce Boyd. "'They're Trying to Wash Us Away': New Orleans Musicians Surviving Katrina." *Journal of American History* 94 (December 2007): 812–819.

Ratliff, Ben. "New Orleans Musicians Ask If Their Scene Will Survive." *New York Times,* September 8, 2005, p. B1.

Rebennack, Jack (Dr. John), with Jack Rummel. *Under A Hoodoo Moon: The Life of the Night Tripper.* New York: St. Martin's, 1994.

Reckdahl, Katy. "A Colorful Farewell for the Chief of Chiefs." *New York Times,* July 11, 2005, p. A1.

Reed, Denise Pamela. "From the Freedmen's Bureau to FEMA; A Post-Katrina Historical, Journalistic, and Literary Analysis." *Journal of Black Studies* 37, no. 4 (March 2007): 555–567.

Reed, Ishmael. *Conjure: Selected Poems, 1963–1970.* Amherst: University of Massachusetts Press, 1972.

———. *Shrovetide in Old New Orleans.* Garden City, N.Y.: Doubleday, 1978.

———. *The Last Days of Louisiana Red.* Normal, Ill.: Dalkey Archive Press, 2000 [1974].

Reich, Howard. "Katrina Silences Legendary Jazz City." *Chicago Tribune,* August 31, 2005, p. 5.

———. "At Jazz Festival, a Requiem for New Orleans." *Chicago Tribune,* September 5, 2005, p. 6.

———. "Thousands of Famed Photos Ruined." *Chicago Tribune,* September 12, 2005, p. 5.

———. "Why New Orleans Matters." *Chicago Tribune,* September 18, 2005, sec. 7, p. 1.

———. "Living, Breathing Musicians Are What Make NOLA Memorable." *Chicago Tribune,* September 18, 2005, sec. 7, p. 5.

———. "New Orleans Urges Effort to Resurrect Cultural Soul." *Chicago Tribune,* January 17, 2006, p. 5.

Reinders, Robert C. "The Church and the Negro in New Orleans, 1850–1860." *Phylon* 22 (1961): 241–248.

Rhodes, Jewell Parker. *Voodoo Dreams: A Novel of Marie Laveau.* New York: Picador USA, 1993.

Rice, Anne. "Do You Know What It Means to Lose New Orleans?" *New York Times,* September 4, 2005, sec. 4, p. 11.

Rickels, Patricia K. "The Folklore of Sacraments and Sacramentals in South Louisiana." *Louisiana Folklore Miscellany* 11, no. 2 (1965): 27–44.

Rigaud, Milo. *Secrets of Voodoo.* San Francisco: City Lights Books, 1985 [1953].

Roach, Joseph. *Cities of the Dead: Circum-Atlantic Performance.* New York: Columbia University Press, 1996.

Roberts, John Storm. *Black Music of Two Worlds: African, Caribbean, Latin, and African-American Traditions.* 2nd rev. ed. New York: Schirmer Books, 1998.

———. *Latin Jazz: The First of the Fusions, 1880s to Today.* New York: Schirmer Books, 1999.

Robertson, Clyde C., and Joyce E. King. "Bon Feerey: A Teaching and Learning Methodology for Healing the Wounds of Distance, Displacement, and Loss Caused by Hurricane Katrina." *Journal of Black Studies* 37, no. 4 (March 2007): 469–481.

Rogers, Karen Lacy. *Righteous Lives: Narratives of the New Orleans Civil Rights Movement.* New York: New York University Press, 1993.

Rose, Al. *Storyville, New Orleans: Being an Authentic, Illustrated Account of the Notorious Red-Light District.* Tuscaloosa: University of Alabama Press, 1974.

Roussève, Charles B. *The Negro in Louisiana: Aspects of His History and His Literature.* New Orleans: Xavier University Press, 1937.

Salaam, Kalamu ya. "An Interview with and Portfolio of Paintings by John Scott." *African American Review* 27, no. 2 (summer 1993): 257–276.

Sandmel, Ben. *Zydeco!* Jackson: University Press of Mississippi, 1999.

———. "I Get the Blues When It Rains." *Louisiana Cultural Vistas* 16, no. 3 (fall 2005): 70.

Sanneh, Kelefa. "Rapping for a Hometown in Hurricane Crisis." *New York Times,* September 19, 2005, p. B1.

———. "Trying to Revive the City That Care Forgot." *New York Times,* September 22, 2005, p. B5.

———. "Gangsta Gumbo." *New York Times,* April 23, 2006, sec. 2, p. 1.

Saxon, Lyle, Edward Dreyer, and Robert Tallant. *Gumbo Ya-Ya: A Collection of Louisiana Folk Tales.* Gretna, La.: Pelican, 1998 [1945].

Schafer, William J. *Brass Bands and New Orleans Jazz.* Baton Rouge: Louisiana State University Press, 1977.

Scherman, Tony. *Backbeat: Earl Palmer's Story.* New York: Da Capo, 2000 [1999].

Schmidt, Leigh Eric. *Consumer Rites: The Buying and Selling of American Holidays.* Princeton, N.J.: Princeton University Press, 1995.

Schuman, Jamie. "Southern U. at New Orleans May Have to Rebuild from Scratch." *The Chronicle of Higher Education,* September 23, 2005, p. A16.

Scott, Rebecca J. "The Atlantic World and the Road to *Plessy v. Ferguson.*" *Journal of American History* 94 (December 2007): 726–733.

Scott, Saul. *Freedom Is, Freedom Ain't: Jazz and The Making of the Sixties.* Cambridge, Mass.: Harvard University Press, 2003.

Shack, William A. *Harlem in Montmartre: A Paris Jazz Story between the Great Wars.* Berkeley: University of California Press, 2001.

Sharkey, Patrick. "Survival and Death in New Orleans: An Empirical Look at the Human Impact of Katrina." *Journal of Black Studies* 37, no. 4 (March 2007): 482–501.

Sidran, Ben. *Black Talk*. New York: Da Capo, 1981 [1971].

Smith, Michael P. *New Orleans Jazz Fest: A Pictorial History*. Gretna, La.: Pelican, 1991.

———. *Spirit World*. Gretna, La.: Pelican, 1992.

———. *Mardi Gras Indians*. Gretna, La.: Pelican, 1994.

Smith, Theophus H. *Conjuring Culture: Biblical Formations of Black America*. New York: Oxford University Press, 1994.

Somé, Malidoma Patrice. *Of Water and the Spirit: Ritual, Magic, and Initiation in the Life of an African Shaman*. New York: Penguin Arkana, 1994.

Souther, Mark J. "The Disneyfication of New Orleans: The French Quarter as Façade in a Divided City." *Journal of American History* 94 (December 2007): 807–811.

Spence, Patricia R., Kenneth A. Lachlan, and Dongale R. Griffin. "Crisis Communication, Race, and National Disasters." *Journal of Black Studies* 37, no. 4 (March 2007): 539–554.

Spencer, Jon Michael. *Blues and Evil*. Knoxville: University of Tennessee Press, 1993.

Stannard, David E., ed. *Death in America*. Philadelphia: University of Pennsylvania Press, 1975.

Starr, S. Frederick, ed. *Inventing New Orleans: Writings of Lafcadio Hearn*. Jackson: University Press of Mississippi, 2001.

Stearns, Marshall, and Jean Stearns. *Jazz Dance: The Story of American Vernacular Dance*. New York: Da Capo, 1994 [1968].

Steptoe, Sonja. "The City Tourists Never Knew." *Time*, September 12, 2005, 116.

Suhor, Charles. *Jazz in New Orleans: The Postwar Years through 1970*. Lanham, Md.: Scarecrow, 2001.

Tademy, Lalita. *Cane River*. New York: Warner Books, 2001.

Tallant, Robert. *Voodoo in New Orleans*.Gretna, La.: Pelican, 1994 [1946].

Taylor, Allan. *American Colonies*. New York: Viking, 2001.

Teish, Luisah. *Carnival of the Spirit: Seasonal Celebrations and Rites of Passage*. New York: Harper San Francisco, 1994.

Teissl, Helmut. *Carnival in Rio*. New York: Abbeville, 2000.

Thompson, Robert Farris. *Flash of the Spirit: African and Afro-American Art and Philosophy*. New York: Random House, 1983.

———. *Face of the Gods: Art and Altars of Africa and the African Americas*. New York: Museum for African Art, 1993.

Toole, John Kennedy. *A Confederacy of Dunces*. New York: Wings Books, 1980.

Touchet, Leo, and Vernel Bagneres. *Rejoice When You Die: New Orleans Jazz Funerals*. Baton Rouge: Louisiana State University Press, 1998.

Turner, Frederick. *Remembering Song: Encounters with the New Orleans Jazz Tradition*. Exp. ed. New York: Da Capo, 1994.

Tyler, Pamela. "The Post-Katrina Semiseparate World of Gender Politics." *Journal of American History* 94 (December. 2007): 780–788.

U.S. House of Representatives. *A Failure of Initiative: Final Report of the Select Bipartisan Committee to Investigate the Preparation for and Response to Hurricane Katrina*. Washington, D.C.: U.S. Government Printing Office, 2006.

Usner, Donald H., Jr. "From African Captivity to American Slavery: The Introduction of Black Laborers to Colonial Louisiana." *Louisiana History* 20, no. 1 (winter 1979): 25–48.

———. *Indians, Settlers, and Slaves in a Frontier Exchange Economy: The Lower Mississippi Valley before 1783*. Chapel Hill: University of North Carolina Press, 1992.

Vega, Marta Moreno. *The Altar of My Soul: The Living Traditions of Santeria*. New York: One World Books, 2000.

Ventura, Michael. *Shadow Dancing in the U.S.A.* New York: St. Martin's, 1985.

Voeks, Robert A. *Sacred Leaves of Candomblé: African Magic, Medicine, and Religion in Brazil*. Austin: University of Texas Press, 1997.

Vogel, Carol. "Artists on the Run, Their Art Left Behind." *New York Times*, September 13, 2005, p. B1.

Wafer, Jim. *The Taste of Blood: Spirit Possession in Brazilian Candomblé*. Philadelphia: University of Pennsylvania Press, 1991.

Wakin, Daniel J. "Toll Is Also Exacted on Gulf Region's Historical and Cultural Treasures." *New York Times*, September 4, 2005, p. A26.

Walker, Daniel E. *No More, No More: Slavery and Cultural Resistance in Havana and New Orleans*. Minneapolis: University of Minnesota Press, 2004.

Walker, Harry Joseph. "Negro Benevolent Societies in New Orleans: A Study of Their Structure, Function, and Membership." Ph.D. diss., Fisk University, Nashville, Tennessee, 1937.

Ward, Martha. *Voodoo Queen: The Spirited Lives of Marie Laveau*. Jackson: University Press of Mississippi, 2004.

Washington, Tracie L., Brian D. Smedley, Beatrice Alvarez, and Jason Reece. *NAACP Reports Housing in New Orleans: One Year after Katrina, Policy Recommendations for Equitable Rebuilding*. NAACP, Gulf Coast Advocacy Center, Opportunity Agenda, and Kirwan Institute for the Study of Race and Ethnicity, 2006.

Werner, Craig. *A Change Is Gonna Come: Music, Race, and the Soul of America*. New York: A Plume Book, 1999.

Wessinger, Catherine, ed. *Women's Leadership in Marginal Religions*. Urbana: University of Illinois Press, 1993.

White, Ismail K., Tasha S. Philpot, Kristin Wylie, and Ernest McGowen. "Feeling the Pain of My People: Hurricane Katrina, Racial Equality, and the Psyche of Black America." *Journal of Black Studies* 37, no. 4 (March 2007): 523–538.

White, Michael G. "Evolution of a Cultural Tradition: Contrary to Custom, Modern New Orleans Jazz Players Are More Likely to Praise and Absorb Styles of Past Jazz Greats." *Louisiana Cultural Vistas* (winter 1991): 18–38.

———. "The New Orleans Brass Band in the Twentieth Century." *Xavier Review* 4, nos. 1 and 2 (1984): 23–35.

———. "Reflections of an Authentic Jazz Life in Pre-Katrina New Orleans." *Journal of American History* 94 (December 2007): 820–827.

Wilcken, Lois. *The Drums of Vodou*. Tempe, Ariz.: White Cliffs Media, 1992.

Wilder, Craig Steven. *In the Company of Black Men: The African Influence on African American Culture in New York City*. New York: New York University Press, 2001.

Wilkinson, Christopher. *Jazz on the Road: Don Albert's Musical Life*. Berkeley: University of California Press, 2001.

Wimbush, Vincent L., ed. *African Americans and the Bible: Sacred Texts and Social Textures*. New York: Continuum, 2000.

Wycliff, Don. "Refugees, Evacuees, Victims or Survivors?" *Chicago Tribune*, September 8, 2005, p. 11.

Zander, Marjorie Thomas. "The Brass Band Funeral and Related Negro Burial Customs." Master's thesis, University of North Carolina, Chapel Hill, 1962.

INDEX

Italicized page numbers indicate illustrations.

RICHARD BRENT TURNER is Professor of Religious Studies and African American Studies at the University of Iowa and author of *Islam in the African-American Experience,* 2nd ed. (Indiana University Press, 2003).